HOW DOES IT

FEEL TO BE

A PROBLEM?

THE PENGUIN PRESS   NEW YORK   2008

HOW DOES IT

BEING YOUNG AND

FEEL TO BE

ARAB IN AMERICA

A PROBLEM ?

MOUSTAFA BAYOUMI

THE PENGUIN PRESS
Published by the Penguin Group
Penguin Group (USA) Inc., 375 Hudson Street, New York, New York 10014, U.S.A. • Penguin
Group (Canada), 90 Eglinton Avenue East, Suite 700, Toronto, Ontario, Canada M4P 2Y3
(a division of Pearson Penguin Canada Inc.) • Penguin Books Ltd, 80 Strand, London
WC2R 0RL, England • Penguin Ireland, 25 St. Stephen's Green, Dublin 2, Ireland (a division of
Penguin Books Ltd) • Penguin Books Australia Ltd, 250 Camberwell Road, Camberwell,
Victoria 3124, Australia (a division of Pearson Australia Group Pty Ltd) • Penguin Books India Pvt
Ltd, 11 Community Centre, Panchsheel Park, New Delhi – 110 017, India • Penguin Group (NZ),
67 Apollo Drive, Rosedale, North Shore 0632, New Zealand (a division of Pearson
New Zealand Ltd) • Penguin Books (South Africa) (Pty) Ltd, 24 Sturdee Avenue,
Rosebank, Johannesburg 2196, South Africa

Penguin Books Ltd, Registered Offices:
80 Strand, London WC2R 0RL, England

First Published in 2008 by The Penguin Press,
a member of Penguin Group (USA) Inc.

Copyright © Moustafa Bayoumi, 2008
All rights reserved

Page 292 constitutes an extension of this copyright page.

LIBRARY OF CONGRESS CATALOGING IN PUBLICATION DATA
Bayoumi, Moustafa.
How does it feel to be a problem? : being young and Arab in America / Moustafa Bayoumi.
p. cm.
Includes bibliographical references.
ISBN: 978-1-59420-176-9
1. Arab American youth—Interviews.   2. Arab American youth—Race identity.
3. Arab American youth—Psychology.   4. Arab Americans—Social conditions.
5. Race awareness—United States.   6. United States—Race relations.   I. Title.
E184.A65B35   2008
305.892'7073—dc22   2007049272

Printed in the United States of America
1   3   5   7   9   10   8   6   4   2

DESIGNED BY MEIGHAN CAVANAUGH

To my parents

Between me and the other world there is ever an unasked question: unasked by some through feelings of delicacy; by others through the difficulty of rightly framing it. All, nevertheless, flutter round it. They approach me in a half-hesitant sort of way, eye me curiously or compassionately, and then, instead of saying it directly, How does it feel to be a problem? they say, I know an excellent colored man in my town; or, I fought at Mechanicsville; or, Do not these Southern outrages make your blood boil? At these I smile, or am interested, or reduce the boiling to a simmer, as the occasion may require. To the real question, How does it feel to be a problem? I answer seldom a word.

—W.E.B. DU BOIS, *The Souls of Black Folk*

CONTENTS

PREFACE   1

RASHA   13

SAMI   45

YASMIN   81

AKRAM   115

LINA   149

OMAR   187

RAMI   219

AFTERWORD   259

ACKNOWLEDGMENTS   271

NOTES   273

PREFACE

Sade and four of his twenty-something friends are at a hookah café almost underneath the Verrazano-Narrows Bridge in Brooklyn. It's late, but the summer heat is strong and hangs in the air. They sit on the sidewalk in a circle, water pipes bubbling between their white plastic chairs.

Sade is upset. He recently found out that his close friend of almost four years was an undercover police detective sent to spy on him, his friends, and his community. Even the guy's name, Kamil Pasha, was fake, which particularly irked the twenty-four-year-old Palestinian American. After appearing as a surprise witness at a recent terrorism trial in Brooklyn, Pasha vanished. That's when Sade discovered the truth.

"I was very hurt," he says. "Was it friendship, or was he doing his job?" He takes a puff from his water pipe. "I felt betrayed." The smoke comes out thick and smells like apples. "How could I not have seen this? The guy had four bank accounts! He was always asking for a receipt wherever we went. He had an empty apartment: a treadmill, a TV, and a mattress. No food, no wardrobe." He shakes his head. "We were stupid not to figure it out.

"You have to know the family," Sade says. He points to those around the circle. "His mother is my aunt. I've known him since I was in second grade. I know where his family lives, and he's also my cousin," he says, ticking off each person in turn. He gets to me. "You I'm not so sure about!" he says, and all the young men laugh loudly.

Informants and spies are regular conversation topics in the age of terror, a time when friendships are tested, trust disappears, and tragedy becomes comedy. If questioning friendship isn't enough, Sade has also had other problems to deal with. Sacked from his Wall Street job, he is convinced that the termination stemmed from his Jerusalem birthplace. Anti-Arab and anti-Muslim invectives were routinely slung at him there, and he's happier now in a technology firm owned and staffed by other hyphenated Americans. But the last several years have taken their toll. I ask him about life after September 11 for Arab Americans. "We're the new blacks," he says. "You know that, right?"

HOW DOES IT FEEL to be a problem? Just over a century ago, W.E.B. Du Bois asked that very question in his American classic *The Souls of Black Folk,* and he offered an answer. "Being a problem is a strange experience," he wrote, "peculiar even," no doubt evoking the "peculiar institution" of slavery. Du Bois composed his text during Jim Crow, a time of official racial segregation that deliberately obscured to the wider world the human details of African-American life. Determined to pull back "the veil" separating populations, he showed his readers a fuller picture of the black experience, including "the meaning of its religion, the passion of its human sorrow, and the struggle of its greater souls."

A century later, Arabs and Muslim Americans are the new "problem" of American society, but there have of course been others. Native Americans, labeled "merciless Indian savages" by the Declaration of Independence, were said to be beyond civilization and able to comprehend only the brute language of force. With the rise of Catholic immigration to the country in the nineteenth century, Irish and Italian Americans were attacked for their religion. They suffered mob violence and frequent accusations of holding papal loyalties above republican values. During World War I, German Americans were loathed and reviled, sauerkraut was redubbed "liberty cabbage," and several states banned the teaching of German, convinced that the language itself promoted un-American values. Between the world wars, anti-Semitism drove Jewish Americans out of universities and jobs and fueled wild and pernicious conspiracy theories concerning warfare and world domination. Japanese Americans were herded like cattle into internment camps during World War II (as were smaller numbers of German, Italian, Hungarian, and Romanian Americans). Chinese Americans were commonly suspected of harboring Communist sympathies during the Mc-Carthy era, frequently losing careers and livelihoods. And Hispanic Americans have long been seen as outsider threats to American culture, even though their presence here predates the formation of the present-day United States.

But since the terrorist attacks of September 11 and the wars in Afghanistan and Iraq, Arabs and Muslims, two groups virtually unknown to most Americans prior to 2001, now hold the dubious distinction of being the first new communities of suspicion after the hard-won victories of the civil-rights era. Even if prejudice continues to persist in our society, the American creed of fairness was now supposed to mean that we ought to be judged not by our religion, gender, color, or country of origin but simply by the content of our individual characters. The terrorist attacks, the wars in Afghanistan and Iraq, and the explosion of political violence around the world have put that dream in jeopardy for American Arabs and Muslims. In the eyes of some Americans, they have become collectively known as dangerous outsiders. Bias crimes against Arabs, Muslims, and those assumed to be Arab or Muslim spiked 1,700 percent in the first six months after September 11 and have never since returned to their pre-2001 levels. A *USA Today*/Gallup Poll from 2006 shows that 39 percent of Americans admit to holding prejudice against Muslims and believe that all Muslims—U.S. citizens included—should carry special IDs. Different studies from

the University of Illinois at Chicago, Harvard, and Purdue have each concluded that the more positively one feels about the United States, the more
likely one is to harbor anti-Arab feelings. Hostility remains high.

Government policies certainly haven't helped the situation. Mass arrests following the attacks increased generalized suspicion against Arabs
and Muslims in this country. The government demanded that nonimmi-
grant males from twenty-four Muslim-majority countries register their
whereabouts in this country, leading to deportation proceedings against
almost fourteen thousand people. And racial profiling, almost universally
loathed prior to 2001, assumed a new lease on life in 2003 when President
George W. Bush ordered a ban on the practice but included "exceptions
permitting use of race and ethnicity to combat potential terrorist attacks."
While it could now be said that profiling other groups was officially and
legally un-American, profiling Arabs and Muslims made good national-
security sense.

But what exactly is a profile? It's a sketch in charcoal, the simplified
contours of a face, a silhouette in black and white, a textbook description
of a personality. By definition a profile draws an incomplete picture. It
substitutes recognition for detail. It is what an outsider from the street ob-
serves when looking through the windowpane of someone else's life.

Profiling Arabs and Muslims has in reality expanded far beyond the
realms of law enforcement. Arab and Muslim Americans are now routinely
profiled in their places of employment, in housing, for public-opinion polls,
and in the media. Yet they remain curiously unknown. Broadly speaking,
the representations that describe them tend to fall into two types, the exceptional assimilated immigrant or the violent fundamentalist, with very little
room in between. The questions they are asked in the media and in real
life constantly circle simplistically around the same frames of reference—
terrorism, women, and assimilation—fixations that may be understandable in this age but frequently overlook the complex human dimensions of
Muslim-American or Arab-American life. Terms such as "moderate" and
"radical" are bandied about so freely as to mean next to nothing, and cli-
chéd phrases like "sleeper cells," "alienated Muslims," "radicalization,"

and "homegrown terrorists" degrade the language to the point that they structure the thinking about the Muslims living among us.

It seems barely an exaggeration to say that Arab and Muslim Americans are constantly talked about but almost never heard from. The problem is not that they lack representations but that they have too many. And these are all abstractions. Arabs and Muslims have become a foreign-policy issue, an argument on the domestic agenda, a law-enforcement priority, and a point of well-meaning concern. They appear as shadowy characters on terror television shows, have become objects of sociological inquiry, and get paraded around as puppets for public diplomacy. Pop culture is awash with their images. Hookah cafés entice East Village socialites, fashionistas appropriate the checkered kaffiyah scarf, and Prince sings an ode to a young Arab-American girl. They are floating everywhere in the virtual landscape of the national imagination, as either villains of Islam or victims of Arab culture. Yet as in the postmodern world in which we live, sometimes when you are everywhere, you are really nowhere.

Frankly, it's beleaguering; like living on a treadmill, an exhausting condition. University of Michigan anthropologists Sally Howell and Andrew Shryock succinctly describe the situation when they write that "in the aftermath of 9/11, Arab and Muslim Americans have been compelled, time and again, to apologize for acts they did not commit, to condemn acts they never condoned and to openly profess loyalties that, for most U.S. citizens, are merely assumed." Yet despite the apologies, condemnations, and professions, their voices still aren't heard. And while so many terrible things have happened in the past years, plenty of good things have also occurred, from Japanese-American groups speaking out against today's wartime policies, to prominent civil-rights activists fighting for due process for Muslim and Arab clients, to ordinary people reaching out to one another in everyday encounters. Much of this happens quietly in church basements, in mosques holding open houses, in Jewish centers, or in university or community halls, but such events too are often obscured, drowned out by the ideology of our age. Yet what most remains in the shadows today are the human dimensions to how Arabs and Muslims live their lives, the rhythms of their work and days, the varieties of their religious experiences, the obstacles they face, and the efforts they shoulder to overcome them. In other words, what is absent is how they understand the meanings of their religion, the passions of their sorrow, and the struggle of their souls. But in today's landscape, none of that seems to matter. One could say that in the dawning years of the twenty-first century, when Arabs are the new chic and Islam is all the rage, Muslims and Arabs have become essentially a nagging problem to solve, one way or another.

And being a problem is a strange experience—frustrating, even.

THIS BOOK WAS CONCEIVED out of my frustrations, but it is not about me. It is about the generation behind me, twenty-something Arab Americans who since 2001 have had to navigate a rocky terrain somewhere between expectation and frustration. I know what it is like to be Arab and Muslim today, but what is it like, I wondered, to be young, Arab, and Muslim in the age of terror? I began exploring this question in early 2005, spending my time with Brooklyn's Arab-American youth, and this book is the answer to my question. In it I have attempted to employ the power of narrative, to tell the stories of seven different Arab Americans from Brooklyn as richly and accurately as I could.

The main character in this book is youth. To be young is to be at a crossroads in life. It is a time to discover who you are, what values you hold, and which friendships you will cherish. This is true for all young people. But for young Arab Americans today, to be young is also more complicated, for it means that you are living a paradox. On the one hand, the older generation looks hopefully to you with the belief that you will produce a better world for yourself, for your family and community, and for your nation. On the other, the culture at large increasingly spies you with mounting levels of fear, aversion, and occasionally outright hostility. Today's young Arab Americans often live uncomfortably between these expectations.

Moreover, there are many of them. Like most immigrant populations, both Arab and Muslim Americans are younger than the general population. Twenty-one percent of the American public is between eighteen and thirty years of age, but 30 percent of American Muslims are. The median age of Arab Americans is thirty-one, compared to thirty-five for the whole of the United States. This also means that many young Arabs and Muslims have no adult experience of the world prior to September 11. And while, nationally, Arabs and Muslims are generally more affluent than average Americans, in Brooklyn, the setting of this book, many come from working-class backgrounds, where they are driving their way through the maze of the American dream on paths that have become more complicated for all those who are young, Arab, and Muslim. They are often anxious about their futures, and their anxieties reveal much, not only about their own personalities but also about the tensions evident in contemporary American society.

This book concentrates on Arab Americans and focuses on Arab Muslim Americans for the simple reason that the Muslim-American experience is capacious and sprawling. It contains many different moments of arrival and dozens of different ethnic histories. The Arab-American story, on the other hand, is more coherent and self-contained. It relates a community to the specific overseas geography of the Arab world, where much of the "war on terror" is raging. It is true and necessary to point out that the Arab-American community is a majority Christian population, but it is also true that Arab-American Muslims are at the eye of today's storms. They are the ones forced to reconcile particular American foreign policies that affect their countries of origin with the idea that their faith poses an existential threat to Western civilization. Even the one chapter in this book that tells the story of an Arab-American Christian, Sami, relates how he must navigate the minefield of associations the public has of Arabs as well as the expectations that Muslim Arab Americans have of him as an Arab-American soldier.

If youth is the central character here, Brooklyn is the setting. Abstractions thrive when people are removed from their contexts, but grounding a story in one place has allowed me to explore the concrete details of lived experience within a single geography. My reasons for choosing Brooklyn are multiple. Besides its proximity to what is now known as Ground Zero, Brooklyn has the largest Arab-American population in the nation. According to the 2000 U.S. Census, close to 36,000 live in Brooklyn, about half of New York City's total Arab-American population. Dearborn, Michigan, the unofficial capital of Arab America, may have a much higher concentration of Arab Americans by orders of magnitude, but Brooklyn's Arab population is more numerous than even Dearborn's (at around 30,000). (The Arab-American Institute believes that the census underreports Arab Americans and puts Brooklyn's Arab Americans at around 120,000 people.)

Yet far more important than base numbers is the borough itself. Brooklyn is "chiefly no whole or recognizable animal," writes James Agee, "but an exorbitant pulsing mass of scarcely discernible cellular jellies and tissues." With more than 2.5 million residents, it is the third-largest metropolitan area in the country. Size alone does not account for its energy. Robber barons, refugees, free blacks, and the international working class have all settled here, whether in leafy Victorian mansions or in limestone, brownstone, or Federal-style row houses, making the story of Brooklyn a short history of human escape and reinvention flattened through geography and narrated through architecture. Walt Whitman once called it the city of "homes and churches," and yet it is more. A country on its own, Brooklyn continuously repopulates itself, first by boat and ferry and now by planeloads of the world's exiles and émigrés, and it brims with the rhythms and pageantry of twenty-first-century American life.

Today Brooklyn is Prospect Heights with its late-night barbershops, all fabulous hair and atomic white light at 12:00 A.M., or Coney Island, a seasonal experiment in radical democracy held in a riot of colors and soundtracked to amusement-park songs. It's the Friday-afternoon call to prayer in Bedford-Stuyvesant. Brooklyn is a tourist-free Chinatown in Sunset Park or the dollar stores of Flatbush Avenue that spill their wares onto the noisy street and away from their weeping, scarred, and aching buildings. It's dreadlocked West Indians flying kites in Prospect Park or the colony of Middle American defectors in Williamsburg, urban hipsters costumed in androgynous jeans and monotonous tattoos. It's the bourgeoisie of Brooklyn Heights, living in stately grace but with barely suppressed feelings of self-loathing for not owning a 212 area code. Brooklyn is the slowly dissolving Italian hub of Bensonhurst, the Syrian Jews of Ocean Parkway, and the Pakistanis of Coney Island Avenue. It is the birds of Green-Wood Cemetery singing their songs to the Civil War dead, upper-crust Haitians living well in Midwood Estates, and intrepid diners visiting Bay Ridge's transplanted Mediterranean coast, where, high on the old Nordic Third Avenue, sea air mingles with the garlic aromas floating out of the Arab, Greek, and Italian eateries that line the street. Brooklyn is the informal urban apartheid of Eastern Parkway, the soft socialism of Park Slope, the Russian capitalism of Brighton Beach. It's the Salt Marshes of Marine Park, the roast beef sandwiches on Nostrand Avenue, Di Fara's Pizza, Vox Pop, and Vinegar Hill. Brooklyn is the dangerous rush of traffic on Atlantic Avenue, where bus exhaust mixes with the smells of fresh bread and Arabic spices; it is the madness of Pacific Street, where parents seek refuge from the urban cacophony in its tiny community garden, and Dean Street, where the Chinese food is halal. Brooklyn is the concentrated, unedited, twenty-first-century answer to who we, as Americans, are as a people.

After deciding on the setting, I began asking friends what stories they knew about the contemporary Arab-American existence here, and those friends were soon asking their friends on my behalf. I talked to community leaders and introduced myself to imams at local Islamic centers. Although my own background is both Arab and Muslim, I don't live in Bay Ridge, the neighborhood in Brooklyn with the highest concentration of Arab Americans, and most of my Arab and Muslim friends and associates prior to my writing this book were older and came from the academic world. I was, in other words, both an insider and outsider to the community. Since Muslim communities around the country now often feel under the blunt hammer of suspicion, I was concerned that those I spoke to might be leery of me and my interest, but my worries were quickly allayed. One Friday after prayer, for example, an imam invited me to his office upstairs, sat me down, and pulled out his little book. Instead of reading off problems or lecturing me about how I should represent the community, he began telling me about a Muslim woman he knows. "She's Egyptian, with a master's degree from Denmark," he told me. "Do you want to meet her?" He was trying to marry me off. I smiled and thanked him gently. *"Ley, ya Moustafa?"* he asked me. *"Heya helwa, ezzay al besboosa."* Why, Moustafa? he asked. She's sweet, like Egyptian honey cake!

Before long my efforts were paying off, even if the imam's didn't. I gained enough confidence with the community to attend a closed-door meeting between community leaders and the FBI. These were the first FBI agents I'd ever met, and they looked as if they had just walked out of a movie. They stared you in the eye and repeated your name while shaking your hand. They all had similar, almost military-tight haircuts. And, except for the Moroccan agent with them (inexplicably dressed in brown), they all wore sharp suits in navy blue and spoke with the same diction of officialdom. Later I realized how the twelve community leaders present—speaking with accents and in Arabic with each other, mostly darker-skinned, accompanied by a mystical-looking sheikh, and breaking in the middle of the meeting for prayer—must have looked like movie characters to them. But, as everyone knows, in the movies we are the bad guys.

The three-hour meeting was an example of the failed communication that marks our era. Seemingly unaware of the irony in their statements, the FBI told the community leaders, a group of successful physicians and businessmen who had already contributed much to multicultural America, that the Bureau wanted to "bring the Arab Muslim community to this melting-pot country" and "to instill a sense of love for our precious freedoms." They demanded that the community leaders condemn terrorism in front of them, which they willingly did. Meanwhile, the community leaders wanted to talk about other issues, like the crisis in local charitable donations, fallen sharply since the government shut down several national charities, and how government surveillance was scaring people away from community activities. They wanted to know how to get off the no-fly list. To these the FBI had little to add. ("Our only answer is to get to the airport early," they said about the no-fly list.) Everyone was polite and well-meaning throughout, but in their clash of priorities, the meeting might have been held in two different languages. I left depressed and frustrated.

My inquiries had spread by word of mouth, and people also began contacting me about the project. I set up rendezvous with people in their favorite locations, usually Brooklyn's busy coffee shops, smoky hookah cafés, quiet mosques, noisy youth centers, and hectic diners. Before long I had the stories that make up this book. Nevertheless, there are gaps, countless other people I did not include, and I make no claims that these seven narratives touch on every detail of Arab-American life. Over the course of writing this book, I heard many other accounts from people, including the young Syrian-American medical student who was unceremoniously detained at an airport, a procedure that has now become a sad routine commonly known as "flying while Muslim" (or sometimes TWA, "traveling while Arab"). Another is the Palestinian-American firefighter who wanted to climb the fire department's ladder of promotion. The study material he needed for his exam is expensive, so he purchased a cheaper copy from an outside vendor. Instead of finding the book in the mail, however, he received a visit to his home. Two investigators from the Joint Terrorism Task Force wanted to know why a man with an Arab name was interested in a book about fires. ("You didn't check to see if I'm a firefighter?" he asked them in frustration.) But the loudest silence in the book concerns those young Arabs, a minority, who have abandoned their ethnic roots or religion out of either shame or fear or both. They have changed their names and try to pass as other-than-Arab—Latinos most often. Perhaps it is fitting that "The Biography of the Ex-Arab Man or Woman" is present here only by its absence.

What you will find are seven Arab-American narratives that are in the end very American stories about race, religion, and civil rights and about how the pressures of domestic life and foreign policy push on individual lives. Some of the young people in this book are friends with one another, but only I know all of them. I have changed the names of some people to protect their privacy. They are students and grocery-store clerks, teenagers and twenty-somethings, community workers and soldiers. They are religious and secular, male and female. What they want most is what the ma-

jority of young adults desire: opportunity, marriage, happiness, and the
chance to fulfill their potential. But what they have now are extra loads to
carry, burdens that often include workplace discrimination, warfare in
their countries of origin, government surveillance, the disappearance of
friends or family, threats of vigilante violence, a host of cultural misunder-
standings, and all kinds of other problems that thrive in the age of terror.

And yet this is far from a gloomy book. In fact, I have developed a great
deal of optimism through its writing. What I have found is that young Arab
Americans understand both the adversities they face and the opportunities
they have with an enviable maturity. They have a keen awareness about their
lives, an acute kind of double consciousness that comprehends the widening
gap between how they see themselves and how they are seen by the culture at
large. They live with their multiple identities and are able to draw connections to the struggles others have faced in our American past. These young
men and women have been raised by immigrant parents and educated in a
post-civil-rights-era America. They bring with them a deep, sometimes firsthand, understanding of the conflicts raging in the Middle East and at the
same time are well versed in the recurring battles for equality in the United
States. They often draw lessons from this past to their own lives, reading
themselves through the pages of American history. This is a remarkable trait
often missing today, where telling someone she's "history" is the equivalent
to telling her that life is over. But their lives are just beginning.

Stories connect us to each other. In ways that polemics and polls cannot, they can reveal our conflicts within ourselves and our vulnerabilities
to each other. Stories can describe why certain choices are made and others
are passed over, and they can reveal the colors of our emotions. Stories
have the capacity to convert a line drawing into flesh, to dislodge the power
of the presumption and prejudice. Perhaps this explains why I responded
the way I did to the many inquiries I heard from friends and associates after
I described the project of this book to them. "Oh, you're writing profiles,"
they would say.

"Portraits," I would answer. "Hasn't there been enough profiling already?"

RASHA

Ah, Rasha's
    foot on the stair.
She moved slowly, as if she carried
the snake around her body
always.

—RITA DOVE, "Agosta the Winged Man
    and Rasha the Black Dove"

The subway tunnel is dark as night. A train rushes through it, and the interior lights of the car blaze like July. Rasha steadies herself on the hard plastic seat as the train rocks back and forth. In a flash the swaying movement comes back to her, and its familiarity is comforting.

It's May 2002, and Rasha's on her way to university. It's also afternoon, but she's deep underground, and it's hard to know what time it is. The subway is almost empty. One older businessman sits quietly across from her. A group of teenagers down the car are screaming at each other, their shrieking laughter filling the car with adolescent self-importance, but even their noise doesn't bother her. Off to her side is a homeless man, covered in all the dirt and odors that street living brings. Rasha finds herself unexpectedly staring at him, and he peers back at her through his tent of hair. For a second their eyes lock, but Rasha's not frightened. Instead she finds the connection rapturous.

Later that night she would write about the moment in a reversible midnight blue notebook labeled "Day Dreams" on one cover and "Night Dreams" on the other. This is where she composes her own poetry and collects her favorite aphorisms. On one page, for example, she has quoted from Kahlil Gibran: "The deeper that sorrow carves into your being, the more joy you can contain." On another she has written out a line from Booker T. Washington: "I will permit no man to narrow and degrade my soul by making me hate him." And in the middle of "Night Dreams" is her prose poem, dated May 8, 2002, called "This man." It ends this way:

> *I saw a man today, and his captivity reminded me that I was free. My mind no longer worrying, my hands no longer tied. I could see my mother, my father, and the world again. I can breathe and taste freedom. But most importantly, I can live & know that I am free. I saw a man today and that man . . . saw me.*

Rasha was nineteen years old when she penned this. She had just spent almost three months in prison with her family. Suddenly free, she was now visible to the world again. She was no longer one of the disappeared.

RASHA IS A PETITE five feet four. She walks with a feather step and looks at you with penetrating, obsidian eyes. Her lips are often lightly glossed in pink, and her serious brown hair is commonly tied in a librarian's bun. She has an aura of modesty around her delicate frame. If she leans over to tie her shoes, she makes sure to cover herself chastely with one of her hands. She's fine-boned, with porcelain features that give her what you think is sparrow innocence, but soon you'll realize that it's more akin to a hard fragility. If you drop her, she'll break, but she'll cut you, too. She's tough and tender, enraged and exhausted, withdrawn and outgoing, a pessimist brimming with humanist hope.

She has also lived in the United States for more than eighteen years, almost all of them in Brooklyn, and to understand her story we need to turn back the pages of her history. Rasha was born in 1983, in Damascus, Syria, but when she was five years old, her family was granted a tourist visa to the United States, and they moved from the Fertile Crescent to Avenue U in

Gravesend. At the time Hafez al-Assad's Syria was anything but fertile. Embroiled in violence, the nation saw Assad's iron fist battering his growing and increasingly daring opposition. Bombings against the regime were frequent, as were mass arrests and torture. It all culminated in the 1982 massacre in the city of Hama, where tens of thousands were viciously killed. Rasha's father wanted better things for his family, so as soon as they arrived in the United States, he applied for their political asylum. He also began working at a discount clothing store on Fourteenth Street in Manhattan, eventually moving up to manager and then partner. Five-year-old Rasha assumed an American life.

Some of her earliest memories involve asking her mother little-girl questions about the world. One December when she was about ten years old, she was jealous of her friends with their gifts and sparkling Christmas trees. *This house sucks!* she thought. *Why don't we get a Christmas tree? Why are we so primitive?* So she resolved to ask her mother. "Mama," she broached the question one day, "are we going to get presents this year?" Her mother sat her down and explained to her in Arabic that they were not *mesihayeen,* Christians, and that's why they don't celebrate Christmas. Rasha rolled her eyes in confusion and walked away. She had confused *mesihayeen* with the word *mesrahayeen,* "stage actors," and for a long time afterward tried to figure out what exactly acting had to do with Christmas.

She eventually learned the differences between religions and nations and about where she came from. Her mother was her guide, and she taught little Rasha how to be a proper Arab Muslim girl in the United States. Rasha's parents were not particularly religious, so the lessons revolved less around points of faith and theology and more around the simple values of honesty, compassion, and protection of her honor. She had three siblings: Reem, an older sister; Munir, an older brother; and Wassim, a younger brother. None of them was much of a model for Rasha. Reem was five yars older than Rasha, and half a decade is a large span of time at that age. The two girls fought often.

The family stayed in the New York area until 1996, still without having adjusted their immigration status. The asylum claim had been unsuccessful, but Rasha's father had hired a lawyer and was appealing the decision and looking for other legal ways to remain in the country. Meanwhile, her mother had given birth to two more little brothers. Since they were born in Brooklyn, the two infant boys were, unlike the rest of the family, citizens of the United States. But the pace of progress in the immigration proceedings was like washing your hair from a leaking faucet. Nothing was moving except for Congress, which in 1996 legislated even more draconian anti-immigrant legislation in the wake of Timothy McVeigh's bombing of the Murrah Federal Building in Oklahoma City. Rasha's father gave up and moved them all back to Syria that year.

By the time they returned to Syria, Rasha was in sixth grade, going on seventh, and she found her new environs hard going. She was crashing into puberty, which is hard enough without having to adapt to a brand-new country. She spoke Arabic but could not read and write the language, so school was difficult. At first her father put her in a public girls' school, and Rasha loathed it. Hitting students who acted up was formally forbidden but still routinely practiced, and Rasha, who has a proud streak at her core, talked back to her teacher one day. The slap came, and she was stunned silent at first and then came home crying. Her father gangbusted his way to her school, screaming at the female teacher never to lay a finger on his daughter again, then promptly moved his daughter to a private girls' school.

After a couple of months, Rasha's father received word from his American lawyer that they finally had an interview scheduled for their green-card application, one of the final phases before gaining residency. But, the lawyer explained, it was nothing to get excited about. Since the family had already returned to Syria, the victory was abstract. If you leave the country, you give up your claim to naturalization. It was too late.

Private school wasn't much easier for Rasha. The biggest difference here was that there were more Christian and Jewish students. (In thinking back to that time, Rasha told me, she is struck by how Jewish Syrians were not nearly as ostracized as we are led to believe.) But Syria was still a stifling place for the family. For Rasha it was airless because of her age and her school. Her family was constantly watching were she was going, and she felt suffocated. For her father, Syria was a failure due to its flailing economy and miserable political environment. No one was happy.

It was time to make a change, so they applied again for a visa to visit the United States, and they were approved. It felt like a miracle. Reem, Rasha, and Munir were literally jumping for joy in their living room when they found out. They had been in Syria for only seven months, and already they were saying their good-byes to family. They boarded a plane and, half a day later, landed at JFK. They stayed at the Golden Gate Hotel in Sheepshead Bay for three days until they found an apartment. Now that they were back in Brooklyn, Rasha was again happy. This is what she knew. This was home. Once again her father applied for adjusted status. And once again he began working, this time opening his own restaurant. Over time Rasha started high school.

JAMES MADISON HIGH SCHOOL was good for Rasha. Rising up in red brick, the crowded school is set in a prosperous area of Midwood, with its large houses and green lawns. It has an elegant exterior but caged windows and metal detectors. It also has a quote from President Madison carved on its edifice. "Education," it reads, "is the true foundation of civil liberty."

At Madison, Rasha met her best friends, Gaby and Nicky. Gaby is from Ecuador, and Nicky is from Azerbaijan. Befriending Nicky was easy and obvious. They both came from Muslim backgrounds and shared a lot of similar stories and values. And Rasha got close to Gaby because both of their families were traditional. They were talking about boys one day, and Rasha told Gaby that she wasn't allowed to date. "Yeah." Gaby nodded out of Catholic correspondence. "Neither am I." Rasha looked at her with disbelief. "You're not even Arab!" she said. "Or Muslim!" The three of them became an international posse and an inseparable trio.

When they weren't in school, they were everywhere else—on the subway to the city, at one another's houses, at the movies, shopping, or eating.

They were especially fond of Times Square, miles away from Brooklyn and full of tourist glitz and cheap madness. Gaby was a year younger than Rasha, so Rasha, who felt herself growing into her own skin with her friends, became a big sister to Gaby. All three spent so much time together that they became like their own family. When, in the spring of 2000, Rasha and Nicky graduated from Madison, Rasha moved, but not far away. Her father had now saved enough money that they could afford to buy a place in Bay Ridge, Brooklyn, with its limestone row houses and numerous Arabs. This was the first property the family had owned, and her parents were very proud of the accomplishment. The girls came over to see the new house. Rasha shared a room with her sister, Wassim and the two little brothers had another bedroom, and Munir slept downstairs. Two Egyptian tenants, whose rent helped with the mortgage, lived in a separate apartment carved into the basement. The friends stayed close after high school, and Rasha started college in September 2001.

On the morning of September 11, 2001, Rasha was sleeping late. Her mother opened her bedroom door and peeked in. "Rasha," she said. "You can't go to school. The subway's not working." Half asleep, Rasha raised her head. "Why?" she asked. "Accident," her mother explained, shrugging her shoulders. "With a plane." Rasha put her head back down and went back to sleep.

ONE FEBRUARY NIGHT in 2002, just a week after her nineteenth birthday, Rasha *couldn't* sleep. She didn't know why. The spring semester was under way at school, and she had classes to attend in the morning, but for some reason sleep was a gold coin in the water just beyond her grasp. She went downstairs and turned on the TV, mindlessly changing channels until 4:00 A.M. She turned off the set and trudged back to her bedroom. On her way up the stairs, she noticed a bizarre reflection of lights shimmering in the mirror that sat right on top of the fireplace. *I'm just seeing things,* she thought, and continued up to bed. After a few minutes, she had mercifully dozed off.

But half an hour later, Rasha suddenly opened her eyes. A female officer was shaking her, telling her in gray, official tones to get dressed. *Oh, my God,* Rasha thought, *somebody's died,* and she felt her heart drop and crack. She immediately glanced over to her sister. "What the hell's going on?" she asked, but Reem just looked frightened. Shock and fear paralyzed Rasha, and her knees locked. "Ma'am, just get up," repeated the female officer. "Get up and get dressed." Disoriented, Rasha forced herself to slowly rise. She walked downstairs in her pajamas, a few steps behind her sister. She couldn't feel her legs.

In the living room, she saw her entire family sitting awkwardly on the couch, and she sighed with relief. *Thank God,* she thought, *they're all okay!* She sat beside her sister, and then noticed that her brother Munir's legs were shackled. Shock turned to confusion, as she realized that about fifteen law enforcement officers—INS officials, U.S. Marshals, and FBI agents— had taken over their residence. The strangers, some with guns, walked through her house as if they owned it. Out the window she saw that it was the lights from their vehicles that had been shining into the living room. Fear began to bubble through her again.

An FBI agent, the apparent leader of the group, stood in front of the family. He identified himself and asked each of them their names. He told them they were being investigated for possible terrorism connections and that they were going to be taken to Federal Plaza. He told them that due to their immigration status they could be deported. If that were the case, they might be detained beforehand. And he told them that the detention would last only two or three days. At this point Rasha's mother became frantic, crying and screaming out questions. But the man's flat monotone reiterated that everything would be explained to them at Federal Plaza.

This was no accidental arrest. The man seemed to know everything about the family, including the fact that Rasha's two youngest brothers, both minors, were U.S. citizens. He turned to Rasha's father and told him to arrange custody for the boys. Rasha's father suggested that his brother, who lives in New York City, could take care of them. He asked to call him, suggesting that the authorities wait before transporting them to Federal

Plaza until his brother could arrive. But the agent torpedoed the idea. That would take too long, he said, and instructed him instead to wake the tenants below and leave the boys there. Rasha's father had no choice but to comply, and when they were ready to go, the agent turned to the entire family and said, "We're going to handcuff you now."

(Later Rasha learned why her eldest brother had already been not only handcuffed but shackled. Munir is a deep and stubborn sleeper, and when an agent went to his downstairs bedroom to wake him, Munir was uncooperative. "Why?" he kept asking. "Come on, get up," the agent said. "Why?" "Just get up," the man repeated, and Munir asked why again. "Get up!" the agent yelled. "Get up and put your hands together, like the way you pray!" Munir swore at him and told him to get the hell away. "So they shackled him," Rasha told me, "you know, to tame him.")

Outside, the official vehicles had closed off the entire street. The agents shepherded the family into a van, and they sat on benches in the back, riding in silence except for Rasha's sobbing mother, until they arrived at Federal Plaza in Manhattan. The ride was bumpy and disorienting, affording them no view of the road. When the van stopped and the back doors eventually swung open, they were all pulled from the vehicle into the building, where they were led to a room and then searched and fingerprinted before being dumped in a holding cell. They sat in the cell for what felt like half their lives.

Eventually the cell door opened and two FBI agents walked in. One was the man who had been in charge at their home. The two agents passed out flyers of alleged terrorists and wanted men, instructing them all to look at the pictures. The papers moved down the line of the family. Do you know any of them? the head agent asked. No, everyone responded in turn. And Rasha realized that they themselves were being investigated as terrorists.

Each family member was then escorted individually into a separate room. When Rasha's turn came, she was taken in handcuffs to a bare room furnished with a simple desk and a few chairs. They began questioning her. Where was she on X day? When did she go to Y place? She looked at her interrogators. How did they know where she had been? She answered their questions, realizing that they already knew what she was going to say. Her interrogators were neither rude nor abrasive. They were polite, and why shouldn't they have been? There was nothing she could tell them that would help their investigation. After a few minutes, they even seemed to be feeding her the answers to their questions. None of this lessened her fear— Rasha was scared to death about what was happening and what was going to happen—but the whole drama seemed stupid, scripted, and pro forma, a badly choreographed dance of bureaucracy and dread.

YEARS BEFORE, when she was in Syria and studying in the seventh grade, Rasha learned how to shoot a rifle. It was part of the curriculum in the public girls' school she attended. They had mandatory classes in military history that were taught by a female officer who made them sing patriotic songs and memorize the details of Syria's various military escapades. The regime demanded devotion—All hail Hafez, the lion of Syria—and Rasha had to comply. There she was, a thirteen-year-old girl—awkward, dislocated, going through puberty, and half a world from what she knew—loading and unloading a rifle with a bunch of other girls in a class at school.

Outside class she would repeat to her school friends what she heard about their dear president at home, and they would stare at her with their mouths dropping, and then they would shush her up. "What are you doing?" they would whisper. "No. You never, ever, *ever* say anything about the president!" She would become even more pro-American then, seeing with a teenage girl's perspective what things like freedom of speech, arbitrary detention, and human rights mean. She realized that she took so much for granted. At times like these, she missed her American life.

THAT NIGHT THEY PRAYED as a family in the holding cell at Federal Plaza. Her father led the prayer, and the women covered their hair as best they could. When the authorities came back in the morning, her father pleaded with them. Enough of this, he said. Just deport us. It would be a lot more dignified than having to go to jail, he said. Take us to the airport right now and just put us on a plane. But the FBI man wouldn't hear it. No, he said. We are turning you over to the INS. You have to be investigated, and you will be held in detention meanwhile. Another agent told them in more private tones that they should have expected to be arrested, in times like these, and that they would be deported within three days, but that they would have a better life over there. Rasha glared at him. He was so cavalier, so offhand, she felt. And he sounded like he was lecturing them, telling them with a kind of official nonchalance that we're cleaning out the country and you're the dirt. Right there Rasha's anger toward how immigrants are treated in the United States was sparked. The feelings would deepen.

When the cell door swung open again, the agents told them that they were now being taken to separate facilities. Rasha's father and Munir were being sent to a male prison in Brooklyn. The women would be taken to a women's prison in New Jersey, and Wassim, who was under eighteen years of age, to a juvenile detention center in Pennsylvania. The agents told them to stand up, because they were now going to be shackled and led to different vehicles to transport them to their various locations. This was the most unbearable news, and horror set in that the family really was being split up. Through her own waterlogged eyes, Rasha watched every person in her family collapse in tears.

UNDER ARMED ESCORT, the three women were driven to Bergen County Jail. The van parked in the prison's sally port, and Rasha, her mother, and sister were met by the prison's correctional officers and led in handcuffs from the vehicle where they were strip-searched and photographed before being taken to one of the prison's holding areas. Rasha had barely recovered from the violation of the strip search when she found herself staring at the scene in front of her. The holding cell was filthy, disgusting, and overcrowded. People milled about waiting to hear their cell assignments, and everybody seemed nasty or catatonic. *This is just like prison on television*, Rasha thought, and she was frightened for herself and for her mother. A correctional officer opened the door and told them to get inside. The door locked behind them.

For six hours they were stuck waiting in the holding cell, as if "holding" meant a place where you hold on to (a) family or (b) your sanity. It scared her to the white of her bones, and when they finally heard their names called, the women sighed in relief. But their respite was short-lived. They were merely herded into another holding cell, teeming with even more people, the most crowded place Rasha could imagine, and they would stay there for two days. Rasha broke down and sobbed.

During this time Rasha's mother raged and yelled until she was able to place a call to her brother-in-law about her youngest sons. She looked so relieved to hear that her children were managing, and she related in detail to her brother-in-law how she and the family were being held. Rasha, Reem, and their mother were eventually moved again to a larger space, a wing of the facility, where they were again strip-searched, then given beige jumpsuits and black-and-white Converse shoes, and assigned to cells. Rasha kept thinking about what the INS official had told them at Federal Plaza: that they would be detained for three days tops, then deported. But when they joined the general population, another realization hit her. They were going to be staying for a while.

When Rasha looked at her new address, she saw a huge room with cells lining the wall. Correctional officers stood in a separate area that was elevated, behind glass, and in front of the cells. From their perch they could watch the inmates constantly. Rasha looked at the arrangement and thought, *They keep us like lab rats.* She and Reem were assigned to the same cell: two unhappy beds and a stainless-steel toilet.

They were given blankets, thick, itchy blankets made of some kind of Stone Age material that didn't even seem to bend. It was like sleeping under hairy cardboard.

And they began to live, or at least survive, there. It was so much to deal with, and it had all happened so fast, and Rasha became extremely depressed. Prison was mostly a terrible tedium that promoted an inconsolable apathy. You stopped caring. She would lie on her bed for days on end, thinking about her feelings. She felt demeaned and humbled. She'd had setbacks in the past, but she had never been this sad, this powerless, this misunderstood. She contemplated hurting herself. She considered suicide. She had never felt more human, and she discovered that being human means being vulnerable.

For a while she stopped eating. She would lie on her bed sometimes for two or three days continuously, finally lugging herself out of bed one day when the cell door opened so she could join the others and eat. *Like lab rats,* she thought.

She slowly snapped out of her depression, but she couldn't stop feeling angry. She tried to transform her anger into a life lesson, to believe that God was trying to show her the nature of her humanity. But she felt wronged. Never in her life had she thought that she would end up in jail unless she had committed a crime. So why was she here? For what? Because she had overstayed her visa and was now undocumented? She didn't commit a crime, and she was being punished for someone else's acts. For someone else's crime. She hadn't been convicted. She had been abducted.

This wasn't justice. It was revenge.

She watched her mother become a praying machine.

She began to observe the little things the inmates would do for survival, to keep a sense of autonomy, in whatever small fashion, over their own destiny. One woman would swipe the pint-size milk cartons from her meals and store them in the toilet because they stayed colder that way. When Rasha's mother saw this, she freaked out. "Oh, my God," she told her daughters at a meal one day. "They put milk in the toilet! Why? Why do they put milk in the toilet!"

And Rasha saw her mother slowly begin to mingle with the other inmates, which relieved her as she never expected it would. Her mother shared a cell with another woman, and Rasha, in her cell, was becoming closer to her sister. They had often fought while growing up, but now they were close. The two girls held each other's sanity like a locket, and Rasha felt the life breathing back into her. She and Reem began cracking all kinds of jokes about prison life (jokes that Rasha has since blocked out). They played games with each other. They looked down at their prison-issue jumpsuits and Converse shoes and resolved never to wear Converse shoes again.

Over time they met the rest of the inmates: Pakistani women, Arab women, and other Muslims detained under similar circumstances; Russians and Israelis were also there, usually for immigration reasons; a smaller group of Asians and a much larger population of Latinas and African-American women held mostly on drug-related charges. They found out that the other immigration detainees had been incarcerated for days, weeks, and sometimes months. This discovery was not comforting.

But if the holding area reminded her of TV prison, the prison wing was different. On TV, inmates are constantly in your face, goading you into fights, organizing into gangs, and carving out turf. But at Bergen, Rasha eventually found out that the women were there because of crimes they'd committed just to get on with their lives, to make money, to survive. Petty theft, smuggling, and dealing were their offenses. It didn't matter if the women were serving criminal sentences or were detained for immigration violations. Everyone was incarcerated together. And slowly Rasha and her sister and mother learned that the women in jail, both immigrant and criminal prisoners, were kind with each other. The system had turned all of them into caged specimens, and as a way of defeating it, the inmates shared in a surplus of goodwill for one another. Being treated as beasts grew their humanity to one another. It was how everyone survived.

The situation was different with the correctional officers. They spoke to the inmates as if they were gods and the inmates a subhuman species. Rasha found them ignorant and abusive. They carried their authority like a truncheon. They walked around like Mack trucks shaking the highway, and they steamrolled over you like you were a fly stuck in hot tar. They yelled at you. They ignored you. They terrified you. Here the gods were the beasts.

GABY WAS CONFUSED. Rasha had just disappeared. They had made plans a couple of days ago to hang out after school, but Rasha never showed up. Gaby called her cell phone, but Rasha wasn't picking up. She called

Nicky, and Nicky said the same thing had happened to her. They both called her house, and no one answered there either. They began worrying. Where is Rasha? Where is her family?

Gaby was on her computer one night a few days later when someone instant-messaged her out of nowhere. ARE YOU GABY? the message read. YES, THIS IS GABY, she wrote back, confused. A message popped up on her screen: GIVE ME YOUR PHONE NUMBER. I HAVE TO TALK TO YOU. It was Nada, a friend of Rasha's family. Gaby had met her before, although they weren't close. But Nada knew that Gaby and Rasha were best friends. Through Rasha's uncle, Nada and her family had learned what had happened, and Nada explained the situation to Gaby. "Oh, my God," Gaby said. "But you can't tell anybody," Nada warned. "Don't contact anybody." Gaby agreed, and she hung up the phone. She was so scared for Rasha.

THEY WERE MORE FORTUNATE than many of the post–September 11 detainees. They had an attorney. One of Reem's friends learned about their ordeal and called various legal and community organizations on their behalf. After being incarcerated for two weeks Rasha and her family received their first visit from an attorney affiliated with a local Arab-American association. (Later, a well-known civil-rights attorney took up their case, and one of his associates would visit them regularly and update them on progress.) Meanwhile, they watched attorneys affiliated with the Council on American-Islamic Relations float by the prison, trying to locate others who had been swept up in the mass arrests.

But prison still terrifies. It didn't take Reem long to develop a horrible rash all over her body from those blankets. One night, when everyone was asleep, Reem couldn't take the itch and pain any longer, and she began knocking on the glass. Two officers were talking on the other side, and Reem began pleading with them to come out. "I need to tell you something," she said. "Come out." The glass moved sound only in one direction. The officers could hear her, but she couldn't hear them. One officer looked up, stared at Reem, and motioned for her to go back into the interior of her cell. But Reem wouldn't give up. She kept knocking, louder and louder. "Come here!" she yelled. She opened her jumpsuit to show her rash to the female officers. "Come here!" she yelled again. "I need to show you something right now!"

The officer leaned over and pressed a button. "I'm in the middle of a conversation," she lectured. "You wait till I'm done." But Reem just wouldn't stop banging. "You come out right now!" she yelled frantically. "You come out right now!" She was sobbing. Seeing her older sister desperate for some kind of medical attention, Rasha began crying, too, and later she would thank God that her mother wasn't around to see this, because she was sure it would have given her a heart attack.

The officer finally came out to see Reem and began yelling at her. "What the hell is your problem?" she shouted. Reem was screaming hysterically. "I have a rash! My whole body is red! I need attention!" Rasha watched the officer. She wasn't the least bit sympathetic, she thought. Eventually she made a medical call.

But the incident stayed with Rasha. She couldn't get it out of her head. She kept seeing the officer's reaction replay when she closed her eyes. The only reason she'd made the call was because it was her duty, Rasha thought, because her job told her she had to do something. It was not out of any feeling for Reem's suffering. Not because she, too, was a human being. Beasts acting like gods.

THEY STAYED IN COUNTY JAIL for three weeks, after which they were transferred to a female wing in the Metropolitan Detention Center (MDC) in Brooklyn. This is a federal prison on the outskirts of Sunset Park, a working-class neighborhood of barren warehouses, low-rent town houses, desperately few trees, and crowded immigrant families. The prison is recessed under the Gowanus Expressway and in a bombed-out industrial area hosting strip clubs and a Costco nearby. But it was also the same facility that was holding Rasha's brother and father.

Getting there was the same routine. They collected their belongings, then were shackled and driven under armed guard to Brooklyn. There,

they were again led out of the Bureau of Prisons van, given jumpsuits, photographed, and searched. But, compared to Bergen, MDC was a step upward. The female wing was much cleaner than the New Jersey jail and
arranged more like dormitory living than lab-rat cages. The women were
assigned to a huge room with bunk beds and lockers. The wing had a simple common kitchen, and its architecture facilitated much more opportunity to commune with others. Maybe life was getting better.

The women held at MDC were just as resourceful, especially again with
food. They would collect all the leftover food and find ways preserve it: jerk
the meat, collect the vegetables and store them. When they were given plain
pasta for dinner one night, some of the Asian inmates took over, reaching
for the old vegetables, chopping them up, and mixing them with the pasta
for dinner. Rasha was impressed.

But, just as at Bergen, time at MDC dragged on, and Rasha began to feel
that they were never going to get out, that she wasn't going to see her
friends again, that she was not going to graduate college, get married, and
move on to the next phases of her life. She slowly resigned herself to these
facts. At least if she had committed a crime, she would have stood in front
of a judge and answered the charge against her. If convicted, she would
have been properly sentenced, and then she would know exactly how long
she was to be here. But as a detainee she had no idea when she would be let
out. It was enough to drive her crazy.

What saved both her and her sister from madness was a feeling of responsibility for their mother. The living arrangements allowed the daughters to look out for her. This usually meant standing up for her with the
correctional officers, who often treated Rasha's mother, since she couldn't
communicate in English as easily as her daughters, with impatient con-
tempt. The conflict reached a head one day when Rasha's mother went to
a room assigned to their wing's correctional counselor. A correctional
counselor's job is to assist in the smooth running of the facility, in part by
hearing and assisting inmates' concerns and requests. She asked him to call
her son, who was being held in Pennsylvania.

Rasha didn't like this counselor. He had all the capricious behavior and arbitrary mood swings of a dictator. On some days he would look at you with these large, gentle cat eyes. He would listen to your problems and help you out as he could. Then you'd feel so grateful, as if you owed him more than you would ever be capable of repaying. But most of the time, he was just lecturing and insolent. He would look at Rasha and her family, in their prison jumpsuits, and treat them like the dust hiding under dust. He didn't know the reasons for people's incarceration, and he didn't care anyway. He was always shaking his head at the inmates, telling them they shouldn't expect anything at MDC and that they deserved everything they got. Since they all had done something terrible, they all deserved to be here. That's how he treated Rasha, but she had committed no crime, and she knew she didn't deserve to be there. She hated him.

Rasha's mother had the right to call Wassim in juvenile detention on regular occasions, and she always counted down the days when she would next be able to hear his voice. One day, when it was time, she walked into the counselor's office and asked him to call. For reasons that were unclear to Rasha, he denied her mother's request and summarily dismissed her like a kindergarten child. Rasha's mother walked out of his office believing she would never be able to call her son. She was in tears, and the two girls ran up to their mother to ask her why she was crying. They got the story, and turned their mother around, walking her back into the counselor's room. They started yelling at the counselor, and eventually he relented. Rasha's mother felt so much better, because she got to make the call and talk to her son. But Rasha looked at the counselor and could feel the acid bubbling in her stomach for this man who made her mother cry for no reason.

FOR A WHILE they were the only immigration detainees in their wing of MDC. Everyone else was being held on a criminal charge. Some of them were so young. One baby-faced Latina girl seemed so childlike to Rasha that she felt her heart crack every time she looked at her.

One day a woman was newly deposited in their wing. Rasha later discovered that she had been delivered directly from the airport, even though she and her husband had valid entry visas. The prison authorities had taken her belongings and outfitted her in a standard-issue jumpsuit, and the lady walked in looking like she was already dead, holding a towel wrapped around her head as an impromptu *hijab,* her hand clasping it tightly under her chin. Rasha's mother spotted her. "I think she's Muslim," she whispered to Rasha before going over to the woman. She started to speak to her in English but received only a blank stare. So she tried Arabic, and the woman, who turned out to be Egyptian, exhaled an enormous sigh of relief. Speaking in a flurry of their mother tongue, they both broke down crying.

Rasha's mother also befriended another woman, Dora, a middle-aged Nigerian woman. She was tall and round and spoke a lilting West African English. When she talked, it was as if the words were bouncing like a stone skipping over water. She had half a dozen kids in Nigeria and was now stuck in MDC on drug charges. She was also a born-again Christian, and she had a mission to heal the whole jail and save everyone's soul. She would move from person to person and channel God's good graces to them all. She did it with such sweetness and conviction, though, that you couldn't help but be bowled over by her. She had a lot of faith.

Rasha's mother liked that about her, and Dora was eventually very helpful. Before they had been arrested, Rasha's mother had had surgery scheduled. She was having gallbladder problems, but the incarceration had forced her to miss her appointment. At MDC her gallstones flared up again, painfully. The prison doctor prescribed some painkillers, but they had little effect. To leave the facility for a medical procedure was a bureaucratic nightmare and would take months of wrangling and paperwork. Rasha's mother intensified her own prayers in an effort to help ease her own suffering.

For three nights Dora would visit her. She would come with a cup of water. "I've prayed over this water. Drink it," she would say. Rasha wondered what her mother would do, but in prison, or in any desperate moment in your life, you are going to hang on to anything, she realized. Her mother drank the water, and Dora then gave some to her and her sister. They all drank the water, and for whatever unknown reason the pain subsided. Everyone loved Dora.

Another day a group of women, including the three of them, were sitting around the bottom bunk of one of the beds talking. Suddenly Rasha heard sounds coming from the lockers behind the beds, weird noises, an amorous racket being exchanged between two of the inmates. She turned to her sister, and they realized in a silent look between them what was going on. Their mother was talking to another woman, and they tried to get her attention, to distract her so she wouldn't hear the same thing they did. It would have been altogether too awkward, Rasha thought. "Come on, *Ummi*. It's time to go," Rasha said to her mother. They moved away to another part of the room, saving their mother, they thought, from the shock of prison sexuality. Later, when they were without their mother, they laughed about the whole matter.

And then after about a month at MDC, Rasha received her first piece of mail from Gaby, who had found out from Nada that Rasha had been transferred to MDC and that she could now receive mail. Rasha couldn't believe it. She said it was like Christmas when the mail came! She read Gaby's letter over a hundred times, even though she knew it by heart after seventeen readings. Gaby sent more letters, along with pictures of them when they were in high school. Rasha would cry looking at the pictures. *Damn, what is she trying to do to me? What is she doing to me?* she would think. But it was nice, and she made sure to save each letter like the treasure it was. Rasha, who still has the letters, told me that they gave her "a feeling that I'm being remembered." She added, "You can imagine—well, no, you probably can't imagine—but it was a feeling that somebody knows I'm here."

AS QUICKLY AS THEY WERE TAKEN, they were released. It happened in the first days of May. One morning Rasha heard her name called by one of the correctional officers, then her mother's, and then her sister's. They were told to collect their belongings, because they were free to go. Skeptical but hopeful, Rasha gathered her letters. Once she walked through the metal gate of the women's section with her mother and sister and saw her father and brother waiting for them, she thought, *Oh my God, it really is true. We're finally out!* The entire family was set free at the same time, including Wassim, who was discharged from the juvenile facility in Pennsylvania on the same day. An immigration official was present at their release. He handed Rasha's father some details about an upcoming trial date and the name of their immigration judge. He also looked over their file and remarked, "You know, you have grounds for a residency petition here." No one knew how to balance gratitude with resentment.

An officer was dispatched to accompany Rasha's father as he drove to Pennsylvania to retrieve Wassim. Meanwhile, Rasha's uncle arrived at the facility to take them home. They walked out of prison, and as soon as they were beyond MDC, Rasha fell to the ground and kissed the pavement. She looked up. She hadn't seen sky for almost three months. It was the same sky, and it looked glorious and familiar.

They entered their own house like strangers, which was creepy. Everything was just as they had left it, except that the food in the fridge had turned moldy and dust had snowed over the furniture. Her uncle had also brought her two youngest brothers with him, along with some groceries, and when her father arrived a few hours later with Wassim, the family was quietly reunited. Rasha felt numb and dislocated. It was hard to believe that the nightmare was over. She watched Munir disappear downstairs and heard him calling his friends, and then she too began plotting about how she would surprise Gaby and Nicky and the rest of her friends with the news that she was free. She was free! Surprising them became the only thing to look forward to at that moment. She didn't want to think about the past. She found that she could think only in one direction, to the future.

The family had a quiet night. Rasha's mother went to the kitchen and cooked a simple meal. They ate dinner together, and over the meal Rasha and her siblings exchanged a few stories about their experiences. Her parents were mostly quiet, and then everyone went to bed early.

THE NEXT MORNING Gaby ran into some of Munir's friends on her way to college, and they told her that Rasha's family was finally home.

"You're lying," she told them, "you're lying!" No, it's true, they said. Munir called us yesterday, they explained, and Gaby turned hopeful and then totally excited by the news. She pulled out her phone and called Nicky. "Nicky, Rasha's back!" she screamed into her cell, and Nicky, who was going up the escalator at her Manhattan college when she heard Gaby's news, couldn't believe it either. She froze at the top of the stairs, and the people behind her bumped into her like groceries on a faulty checkout belt. They began yelling at her to move out of the way while she stood absolutely still, absorbing what she'd just heard.

Gaby hung up the phone but was so overwhelmed with the anticipation of seeing Rasha that she couldn't wait for Nicky. So she blew off her first class and beelined for the house. But then it struck her: "I can't go empty handed!" She made a pit stop at a corner store and quickly scanned around for a gift. Outside the front door of the store was a potted plant for sale. She grabbed it and, trucking the plant in her arms, hustled her way to Rasha's house.

The sound of the doorbell was bizarre to Rasha. *Who the hell is that at 10:00 A.M.?* she thought. In her pajamas Rasha opened the door, and standing there behind a pot full of leaves and flowers was Gaby. She was already crying hysterically. And as soon as she saw Gaby, Rasha burst into tears.

"Oh, man!" Rasha stomped her foot. "The surprise is ruined! I wanted to surprise you!"

They hugged forever.

"I'm sorry," Gaby said, sniffing between her tears. "I didn't call first! I'm so sorry!"

"Get in here," Rasha reprimanded, but the two girls stayed where they were. They just couldn't stop hugging each other and crying.

RASHA'S PARENTS SOLD THE HOUSE. They were behind in the payments, and Rasha's mother was convinced that the place was cursed anyway. Rasha also had to deal with the row of F's on her transcript. Having disappeared from the world for three months, she naturally failed all her classes. She went to speak to her dean and calmly explained her situation.

He listened sympathetically, said he was very sorry for what had happened to her, but then asked if she could provide some documentation to prove what she'd just told him. "What kind of sick person would tell you that she'd spent three months in jail to get excused from her grades?" she asked. "You'd be surprised," he said.

Rasha learned that her sister's classmates had organized around the family's case. Over two hundred people from the school had signed a petition on her behalf, and the president of the university wrote a letter to the INS supporting the family.

Right after her release, Rasha felt freer than she ever had in her life. Normal things like hanging out in Times Square or riding the subway had never been so exciting to her. But everywhere around her was the constant spit of all the 9/11 talk. She bit her tongue repeatedly, and the anger inside her would boil. She now had her own analysis about the way the country is run, and she had proof about the way people are treated. She wanted to scream at people, "You don't know what you're talking about unless you've been in a situation like the one I've been in!" But she didn't say anything. She knew that it was a contradiction, but she felt both stronger and totally drained simultaneously. She thought she had aged ten years in three months.

Her family never really addressed the trauma they had undergone. No one spoke openly about it, and Munir in particular seemed deeply injured. Neither he nor their father told the women very much about MDC's male wing, where later the government's own internal auditor would expose violent abuses that some of the post–September 11 detainees endured. Right after their release, Munir was joyous and full of life. He began praying regularly, five times a day, and was talkative and communicative. That lasted for about a month, and then he began retreating into silence. He became a distant island, hard to reach.

Her mother continued to pray, and her father quit smoking, only to start up again after a bit. Rasha felt so close to and so distant from her family all the time. The closeness came from having emerged on the other side of such an experience. The distance was the inability of anybody to confront it. Only her sister sought outside help by going to a therapist for a while. Rasha put her energies into her future.

She started thinking about all the lawyers and activists who had helped them, and she realized that she had to do something to help others in similar situations. Her interest in international relations and human rights grew, and eventually Rasha interned with a United Nations–affiliated organization on Middle East peace. She was also nominated by her university to be a delegate scholar at an international conference on diplomacy. It was a huge honor, but one she had to turn down. Rasha was still undocumented, so, until her immigration status was resolved, she could not leave the country.

And so she told me, "If there's anything that I've discovered out of this whole thing, it's that people take for granted being a citizen of this country. They don't see the importance of having a privilege like that. I've been in this country for eighteen years, and I'm working hard, and I'm qualified, but I've missed all these opportunities. I feel like it should be a lot easier than this. It's not fun. It's not fun at all."

RASHA WAS ONE of the lucky ones. She had family, both inside and outside prison, supporting her. She may have disappeared from her friends for a while, but she hadn't dropped off the face of the earth. The family had an attorney, friends and relatives, and a growing chorus of advocates demanding their release. That wasn't the case with most of the post–September 11 detainees. Hundreds were arbitrarily arrested in the first months after the terrorist attacks. One man, a Palestinian legal permanent resident, was stopped for driving four miles over the speed limit in North Carolina. He then spent four months in jail. Many of the men—and they were overwhelmingly men—were denied access to counsel, secretly shuffled between facilities, and deported in midnight planes back to their home countries, sometimes without having their families in the United States notified and, in at least one reported case, without even his own clothes.

Human-rights organizations watched with horror as the situation unfolded and then took action. Around the same time that Rasha was freed, in May 2002, Amnesty International released a report that charged the U.S. government with violating "certain basic rights guaranteed under international law. These include the right to humane treatment, as well as rights which are essential to protection from arbitrary detention, such as the right of anyone deprived of their liberty to be informed of the reasons for the detention; to be able to challenge the lawfulness of the detention; to have prompt access to and assistance from a lawyer; and to the presumption of innocence."

By 2003 the Office of the Inspector General (OIG) of the Justice Department completed its own investigation and, in a report of more than two hundred pages, reiterated many of the concerns held by Amnesty International. The OIG recommended, among other things, that the FBI should adopt "more objective criteria . . . in future cases involving mass arrests." Religion and ethnicity, in other words, should not be sufficient grounds for incarceration. The OIG also recommended that future arrests "might require some level of evidence linking the alien to the crime or issues in question." A bold proposal indeed.

The OIG's reports (a supplementary one came later) also corroborated recurring allegations of abuse, particularly of male detainees at MDC. September 11 detainees, the OIG found, were "slammed," "bounced," and "pressed" against the walls of the prison, even though they were compliant. This often happened in the sally port that had taped to its wall a bloody T-shirt embossed with a U.S. flag and the words THESE COLORS DON'T RUN. Twisting a detainee's arms behind his back was routine, as was pulling back his thumbs and bending his wrists forward toward his arms, a practice common enough to be known as "goosenecking." Guards yanked men by their restraints and purposefully tripped them by stepping on their chains as they walked. Detainees' meetings with their attorneys were videotaped, and the men were routinely and randomly strip-searched in efforts to humiliate and punish them. If this sounds like a milder form of the infamous actions performed by American military forces in Iraq, perhaps the resemblance is not merely coincidental. Sergeant Gary Pittman, a marine convicted of brutalizing Iraqi prisoners, had been a guard at MDC, and he reportedly advised a fellow marine that when dealing with Iraqi detainees "you have to establish who is in charge," also telling him that Iraqi prisoners need to be treated the same way as prisoners in New York.

Rasha wouldn't tell me if any physical abuse befell her eldest brother or father, just that they were mostly silent about their experiences after the family was reunited. But by the time they were detained, most of the first wave of people who were arrested had already been deported. We may never know how many were arrested. (On November 5, 2001, the Justice Department announced 1,182 arrested, then stopped providing a tally.) The inspector general's report acknowledges 762 people detained on immigration charges between September 11, 2001, and August 6, 2002, as a direct result of the terrorist investigation (including 24 already in prison before September 11). It also says that of these 762 only 6 percent had received a final deportation order prior to their arrests.

In other words, people were picked up randomly, through traffic stops, or tips by nervous neighbors and "snitches," usually petty criminals offered leniency for any information that would push the September 11 investigation forward. (Such information is often wildly unreliable, and Rasha suspects a snitch in her case.) Prior to September 11, immigration authorities could hold people for only twenty-four hours before charging or releasing them, but by September 20, 2001, Attorney General John Ashcroft had changed the rule to forty-eight hours, with an emergency exception for an unspecified "reasonable" amount of time. Most people detained didn't fight their deportations (which is not surprising, considering the stories coming out of MDC). They should have been deported before the legal limit of thirty days, but they continued to be held long after, because the government would not free them before completing an FBI clearance. The FBI cleared only 2.6 percent of detainees within three weeks. Some languished for hundreds of days in prison. The average length of detention for a post–September 11 detainee was eighty days, about the amount of time Rasha spent in Bergen and MDC.

In 1941, immediately following the attack on Pearl Harbor, a similar hysteria burned through this country. The FBI swept through the Japanese-American community on the West Coast, as a lead-up to Japanese internment, arresting more than two thousand noncitizens. Those detained included community leaders, language teachers, and Buddhist priests. Edward Ennis, the general counsel of the INS, complained at the time that "the FBI was turning many aliens over to the INS without a written statement showing good cause for detention." Herbert Nicholson, pastor of the West Los Angeles Methodist Church, objected that the arrests were arbitrary. Law enforcement "picked up anybody that was the head of anything," he said. And Assistant Attorney General James Rowe Jr. later admitted that "we picked up too many. . . . Some of this stuff they were charged on was as silly as hell." After these arrests the government proceeded to detain over 110,000 people, 70,000 of them American citizens, on the basis of ancestry alone, in internment camps that, in the case of the one at Tule Lake, didn't close until eight months after Japanese surrender. In 1988, President George H. W. Bush formally apologized for Japanese internment.

Fortunately, post–September 11 detentions nowhere approximated the scale and suffering of Japanese internment, but the comparison of politically motivated mass arrests should be drawn. Historians of Japanese internment frequently point out that the Roosevelt administration's choice to intern the West Coast Japanese and Japanese Americans was not driven by military necessity. The administration's own intelligence often confirmed that the community as a whole was not at all a threat to national security. But rather than following the course of justice, the administration exploited the jingoism and racism of the moment. Something similar had happened now. Colleen Rowley, the whistle-blower FBI agent who criticized the Bureau for its pre–September 11 lapses, acknowledged the political and ethnic nature of the post–September 11 sweep in a public letter to the FBI director in March 2003. "After 9/11," she wrote,

*headquarters encouraged more and more detentions for what seem to
be essentially PR purposes. Field offices were required to report daily
the number of detentions in order to supply grist for statements on our
progress in fighting terrorism. The balance between individuals' civil
liberties and the need for effective investigation is hard to maintain
even during so-called normal times, let alone times of increased terrorist
threat or war. It is, admittedly, a difficult balancing act. But from what
I have observed, particular vigilance may be required to head off undue
pressure (including subtle encouragement) to detain or "round up"
suspects—particularly those of Arabic origin.*

I traveled to New Jersey one afternoon to talk to Sohail Mohammed, an
attorney who represented thirty-eight September 11 detainees. He told me
about the difficulties he had reaching clients, talking to judges, and dealing
with the new category of "special interest" detainees created in the wake of
the terrorist attacks. "This is not law enforcement. It's random enforcement. It's capricious and copious," he said. He described how a detention
policy based not on credible leads but on ethnicity or religion provides, at
best, a false sense of security. "I want my children to believe in America,"
he told me. "What do I tell them? That everyone should be treated equally
under the law, but Muslims aren't?" And he offered his own prediction. "In
fifty years," he said, "Congress will apologize."

AFTER THE INITIAL WAVE of arrests, the Bush administration announced a new program, the "absconder apprehension initiative." The administration claimed that it was going after the 314,000 people in the
United States who had "absconded" after having been served deportation
notices, and it began by prioritizing Arab and Muslim absconders. Besides
questions about the selective enforcement of such a program and the fact
that it broke up many families, another problem quickly became apparent.
Many arrested under this initiative either didn't know they had been served

final deportation orders (which can be decided in absentia) or were not "absconders" at all, living out in the open and in full knowledge of the authorities but with appeals pending in their cases (such was the case with Rasha's family). Immigration appeals, with the current backlog of cases, often drag on for five years or more, yet under this program people were often taken into custody regardless.

But immigration law, in the words of law professor David Cole, "affords a convenient pretext for targeting millions of people." Just because the government has "charged a foreign national as deportable," Cole explains, "does not generally authorize his detention, unless the individual poses a danger to the community or risk of flight." But, as with most of the post–September 11 detainees, the administration exploited an already flawed system of immigration detention, one that exists largely out of public view, with the absconder initiative. This way the government could claim success by appearing zealous and "tough on terror," but by using immigration detention as a political tool it was also effectively "blurring the distinction between alien, criminal, and terrorist," as Mark Dow has shown in *American Gulag: Inside U.S. Immigration Prisons.* Dow reveals how immigration detention has exploded in recent years. Since 1996, the year Congress mandated the detention of immigrants who had committed aggravated felonies even after they have served their sentences, the number of people in immigration detention has risen dramatically. In 1995 approximately 5,500 people were held on any given day for immigration reasons. By 2006 the number was over 27,000. The federal government, moreover, doesn't have the resources to house all these people, so they often contract out beds to county jails, such as the Bergen County Jail, which holds about a hundred immigrant detainees at a day rate of $85, raking in a total of more than $3 million annually. Besides being politically expedient, immigration detention is also a growing and lucrative industry.

But what this system means is that you can languish in prison for a long time without ever having committed a crime. And this is what angers Rasha more than anything else. Her liberty was taken away from her for no good reason. She hadn't hurt anyone but was treated like a criminal, and she experienced firsthand the manner in which people in prison are treated. She felt powerless to change her situation and utterly unable to challenge her accusers. And when the presumption of guilt was summarily dumped on her, she felt stripped of her dignity.

Now she realizes the importance of speaking out, of correcting the ills that befell her and continue to befall others, and of being able to talk back to a system orchestrated to pacify you. She wants to grow from her experience and is preparing to pursue graduate work in international relations with a program affiliated with the United Nations. She is ready to dedicate her life to human-rights advocacy, because she believes that the only chance for improving our world lies in greater international cooperation and universal respect for human rights. She wants to move forward in her life. And after living through her ordeal, she believes that it is crucial not to obsess about the past but to look constructively to the future. Nevertheless, Rasha will never allow herself to forget what happened to her and her family.

IT WAS THE FIRST weekend after getting out. Rasha went with her girlfriends to Times Square to celebrate her release. That Saturday they went for dinner at Chili's. Gaby was there, and Nicky, too, and a couple of Rasha's other close friends. They sat a big table, and Rasha savored the freedom of ordering food from a menu.

Halfway through dinner she got up to go to the bathroom. When she was coming back to her table, she froze in shock. *It was him. All the restaurants in New York City, and he's at this one.* There, at another big table, was the counselor from MDC, the very same man who constantly talked down to her and her sister, who treated them like criminals and criminals like animals. The man who'd made her mother cry.

She stood there for a while just watching him. He was with his family, at what appeared to be someone's birthday party. A woman—she looked to be his wife—was beside him, and his children around him, along with several other people. Everyone was standing up at his table, pleasantly socializing.

Rasha stood there and waited. She knew what she had to do, but she didn't want his children around. A couple of minutes later, they were off playing with some kids at the other end of the table, and Rasha strode quickly over.

She tapped his back with her finger. "Hi," she said. Her voice was ball-bearing steady.

He turned around. "Hi," he replied. But there wasn't a hint in his voice that he knew who Rasha was.

"You don't recognize me?" All the scenes when he'd yelled at her, when he'd made her cry, when he'd made her mother cry, flashed in her mind. And yet he didn't say anything. His expression remained changeless. "Remember?" she said, her voice turning up. "MDC? You don't remember me?"

And suddenly she realized, *Of course he doesn't remember me. I'm not in a beige jumpsuit.*

But then he responded. "Ah, wow," he said. "See? You cleaned up your act."

Rasha stared into his eyes. "You know," she said, inhaling deeply, "I wasn't supposed to be there in the first place." She then lectured him about how he should have known that and that he "needed to learn a thing or two about respecting others." She could feel her chest rising the whole time. She ended by telling him, "You are a fucking asshole, and you will always be a fucking asshole." And before he could respond, she twirled deliberately and walked back to her table with a stiff spine and an anxious but triumphal smile growing on her face.

She ran the last steps and was out of breath when she got to her friends. She told them what had happened. "You won't believe who I just saw!" she yelled. She explained who he was and what she'd said. "It was such a satisfying moment," she told them, her voice sounding all brassy, like a trumpet blowing victory. "I would have punched him," she joked, "but he's like seven feet tall!" They all laughed, and Rasha was ecstatic. She couldn't wait to tell her parents. She knew it didn't really change anything, but it didn't matter. It just didn't matter. It was such a satisfying moment. Confronting your jailer. On this side of freedom. Such a satisfying moment.

SAMI

Where elements touch and merge,
where shadows swoon like outcasts on the sand
and the tried moment waits, its courage gone—
there were we

in latitudes where storms are born.

—ARNA BONTEMPS, "Reconnaissance"

In January 2006 and after a four-year absence, Sami—a door-size man with soft eyes, a cliff for a nose, and shoulders the mass of Rhode Island—was finally going back to college. For the last six months, he had been living in his parents' house and surviving on unemployment. The days were slow and the money meager, though he had managed to squeeze in a few side trips with Ana, his girlfriend, and was basically enjoying himself. But he knew that this period in his life was cresting to an end. Now was the time to start some serious planning for the future. He was already twenty-four years old, after all. What he needed was a career.

So Sami enrolled in a sports-management program at a local private university. It's the kind of place that has well-dressed students strolling around green lawns with flat hedges and century-old trees. But instead of the luster of autumnal golds and reds that greet most new students, Sami saw the campus as gray and cold. He had arrived in January, and the leaves had abandoned their trees long before.

When he showed up on campus, the other students were returning from winter break, and he would see them congregating in small groups, sitting down on benches, laughing loudly into cell phones, or hanging out in vestibules with their cigarettes. The air was cold enough to disguise smoke in breath. Sami knew no one here, so on most days he would come and go without much conversation. But he was always smiling regardless, a huge, real, and athletic grin. Sami was fundamentally happy to be in school again. The world—not just school, but the whole world—seemed open and exciting and full of possibility.

One day, after classes had barely begun for the semester, Sami was walking down one of the paths. Out of nowhere he heard two young women calling out to him from a distance. "Yusef! Mohammad!" they yelled, looking right at him. "Yusef!" one called out again. "Mohammad!" the other repeated, and they waved their hands madly in his direction. He looked behind reflexively, but no one was there. Confused, he shrugged them off, figuring they had the wrong guy, and continued walking. It must be a case of mistaken identity, he surmised.

And then, a few days later, he passed them again. There they were, all flowing dark hair and liquid eyes, and so he stopped to talk to them, especially since they were cute, vocal, and charmingly aggressive. He asked them why they were yelling out to him the other day. "We were wondering if you are Arab," one of them replied, smiling straight at him. They were Palestinian from Brooklyn, like him, and they invited him to come to the next meeting of the Arab Students Club.

Sami was surprised. He wasn't accustomed to people identifying him as Arab-American. "Are you Spanish?" is the question he hears most of the time. His Sunset Park high school was populated mostly with Puerto Ricans, Dominicans, and African Americans. All his girlfriends have been Latinas. He's darker-skinned than the rest of his family, to the point that even his father will joke with him by asking, "Are you sure you are part of this family?"

Nor did he particularly identify with his Arab background. Sami's parents are Arab Christians; his Egyptian mother, a waitress at a local diner, came to New York from Cairo in 1974, and his septuagenarian father, a Palestinian from Haifa, arrived in Brooklyn in 1949, mere months after the establishment of the state of Israel, what Palestinians refer to as the *nakba,* "the catastrophe." But that was a long time ago, and his father—a retired cabdriver who owns his own medallion, the official and coveted permit assigned to each taxi by the city, and a brownstone in Park Slope, Brooklyn—doesn't talk about it much. Sami, too, is not particularly political, especially when it comes to the upheavals of the Arab region. He sums up the paroxysms of the Middle East with commonsense talk. "There will never be peace over there while there's tension even between the Arabs," he told me with Christian detachment one spring afternoon. He's a Brooklynite through and through. He spends his days at school and most nights working two jobs: as a security guard at a gym and as a car-service driver, what he jokingly refers to as "a stereotypical Arab job." But lately his circumstances kept bringing him back to the importance of his Arab roots.

So he decided to go to the campus meeting. There he met the other Arab students at his college and began hanging out with them, partly from the ethnic tribalism that pervades much of higher education (and American society at large) and partly in a search for new friends. He's naturally affable, so he got along with everyone immediately, even if most were several years his junior. But after a while, he was finding himself getting into heated arguments with some of the guys, disputes specifically over the war in Iraq and the American military presence there. The quarrels could often become heated, and they would frustrate Sami. But still he would continue to return to the club. It was as if he were looking for something and escaping it at the same time.

"I'm like the most far-off Arab you'll find," he complained to me one day when talking about his relationship with some of the guys in the club. We were sitting in the backyard of a Starbucks in Park Slope. "You have to be a Muslim to be an Arab. You have to listen to Arabic music all the time to be Arab. You have to be in love with going wherever your parents are from. You have to marry an Arabic girl to be Arab. Certain things. You're not a real Arab if you're like me. I don't listen to Arabic music. I don't watch Arabic programming. I hate going to Egypt. I hate going overseas. I date a Puerto Rican female."

Is blood thicker than water? This is the question swirling around Sami.

But his disagreements with the others are less theoretical in character. Rather, they hang like talismans around his neck. When I asked him about these verbal sparrings, he reached under his collar and pulled out his dog tags. "I chill with a lot of Arab guys now, and they hate these!" he said, looking right through me. "They ask me how many Iraqis did I kill, how could I fight in this war." (One of the guys from his university told me, "There are two people whose bodies I will not pray over: Yasir Arafat and that soldier.") Sami doesn't care much for the criticism. He thinks most of it is armchair politics, misplaced and misinformed. He's been to Iraq, and they haven't. He didn't kill anyone, didn't see much direct combat, and now he is strongly critical of the war but solidly behind the troops. Yet Sami is still something quite rare in the United States today. He's an Arab-American soldier, an accidental fighter–turned–proud marine who has been away from his formal education for four years because he has served two tours in Iraq.

THREE YEARS AGO everything was different. In March 2003, Sami was in Kuwait with the Radio Sector of the Headquarters Battalion of the First Marine Division. Like everybody else with him, he was waiting for the order to cross the berm and begin the invasion of Iraq. Also like everyone else, he was full of both dread and desire for the order. The anticipation was making all of them restless, but war—real war, where people lose limbs and die—also scared the crap out of the twenty-year-old and most of his friends, too, even if no one said as much.

They had been in Kuwait since the middle of February, having flown there from their base in Camp Pendleton, California, but everyone had known for months that they were going to war. What they didn't know was when. Now in Kuwait for more than a month, they were stuck waiting in the desert.

When they'd first arrived, all they did in Kuwait was train, then train some more, then train again while they waited. Sami set up radio networks, then took down radio networks. He did drills in the desert. He maintained his equipment. He cleaned his equipment again. He inventoried his equipment, then cleaned the equipment once more. Cleaning was not just a means of distraction. Everything was getting battered constantly by the sand.

For the first month, it seemed as though the enemy were not Saddam Hussein but simply the sand. It was everywhere. Like an omen, a huge sandstorm struck them on their first day in Kuwait, turning the whole world beige. But even after the storm ended, the sand continued to be brutal. Even on normal days, it would hit them in the eyes, which would get all crusty. It would land on their lips, which would dry out immediately. It always blew into their mouths, so all they tasted was sand all the time. It was as if the sand were playing them in a divine game of Rock, Paper, Scissors, but in this version sand trumps everything. Sand defeats water. Sand kills fire. Sand smothers man and all his measly weapons.

They learned eventually to seek refuge from the menace when and where they could. The backs of trucks, like covered wagons, were favored spots in the Kuwaiti desert, and there, during their off-hours, the soldiers spoke to each about their feelings while they traded stories. It was at this time that word got around the division that Sami spoke Arabic. He had tried to use this fact to his advantage Stateside, but he'd failed miserably. Since then he'd told a few other people in the military about his background and language skills, something most people didn't realize at first. They, too, had assumed that he was Latino. But when his Arab roots appeared, the comments came rushing out. He became "al-Qaeda" and "sand nigger." The names just slid off his back. (This was the marines, after all, where profanity is elevated beyond sport to art.) Most people continued to consider him mostly a New Yorker, and Dan, a Puerto Rican from Florida and his closest friend in the service, had long before branded him simply "New York." That was the name that eventually stuck with Sami, but his Arabic language ability was about to come in handy.

One day in Kuwait, while they were waiting to invade Iraq, he was called to the tent of the commanding officer, a major who would become a father figure to the young marine. Several other lower-ranking officers were there. They, too, knew that Sami spoke Arabic, and the officers told him straightforwardly that they didn't want to send him away to become an interpreter. That was a common course of action with Arabic-speaking soldiers, but the officers had decided they wanted to keep him close by. They were assigning him to become the major's driver, they said. The major wanted a driver who knew the local language and customs, he was told, in case something happened. *Hey, this is great!* Sami thought. Weeks later, and only when they crossed the border, did Sami realize what this really meant. He would be riding at the very front of his company, at the head of the cavalry and first in the line of fire.

But after a month, Kuwait had become a bore, a monotony of bad food and no showers. Then, on the night of March 20, the entire company was assembled. They were told that the operation into Iraq would begin the next morning. They were regaled with stories about how vicious the Iraqis were. They were reminded that "the enemy will do everything in his power to kill you." No one questioned the mission, including Sami. The attacks of September 11, eighteen months earlier, were still fresh in everybody's memory and continued to smart like a collective wound. It didn't matter that this was Iraq and not Afghanistan, Saddam Hussein and not Osama bin Laden. Tomorrow, everyone agreed, there would be payback. Sami, too, felt this way. The president had told them to go, and he was their commander in chief, which meant that he was always correct by virtue of rank. "Do what you have to do!" they were told. "And let's do this like marines!"

Everybody screamed. Their blood rushed with excitement, and Sami, too, was pumped. But, even more, he was scared. They were told to point all the vehicles of the company facing north so that tomorrow they could be ready to ride across the border, and then they were sent off to get some sleep. But no one slept. Who could, knowing that tomorrow there would be war? Sami and Dan and a handful of others slipped into the back of one of the trucks, where they smoked cigarettes and talked deep into the night. The conversations covered everything—favorite and missed foods, current girlfriends and past lovers, getting paid and spending money—everything but what was going to happen the next morning. No one wanted to say a word about that.

Around five in the morning, one of the first air campaigns of the war began, and they watched the bombing of Safwan Hill from inside the truck. They put on their night-vision goggles and peered out the back, as munitions lit up the desert sky into fireballs of red and orange. They roared. "They were unloading on that mountain," Sami told me, "and we were cheering like it was the Fourth of July. I'm thinking, Jesus, what are we about to do to these people? I wrote a letter to my dad the next day: 'Dad, they're about to murder everybody in this place.'"

SAMI WAS BORN in Bellevue Hospital in 1982. He grew up in Park Slope, Brooklyn, now a family-oriented neighborhood full of progressive politics and multimillion-dollar real estate. It hosts cafés, bookstores, organic-food stores, and handmade-jewelry stands. (Sami's father bought into the area before it went bourgeois.) Sami went to high school in a crumbling Gothic structure just beyond Sunset Park before he attended Baruch College, a vertical university in Manhattan, for a year on a baseball scholarship, where he was a catcher. At Baruch he studied finance, but his first stab at college was uninspiring. He felt lost. School was easy, he said, so easy that he could manage without even going to class. But his grades suffered from his own self-confessed indolence.

By the spring of 2001, after the school year had ended, Sami felt empty. He found himself thinking about how he hadn't achieved anything and how, on the weekends, he was still asking his mother for money to go out. "Is this how it's going to be?" he would ask himself, referring to college. "Like glorified high school?"

That summer a marine recruiter called him at home. The recruiter had his number from two of Sami's high-school friends who'd recently enlisted. This is one way that the U.S. armed forces fills its ranks, through a network that is essentially a big chain letter. The call caught Sami completely off guard, but it also intrigued him. The man was a professional and could sell the rust off an old bathtub. He talked a lot and promised Sami job skills, money for school, and travel around the world. "I wanted to see something else," Sami told me, bored with life at his parents' house. He didn't tell his parents that he was being courted in a well-worn and well-scripted romance. Sami would go and talk to the man in his spare time. He was constantly flattered and promised the moon. He would ask about joining the reserves, as a part-timer, and the recruiter assured him that that would be just fine. Whatever Sami wanted, he could have.

And Sami had what he later characterized as his "moment of insanity." He decided to throw caution and college to the wind and just sign the contract, on his own, without consulting his parents and without thinking hard about what he was getting himself into. When he sat down at the recruiting station on Fulton Street, he read through the papers while the recruiter kept on showing him where to sign. The man had listed Sami as an active-duty soldier, four years of service and four years of inactive duty, and Sami stopped and asked him why. The recruiter smiled. "Look, let's just list you as active duty," he says. "You can change down to reserves anytime you want." That, it turns out, wasn't true.

Later that evening he told his parents. "I joined the marines," he said after dinner, and his mother blew up. "What! Why?" she screamed, before she started crying. His father sat back stoically. "Good," he said. "It'll teach you how to be a man." But a week later, Sami started having his own doubts. He called his recruiter. "Let me get out of it," he said. "You can't," the recruiter lied to him. (In fact, Sami told me, he could have left, since he still had to sign a second set of contracts at basic training. Until then the military had spent virtually no effort on him, and he would have been able to walk away from his contract without much of a penalty. But, he explained, recruiters routinely draw verbal pictures of stockades and jail to frighten gullible neophytes.) He went back to his father and asked him what he should do. The two of them sat down in their living room, and his father put an end to the speculation. "A man finishes what he started," he said.

It wasn't the facts of war that scared Sami. It was simply that he wasn't going to be living at home for the first time in his life, that he was entering an unfamiliar world, and, as he put it to me, "the unknown is always scary."

He was a teenager, and it was May 2001. To him, the military was about joining a brotherhood, about going through some kind of hellish training, but then there was still some kind of reward: You got to meet foreign girls. What it was barely about was fighting an actual war. Who in his right mind would dare to enter a war with the United States anyway?

On May 28, 2001, Sami boarded a bus for Parris Island, South Carolina, where he was enrolled in boot camp. On that same day, the *New York Times* ran front-page stories about the spread of HIV in China and the declining popularity of manual-transmission cars. The business section boasted a story about how Rosie O'Donnell had made the bold decision to pose without lipstick and in a hospital gown for the cover of her own magazine. May 28 was also Memorial Day, requiring an obligatory editorial in the paper that recalled how, when the United States had entered World War II, "the nation suddenly gleamed with purpose larger than self, larger, somehow, even than peace." Less than four months before the United States was attacked, war stories were well-meant nostalgia, a gray-haired man dressed an ill-fitting suit weighted down with polished brass medals that were now more than fifty years old.

IN BOOT CAMP Sami was formally introduced to the culture of the marines. He met the other new recruits, a lot of young men like himself. "There are some crazy psycho guys" in the Marine Corps, he told me, but that's a tiny percentage. The rest of the Corps is made up of a lot of people "who join because they don't know what they're doing. They're just here because they made a stupid mistake, or because they have a family that they want to provide for, or because they have to do it out of necessity." A large number, in other words, are people who sign up because they are essentially, in his word, "lost."

What the Corps is not like is *Jarhead,* he told me. When I met Sami for the first time in 2006, the film version of *Jarhead* had just been released on video. He told me he was unhappy with the movie, convinced that yet again the marines were being stereotyped as people who have to kill to live. *Full*

Metal Jacket, he volunteered, was a much better film. I had thought that both films shared quite a bit: a grueling basic training that verged on the absurd; a theater of war that was confusing if not ridiculous, at least from an individual soldier's perspective; a likable and intelligent protagonist who is the straight man to the bizarre reaches of military sociology; sentimental camaraderie.

But it was *Full Metal Jacket*'s now legendary depiction of basic training that was scrupulously accurate, Sami said, and that's why he loves the film. As did the recruits in Kubrick's film, Sami trained on Parris Island. And just like the one in the movie, his receiving drill instructor was ruthless. "I didn't want him to kill me!" Sami said. The sergeant was intimidation personified. When the recruits were standing in formation one day, Sami pissed his pants just because he was afraid to tell the drill instructor that he had to use the bathroom.

Boot camp is "the hardest thing you could ever do," according to Sami. Each day left you physically and mentally exhausted. Letters from family become sweet moments of reprieve. The experience was tough enough that he entertained thoughts again of quitting the service, but he was afraid of going to jail, and his superiors made sure to let him and the other recruits know that that is where they would land if they packed up and left. To survive boot camp, he made friends with a group of guys who would be with him for the next four years. He was closest to Dan, his bunkmate. And by the end of boot camp, his time had gone exactly according to the Marine Corps program: He had grown into believing that he could complete anything he set his mind to. He had learned how to plan, execute, and evaluate. He had gained an inner confidence that he'd never had before. And he lost thirty-five pounds.

By the very end of August, he had earned a ten-day vacation before he needed to report back for duty. He went home and enjoyed his time off by doing nothing. Then, reporting for duty, he boarded an overnight bus to Camp Lejeune in North Carolina for his marine combat training.

The bus pulled out of New York City late at night on September 10, 2001.

IT WAS AROUND 10:00 A.M. on September 11 when the bus coasted
into a rest stop on the way down to North Carolina. The driver hopped out
quickly to use the bathroom, and when he came back, he turned around
with dread on his face and told the recruits that the World Trade Center
had just been hit by two planes. *That's not funny,* Sami thought. His
thoughts zoomed to the attacks of 1993 and how people had died then. He
walked up the aisle to the driver and told him that this wasn't something to
joke about. "No, I'm being serious," the driver said soberly, staring at the
road. "The World Trade Center's been hit." Sami was confused and said
nothing else. He went back to his seat, and while everyone else began buzzing with talk, he slouched in his chair, thinking about his family.

As soon as they arrived at Camp Lejeune, Sami ran to use the phone. All
he got was a busy signal droning in his ear. He was frustrated, but he had
no choice except to keep trying during the free time in his training schedule. He went through processing and a week of combat training without
being able to contact his family. One day, in the middle of one of his classes,
a drill instructor screamed out his name, and drill instructors, as Sami told
me, never call you in for something good. He went running. It was his recruiter on the phone.

"Sami, your mom has been driving me crazy!" the recruiter complained.
His mother was standing like a drill instructor herself over the recruiter's
desk on Fulton Street. He handed her the phone.

"I'm fine, Mom," Sami said to her questions. "How are you? How's
everyone?"

Everybody in his family was all right, but everyone—in the family, in
the military, in the world—also knew what the attacks meant. The training
at Camp Lejeune is normally physically demanding, but that wasn't the
half of it now. The atmosphere had immediately intensified as the soldiers
were learning battlefield skills that they and their teachers now expected
them to be using in short order. What everyone understood was the inevi-
tability of war, and the new soldiers all paid very close attention.

Sami was at Camp Lejeune from September 11 to September 24, 2001, and during that period he avoided all television. He simply refused to watch the news, the reports on the attacks, the depictions of the carnage, the latest developments. When the rest of the marines would head to the television room after hours, he would go to the basketball court instead and shoot hoops by himself. He chose not to see it, he said, not because of his Arab heritage and the complications that could possibly create, but out of his New York pride. He couldn't bear to see his city wounded like that, he said.

But he felt destroyed regardless and afraid about the future, and for the first time in his life he started talking to God. He'd never been religious, but now everything was crashing in on him. His nights became solitary hours of sleeplessness. He was worried about dying. He kept mulling over two related questions in his head: "Does my bloodline end here?" and "Am I going to die?"

He made it through combat training and left for six weeks of job school. His options were in California, Hawaii, Okinawa, or on the East Coast. He chose Twentynine Palms, just outside San Diego in the Mojave Desert. He took an aptitude test and was placed in telecommunications, where he was told that he would be in a room, far away from war, working with satellites and state-of-the-art equipment. That also turned out not to be true.

From his time in basic training to Camp Lejeune and then to job school at Twentynine Palms, Sami told no one that he was Arab-American. And until he got to Kuwait, he had never mentioned that he spoke Arabic. He was blessed with a relatively ambiguous-sounding name and dark good looks. Everywhere he went, Dan was with him, and they had bunked together as well. Everyone simply thought he was Hispanic.

What he really was a New York Yankees fanatic, and the World Series was on. The Yankees were battling the Arizona Diamondbacks, and the series went to seven games. Sami watched each game like a chess master, examining every move and hoping for the best. But the Yankees blew it and lost in the final stretch, and that night Sami surprised himself by reacting extremely emotionally. He got up from the TV lounge and went to his room, because he could feel the tears coming. He started sobbing uncontrollably, for what felt like hours. *Why am I crying so much?* he wondered. *It's just a game.* But the stress of a coming war added to his sense of loss. Later that evening he returned to an abandoned TV lounge and flipped through the channels with the remote. He landed on CNN, which was re-broadcasting a special on the September 11 attacks.

Alone and in a dark room, this was the first time he saw the footage, and he found that he couldn't move. He watched the show as if magnetically held by the electric blue of the television screen. As he stared at the images, the tears started to flow once again. *Arabs did this?* he thought. *My own people?* And his emotions began hardening into anger. *Let's go now!* he thought. He was resolved. He was ready to get his war on.

But nothing changed that quickly. He still had training to complete and tasks to fulfill. In November 2001, he was assigned to Camp Pendleton and joined to the First Marine Division. It's "the oldest and most prestigious division of the marines in the history of the United States," he said to his mother on the phone. (The First Marine Division was formed during World War II, when on February 1, 1941, it was put into action aboard the battleship *Texas*. But its history reaches back to March 8, 1911, with the formation of the First Marine Regiment at Guantánamo Bay, Cuba.) He wondered if she could hear the pride in his voice over the phone line and feel her son changing into a soldier, because he was feeling it. With about thirty other people, Sami and Dan were assigned to communications, in the radio sector.

Life at Camp Pendleton was still relatively normal. Sami became a guide, a soldier delegated to lead other soldiers. He carried more responsibility and was on his way to promotion. A few soldiers at Camp Pendleton had been cherry-picked for the Afghan campaign, but not many. Daily life was generally routine, and Sami began earning "combat pay." His parents had bought him a laptop computer that Christmas, and he would go online during off-hours and talk with people around the country in different chat rooms. One of these was Ana, a Puerto Rican from New Jersey, and they began e-mailing each other. He bought a cell phone and would call her when they could coordinate schedules and time zones. He visited her for the first time during a break in his schedule in 2002, and they became a couple.

Late in 2002 he and the other guides from Camp Lejeune who were with him at Pendleton were assigned to work a general's house during a party. They wore dress uniforms and handed out drinks and hors d'oeuvres to the VIP crowd. The party clinked on well into the night until the last guest finally left, and then the general sat down and lit up a cigar. This was the first time Sami had had any casual conversation with a general. They all stood while the general talked to them from his soft leather chair. He asked about their work, but the conversation quickly turned to the future, to Iraq, and to the possibilities for war. "Well, you boys better get ready," the general said. He puffed on his cigar. "It looks like we're going somewhere."

PREPARATIONS WERE NOW MADE every day for transporting soldiers and equipment to the Persian Gulf. Sami became more worried. He made an appointment to see his commanding officers.

"I have a problem, sirs," he said, after saluting. "I have a conflict of interest." He shifted on his feet. "I'm Arab, and I can't fight against my own people."

For the first time, he was telling them about his background. The officers asked him some questions and then stared at him with flinty eyes.

"But they're Muslim, soldier. And you're Christian," one of them said.

It went nowhere. They dismissed him.

A few days later, he was back again. "My parents are having trouble," he said nervously. "I can't leave the country."

It wasn't true, and it didn't work either. When he realized there was no way out, he began feeling regret, like less of a marine, for these feeble attempts at getting out of the war. The Corps had respected him, and he wasn't respecting it. But self-doubt continued to plague him. Was he less of an American because he didn't want to fight? he wondered. Was he like the terrorists who attacked the United States? Who was he helping? He was nervous, young, and afraid.

Back in the barracks, he told Dan and his other friends about what he'd done, and they sat him down for a serious talk. We're going as a team, Dan told him, so you have to go. Besides, you'll hate yourself if you don't go. Dan was pushing him hard, and Sami could hear the relief in Dan's voice when Sami told them that he'd made up his mind. He was going.

He took two weeks off over the Christmas break and went back to Brooklyn to celebrate with his family and spend time with Ana. Park Slope was comforting and familiar. But within three weeks after his return to base in California, his unit was given their orders. Sami started to feel that God was determining his destiny. September 11 had happened while he was on his way to boot camp. He had joined the military before September 11. It all started to seem preordained, and he began reading the Bible. With so many devoutly Christian soldiers from the South around him, the Bible was everywhere.

They were leaving in fourteen days. Cars had to be garaged. Everything had to be packed up. The movers came to his room and took everything, and left a shell of bare walls and echoing sound. Sami turned around in the empty room, and he understood that he really was going. And at 6:00 A.M. on February 14, 2003, Sami boarded a plane with the First Marine Division for Kuwait. It was Valentine's Day. Love had been superseded by war.

"WAKE UP. WAKE UP, New York. We need you out here right now!"

The time was past 2:00 A.M., and Sami was asleep on the top of his truck. An hour earlier, from his perch on the vehicle, he had stripped down to his T-shirt and shorts and climbed into his sleeping bag with his nine-millimeter pistol. The major had mercifully told him to get some rest. Sami had been leading the convoy of twelve trucks for hours.

It had been a month since they'd crossed the Kuwait-Iraq border. Each day they would drive a little closer to their destination, the ancient city of Babylon, set up their equipment, and take it down the next morning. The infantry units were always ahead of them, clearing the areas so that Radio Sector could set up its equipment in safety, and so far Sami hadn't seen any indications of a fighting enemy. In fact, as soon as they had passed the border, they started seeing uniforms lying indifferently on the ground: lace-up boots, military blouses, and even trousers, all tossed and discarded like broken umbrellas in a windy rainstorm. They drove by individual Iraqis and then groups of men, from a drip into a flow, many of them walking without shirts and shoes and in half military uniforms. Sami stared at them from his vehicle, and they looked back at him hard. He recalled what he'd been told before, that these guys were all murderous, that they didn't care about anything but killing, that they'd fight to the last tooth. But then here they were, just walking along the side of the road like farmers. "That was all horseshit!" he decided. "They lied. They were trying to scare the living hell out of me, and there it was!" It eased his mind to know that these Iraqis weren't putting up a fight. Maybe it would be like this the whole way, he reasoned.

The logic was reassuring to a young, scared marine. Crossing into Iraq had already frightened him more than he'd expected. When that had happened, three weeks earlier, Sami had led the formation from his vehicle. Made up of concertina wire, high sand berms, rickety fences and abandoned checkpoints, the country looked like a ghost town in brown, lit only with the lights of the vehicles passing by. As soon as he crossed, he saw the oil wells burning, the dark sky punctuated with huge fireballs circling psychedelic orange around them. *I guess I really am in hell now,* he thought. His nerves were getting to him as he was driving. Behind him in the backseat was an older marine, a twenty-year veteran who was videotaping the whole episode like a home movie of his beach vacation. Sami, meanwhile, had a hard time concentrating. All he could think of was that this was happening for real, and he steered the vehicle right off the road. They were heading straight for the wall of an abandoned building when the major yelled at him. "What are you doing, Specialist? Go this way!" he screamed, and Sami's head cleared right away. The veteran laughed at Sami and just kept filming as if this were all great fun.

They passed peasant kids and their families on the road, and something interesting happened. The landscape began to remind Sami of parts of

Egypt, as did the grinding poverty, which was reminiscent of the streets of some neighborhoods in Cairo. People were walking around on cement in 120-degree heat, without shoes. They lived simply in makeshift houses. He found that the destitution was causing him pangs of regret, and he wanted to give the people he passed something, but regulations barred it, out of fear of starting a riot. Eventually he found ways around this. When he was riding in other open vehicles, he would surreptitiously hand off two-liter bottles of water, cases of MREs, and wrapped Tootsie Rolls to people they passed. As his feelings of dread waned, his notions of kinship with the Iraqis were awakened. He told me later, "I wanted to give them that kind of dignity. If I did that, at least it would show some kind of humane feeling toward them, you know, that we were not just here to murder everybody. That we were here to help."

A few of his fellow marines didn't take well to his sympathies. "Fuck those guys. Get rid of them all," they would say, and then Sami would stop them and ask, "Do you really think we should just kill everybody here?" "Hell yeah, fuck them all!" they replied. Sami would just shake his head, and they would call him "terrorist." With his friends, at least, there was none of this talk.

"Come on, wake up! We need you out here right now."

"What happened?"

"We got like fifty Iraqis coming toward us, and we need to search them all. We need you to speak to them."

Wearing only his T-shirt, shorts, and boots, he climbed down off the truck. And there they were, a group of old men surrounded by marines armed to the teeth. The men were all on their knees in the gravel, looking lost and pathetic. PFC Andrews, a kid with an M16, was so wound up, so stressed out from not yet being able to shoot off his gun, and so pumped up by being this close to his Iraqi enemy that he was yelling and screaming at the elders with massacre in his eyes.

"Don't fuckin' move! Don't move! Don't move!" he screamed, his fingers loose on his weapon.

Sami shook the sleep out of his eyes and saw the situation for what it was. He looked at his fellow soldier in disbelief. "Hey, Andrews," he said. "Relax! These are just some old men. Let me get you on *your* knees on the gravel and see how you long you can take it."

Andrews told Sami to fuck off and mind his own business. Sami was getting more worried by the bloodlust he saw in Andrews's eyes. But at the same time, he worried that if he were seen showing too much mercy to the Iraqis, he would be branded as being soft on the enemy. "I am wearing name tapes that say 'U.S. Marine, United States,' but my parents are Arab, and I can't forget that," he told me. "I wanted to treat them as good as I can without showing bias. It's not like I didn't want us to win the war or to rectify what happened," he said, referring to the September 11 attacks, "I just wanted to be mindful of Arab people, to show some compassion."

He decided to take advantage of his privileged position as the major's driver. Sami had been on excellent terms with the commanding officer since being assigned to him, and he had never met a man like the major before—fair, disciplined, and thoughtful. The man was a born marine. Sami approached him.

"Hey, sir," he said. "Can you tell Andrews to ease off a little bit?" He threw in the request like it was nothing, like asking to be passed the plate of potatoes at the dinner table, but he was scared as to how this would look. "It's not that serious, sir. There are a lot of old guys here. These people are kneeling on gravel. They've already been through enough. Can I get them to sit on their butts and not on their knees?"

"All right, get them to sit on their butts."

"Thank you, sir."

He told the men in Arabic how to sit, and he got what he wanted. He looked at Andrews, but rather than feeling relieved, he felt angry, almost irrationally upset. He could have punched the soldier in the face. He wanted to get in Andrews's face and scream at him, "What wrong with you? You act like you're all big and tough because you have a gun? What if the roles were reversed? What if you were the one on the ground? How would you feel? They've already been through hell. They've probably already had their houses blown up. God knows what happened to their families. And now *you* want to add undue pressure? Was he—this old Iraqi man—a threat to you? You've got thirty other marines with guns here. Are you serious?"

But he didn't want to appear soft on the enemy, so he didn't say anything.

BY JUNE 2003, more than a month after the president's "Mission Accomplished" speech, the company finally made it to Babylon, the first modern city in the world and their final destination. They set up camp, and the upper echelon of the company requested a tour of historical Babylon. Sami was taken along as the major's driver, and he was less astonished by the city's amazing history and more at how wide-eyed and eager the officers were, asking all kinds of questions of their Iraqi tour guide. Their deference and respect for an Iraqi surprised Sami.

Sami's company immediately settled into their base, one of Saddam Hussein's palaces. This wasn't a storybook castle. It was more like a gated community, a series of buildings on a huge plot of verdant land. The unit went to town. For months they'd had no showers, no toilets, and only packaged food. They felt less than human. Now they had a swimming pool, they had volleyball courts, they had electricity, cots and tents to sleep in, showers so they could feel clean again and reenter the world of the living.

Life actually became routine at the palace. After a few days, the schedules were set. Sami worked from eight to four, and after 4:00 P.M., his time was again his own, just like at Twentynine Palms. The company set up a makeshift gym in the palace. After work they either exercised or hung around, as fear was slowly replaced by boredom. They were getting restless. There was nothing else to do, and the war was supposed to be over.

To break up the tedium one day, a unit in the company left the base for a tour of another of Saddam's palaces that was nearby. Sami went with his commanding officer, but the entire company soon joined in. As soon as they arrived there, the marines began acting like little kids, running through the palace and screaming to hear their own echoes. They climbed on top of the diving board and looked down upon the dirty pool. The afternoon was a bizarre kind of stress release, a free-for-all like nothing Sami had ever seen before. They began removing things, taking stuff—furniture, fixtures, anything they could get their hands on. They pillaged the guts out of the complex. Anything that moved, moved right into their hands.

It worked for a day, but after the palace visit the boredom and stress and frustration returned and increased. Leaving became the only acceptable topic of conversation. They were restless, and the rumors swirled. "When are we going home, sir?" they asked every day. "We go home when we're told, soldier," was the answer every time. They were young. It was August, and it was hot. They wanted to hug their parents and make love to their girlfriends or wives. They could think of nothing else.

Finally, in early September, the commanding officers announced that they could expect to leave within a week. Everyone hooted, hollered, and hoo-ahed. But nothing happened. Then two more weeks passed, and still nothing. They were told they had to wait for the army to come in and take over the area, and they began resenting the army. Then marine infantry units began departing, until after a while only a small group of marines was left, all of them in Communications. (Communications had to stay back to help the army with the transition.) Finally, at the end of September, Sami got the word that he and his friends in Communications were leaving, and home became real and not just an abstract noun signifying desire. They couldn't stop smiling and started talking about what they were going to do first thing when they arrived. For Sami that was easy. Eat Chicken Alfredo at Olive Garden.

The day of departure finally arrived, and they packed up their gear and drove to the airstrip. They boarded a transport plane for Kuwait and then changed to a commercial airliner for JFK. On board, Sami tried to sleep but couldn't. He had two CDs that he listened to over and over again while thinking about the last thirty weeks. His tour really had finished, and it had turned out just fine, meaning that he was alive. Eight months earlier, he had left Twentynine Palms scared and worried. Now he had discovered that he was actually a pretty good marine. He regretted trying to get out of his service. In the brutal landscape of war-torn Iraq, he had begun to connect to his Arab side, and he had never felt more like a New Yorker.

They closed off a wing of JFK so the soldiers could change planes for their return to Twentynine Palms. When they arrived in California, they were met right off the airplane by one of the soldiers' girlfriends, who brought them all Marlboros and Budweisers to celebrate their return. Everyone reached for an American cigarette and grabbed a cold can of American beer. They looked at one another, goofy smiles splashed on their faces, and toasted one another and themselves on the tarmac. The cigarettes and the beer tasted like life. "It was like champagne to us," Sami said.

THIS IS WHAT Sami was thinking after being home for four months: "When you find out that you are going back to Iraq for a second tour, you're pissed. It's like a sick slap in the face. The second time around, you don't want to go, but the reasons for your resistance stem this time less from fear—you have a better idea of what to expect, although there will still be unknowns—than from a sense of failure. Why the hell are you going out there again? Didn't they say the war is supposed to be over? Didn't the army guys complete their mission? You begin questioning other branches of the service, which you know is not a good thing to do. You start dreading telling your family that you will be back in Iraq. You get on the phone one night to give your girlfriend in New Jersey the bad news. She starts crying, which makes you want to break something. You want to fight someone. You curse the military. You curse George W. Bush."

Upon their return from the first tour, the workload for Sami and his friends at the base was relatively light. The first thing they had to do involved paperwork. The soldiers needed to cancel the power of attorney that they had signed over to family members before leaving for war and retake ownership of their lives. After that it was a short-lived period of bliss. Their stuff was still in storage, so Sami and his friends immediately headed into town to buy clothes. They had thousands of dollars of combat pay now in their bank accounts, more money than most of them had ever held. Sami squirreled away $5K—he was saving to buy a new car, as a symbol of his wartime accomplishments—and the rest of the money was all for fun.

They went shopping. They bought clothes. They spent money on dinners and on drinks. The staff at the Olive Garden, seeing the loud table of shaved heads, immediately realized that the men had just returned from Iraq, and the manager sent them free rounds. For a while everybody was a hero, and the ordinary seemed extraordinary. Running water was as magical to them as a mythical river. Flush toilets were a new invention. Sami also found that some of his simple war habits died hard. For months afterward he continued to take a packet of baby wipes with him into the bathroom, even though he knew it was totally unnecessary.

That December, Sami went home to Brooklyn for Christmas. Walking into his parents' brownstone in Park Slope, he saw the huge banner they'd hung on the door for their war-hero son. He became like a toy for his younger brother to show off. His father had newfound respect for his first son. His mother was beside herself with joy that he was home. And that was why he couldn't find a way to tell her about the rumors that were swirling around. They were going back. After his return to California, in January 2004, he learned that the company was returning to Iraq in February.

Rumors bounced around that the second time would be a cakewalk. They flew right into Iraq and saw that in one way that was true. They were now stationed in the restive western Iraqi province of al-Anbar, but they reached their camp in Iraq easily. And once they got there, this is what they found: a cafeteria with hot food, Internet stations, hot showers, working toilets, a TV room, a gym, a poolroom, and cots rather than sleeping bags. Sami bunked again with Dan. In the beginning, life in Iraq felt a lot more civilized than the first time around, even more routine than when they were in Saddam's palace. It was a little like being at home. Sami once again knew when his shift would end, and so he could easily plan the rest of this day. That usually meant working out with Dan and the others for two hours, taking a shower, and then going on the Internet, e-mailing Ana or calling home, watching the Yankees play the Red Sox on Armed Forces

Network TV, or talking while sharing cigarettes with the guys until he fell asleep.

He had been in the service for almost three years now, and he was ripe for another promotion. Finally the news came. He was to advance to the rank of corporal, and he was thrilled. Now he would become a supervisor. When Sami told his commanding officer, the major, Sami thought, was more excited about the promotion than even he was. That this was happening near the beginning of the deployment was also a plus. Sami would now have more supervisory roles for the duration of the next eight months or so left in this tour. He would join the supervisors' clique, too. He started anticipating the promotion ceremony where, by tradition, two other marines carrying your new rank or higher "pin" you with your new rank insignia. He chose Dan and the major.

But at the last minute, Sami was sent to Kuwait for a routine mission. He cursed his luck, and the ceremony ended up being held in an aircraft hangar far away from al-Anbar. At least the major was with him, and after he pinned Sami, he said to the young man, "I feel privileged and honored. There has never been a marine who deserved this more than you do." The words were deeply affecting to Sami. The major was the marine of all marines to him. If *God had made a marine,* thought Sami, *it's the major. And for him to say that . . . well, maybe I really am a better-than-average marine.*

He returned to the camp a few days later and saw Dan. The first thing his friend did when he saw the new corporal was to sucker-punch him hard in the gut, and Sami lost his breath. Delivering pain. That's the initiation.

IRAQIS WERE CONSTANTLY FILTERING in and out of the camp, usually as workers of some sort, and Sami was doing all he could to avoid them. He didn't want to have any special relationships with them. He didn't want any of his friends or superiors questioning his loyalties, and he didn't want the Iraqis asking him what he, an Arab, was doing in Iraq. "What do you think I'm doing here? You don't see the blouse?" He had this conversation in his head over and over again, but in fact no one ever asked him.

The pool tables in the rec room were usually occupied by the Arabic interpreters, often civilians who had come from the United States and were utilized by the military for their linguistic skills. Many of them were older, and one of them was an elderly Palestinian man who reminded Sami of his father. Sami and his father had had their differences in the past, but he found himself missing his father more and more. He became drawn to the pool tables in his free time, and he took an automatic liking to the man and the others. They would all hang out, shoot games of nine-ball while talking in Arabic and English about the Arab world and its history and complicated, sad politics.

Perhaps for the first time in his life, Sami started to feel proud of his Arabic heritage. He learned more about his history from the interpreters, especially from this paternal Palestinian, than he had in his entire past. He could talk in Arabic to these guys and leave the marines in the dark, having something on them. "You know, these guys are happy about being Arab," he told me, "Why can't I be happy about being Arab?" He found himself talking more often to his parents on the phone.

"Dad, there's a Palestinian guy here, and he looks just like you, he talks like you, everything like you. He's funny and everything."

"That's good," his father said, as if he didn't know what else to say. "That's good."

Sami's mother was overjoyed. "Oh, my God, Sami!" she said. "Your Arabic is getting so much better, so much nicer. You know exactly what you're saying." He was speaking a lot more Arabic now, and he felt himself changing. How stupid he'd been when he was younger, he told me. "Why did I shy away from my culture?" He reflected a lot on his parents during this period, thinking about their incredible success. They had come to the United States with nothing, and now they have a $4-million house and his father has his taxi medallion. "All this for a man with no high-school education!"

IN THE BEGINNING of their second deployment, the soldiers at the camp were allowed to walk around in regular uniform. But the camp started suffering mortar attacks, assaults that were increasing in frequency and intensity. The mortars were becoming so repetitive that the soldiers were ordered to wear their helmets and vests at all times, and the order only increased their frustration. Unlike during Sami's first tour, the soldiers this time almost never left the camp. "We weren't able to fight back," he said. "We felt like, what are we doing here? We're not fighting anybody. We're sitting here on the radio and watching TV half the day, not doing anything. We can do this at home!" They could hear explosions boom regularly in the distance. "That really frustrated us," he said, "because we felt that we were getting put into the position to fail, to see how long we could be here like this without getting hurt. We felt like sitting ducks."

At seven one morning, Sami awoke to an explosion, the loudest noise he'd ever heard. The building rocked. The bang shook him out of bed. He walked into the open area of his building and saw two men: one lying on his back bleeding and another one staring in shock into his mangled hand. The medics were running to them.

"What the fuck just happened?" Sami yelled.

A mortar had exploded next to the building. Sami went outside and saw an enormous crater in the parking area. He saw the military vehicles, their bulletproof windows riddled with holes. He saw busted tires and fluid leaking out of Humvees. And he saw a blouse, covered in blood, next to the crater.

The blouse belonged to Gunnery Sergeant Lane, one of the first supervisors Sami or his friends in the platoon had ever worked with. He was from upstate New York and, like Sami, a huge Yankee fan. Everyone liked Gunny Lane. He was a man who knew his rank but never flaunted it. A career soldier, he'd been in the service for fifteen years, five years away from his retirement. He was smart and generous, and the mood in the camp immediately pitched down when people heard that he was hurt.

After the commotion subsided and the wounded were removed to medical care, Sami and his friends sat outside, helmets on, to smoke. Nobody said a word for a long time. Everyone seemed to be thinking the same thing, but nobody wanted to talk, until Sami broke the silence.

"For what?" he said.

Someone responded. "For nothing."

"For bullshit," someone else said.

They all shook their heads and stared at the ground. Sami was thinking about how they had become almost cavalier in their attitudes, since nobody they were close to had gotten hurt in the war. They believed that everything was going to be all right, that it was basically work, gym, and TV until they got back to California. And then this happened.

Reality set in. They were still in Iraq. They weren't going anywhere.

The commanding officers soon called the entire company into a meeting. A colonel stood in the middle of the group of soldiers and started talking. "As you know, one of our greatest supervisors was wounded in today's attack," he said, then paused. "We're saddened to say that he's gone."

Like everyone else, Sami felt destroyed, but it was the way the gunnery sergeant had died that gnawed at him. *This is the wrong guy to take,* he thought. And he wasn't even doing anything! He died heading to the bathroom! He had one kid and another one on the way, Sami recalled, and he talked about his son so much. He had a child who wouldn't know who his father was. If you wanted to look at it like he died bravely, like he died for a cause, you could, he reasoned, but you knew it wasn't like that. He died going to the bathroom. It would be different if he died in a firefight, in a shootout. We could've tolerated that, he thought. We could deal with that. But Sami couldn't deal with him just answering the call of nature and then paying for it with his life.

Who wants to die like that?

Am I next?

TIME ROLLED ON, and the shock of losing Gunny Lane also passed, but the pain didn't. Nor did the resentment. Many of the soldiers started hating more and more the fact that they were in Iraq. To some the mission was becoming cloudier and feeling more futile, more ludicrous. Others stuck to the official position, and the company divided, almost evenly, along these lines, one half critical and the other single-mindedly directed. "We're marines," one group would say. "This is what we're trained to do. We go home when we get sent home." But Sami and his clique were more critical. "Why are we even out here?" they would ask, adding, "This is not what marines are supposed to do. Marines are supposed to go to action and fight battles, not watch our friends get picked off without a fight." The division between the two camps came to a head one day with the purchase of a bootleg DVD.

Iraqis were often seen hanging around the entrance to the camp in hopes of selling various items of dubious value, including the latest Hollywood movies on DVD. Movies were among the more desirable purchases by the soldiers, who were often bored and looking for new entertainment in their daily life in the compound. One day one of the soldiers bought Michael Moore's *Fahrenheit 9/11* from one of the Iraqi bootleggers. It was a strange little moment of global culture, watching this movie about the Iraq war in a black-market version in Iraq. The soldier walked into the TV room and slipped the disk into the DVD player, which disappeared like a Communion wafer into the machine's mouth. A moment later the screen went black, the sound of airplanes rang out from the speakers, and the controversial documentary began playing.

Sami and about twenty other soldiers watched *Fahrenheit 9/11* in silence. It had them completely captivated. At first Sami was thinking, *Is this for real?* But as he watched the movie, he started wondering, *Am I out here for somebody's personal gain? Am I out here trying to help somebody else advance? What am I really out here for?* He was convinced by the movie. He and his clique had had questions before, but now they had something to affirm their position, a cultural artifact replete with evidence, documents, statistics, and footage. Occasionally someone would yell, "This is bullshit!" at the screen, only to be hushed into quiet by the rest, until the documentary ended.

As soon as it did, an argument ensued. "We're here for someone else's fuckin' own agenda!" someone said.

"That's crap. He's just trying to attack George Bush," countered another soldier.

"Look, the guy's providing evidence for you. There's paperwork suggesting that his relationships are influencing what's going here. How could you just dismiss this?" Sami said.

"Hey, whatever the president does is right. He's a military guy. He gives us raises, he supports us, he takes care of us. He supports the military."

"Are you serious?"

"Bill Clinton never supported the military like Bush. He's the one who got us into this mess."

"Bill Clinton has nothing to do with this! You know, he was probably one of the best presidents we've had in a while compared to this guy. Are you honestly trying to justify this?"

"I don't care. America was attacked."

"They put fewer troops in Afghanistan than they have police in New York City. Does that make sense to you?"

The argument continued for a while, widening the divide between the two groups, until it petered out somewhere between respectful differences and a bad taste in your mouth. The Marine Corps drills into its troops the idea that they're all green, that a fractured and divided group of soldiers is a liability. Ultimately, that was the value that triumphed. Although some soldiers played the movie over and over, Sami and many others refused to watch it again.

But by now Sami's own position had solidified. "I don't support the war," he told me in 2006. "But I support the men and women in the war. A lot of these guys are young guys. They're eighteen and nineteen years old, and they have no choice. When they're told to go somewhere, they have to go. I understand that. Obligation says they have to go. And being a military guy, I side with them. I'm on their side. I value them more than the war.

"But to keep people out there that long for reasons that make no sense to anybody else except to your inner circle, it just doesn't sit right with me. None of these people making decisions have anybody there. They're playing with house money. They're playing with the youth of this country. They're not playing with *their* families. They're playing with other people's families. And you can't do that. You have to respect these people, first off. Give them back their children.

"I'm not on the side of the president at all. I think he's an idiot! I think his policies are skewed. I think his opinions are skewed. I think he uses religion as a form of control over the country. You hear him? He says God's on our side and God has tapped the United States as the world's police, and I'm always thinking, how do you know that? God tells you everything that happens?"

But at the time, Sami didn't share his opinions widely. "I need these guys," he concluded, "so let me shy away from it." Most everyone followed suit. Especially after the first big fight, the movie was rarely brought up again. People's positions on the war became clear after that, and the issues were seldom discussed. Everyone knew what would happen: more arguments, more dissension, more internal conflict. Only when Sami was in a group of like-minded soldiers would he talk about the movie, about politics, or about the reasons for their presence in Iraq. Otherwise it became an issue to be scrupulously avoided, and the soldiers tried to focus on something else. After the movie had been screened enough times so that everyone who wanted to had seen it, the soldiers quietly retired the film, turning their attention to other entertainment. They played more video games.

BY NOW SAMI HAD less than a year left in his active-duty contract, and by the end of September he read the flight roster and found that he was on the first flight back to Camp Pendleton. His second tour was ending. This time the flight stopped in Italy and Ireland before flying directly to California, and Sami and his friends descended back to earth with none of the bravado they'd felt after their first mission. They walked into an empty shop in Pendleton, since half the men were still in Iraq, and this meant that they had little to do. Sami called his parents, and they flew out to visit him.

As a corporal with no expenses for the last six months, Sami had a sizable little nest egg that he was now itching to spend. He wanted to see his parents, and he knew exactly what car he desired. He took his parents to the dealership with him, and pointed to an Acura, a thirty-six-thousand-dollar model, while his parents tried to talk him out of his choice. "Sami," his mother pleaded, "what are you doing? Why do you want such an expensive car? Do you really want to spend sixteen thousand dollars just on the down payment?"

"Hell yeah!" he roared. The car was his reward, his symbol of achievement, and he had been working toward this goal for three and a half long years. When he had walked into the dealership, he saw his baby: red, 2004, with a light interior, wood-grain paneling, and a kick-ass navigation system. It was love at first sight.

Ana came out a couple of weeks later, and Sami took a week off to spend with her. But he was scared about her arrival. He'd been worrying about their relationship since he was in Iraq and found out that he was coming home. Even though they'd been a couple for two years, he knew that he had never spent more than three weeks together with her. What would it be like now? He was going to be home for good. She had always been so supportive, and he'd missed her so much, but would things change? As soon as she came out, though, and he saw her, it was as if they'd never left each other, not even for breakfast. They drove all around Southern California in his new car, eating too much food and laughing over every silly little thing. Sami felt good. He knew that things with Ana were going to be all right.

But he wasn't so sure about the rest of his life. By May his contract would be up, and he didn't know what the transition to civilian life would be like. "What kind of job was I going to find?" he wondered. "Now I have a car payment. But I need to go to school. I'm twenty-three years old; I don't want to live at my parents' house. I want to live by myself. What am I going to do?" He even thought about an option he had discarded long ago: reenlisting.

His superior officers pushed the idea hard in front of him, and the prospect flashed with attraction. He had learned his equipment-maintenance job from scratch, and he'd been cited for personal achievement for best equipment maintenance in the entire company. He started thinking. "Maybe I can make a career out of this? I could switch jobs, get a more technologically oriented job that would prepare me better for the outside world?" If you reenlist, they promise you better choices, better jobs, better living conditions.

His father thought it was a fine idea, but Sami's mother put her foot down. "Sami," she told him quietly over the phone after she had finished shrieking, "we want you home." She said she understood he was concerned about resuming his life. "But don't worry about it. Whatever you need, we're there to help you."

Then Ana told him of her opposition to the idea, and that put an end to the madness and folly of the moment. He thought about the emotional and mental stability of his family, and that was more important to him than anything the military could offer. Nor did he want to make the same mistake twice. He had entered the marines basically on a whim, and here he was, about to reenlist on a wing and a prayer.

About a year later, his younger brother, in a fit of emulation, also signed up with a recruiter in Brooklyn. When Sami discovered this, he went ballistic. He marched his brother down to the recruiting office and had them undo the signature. "What's the matter?" the recruiter fought with Sami. "Aren't you proud to have served your country?"

"Don't even fucking start with me," Sami flung back. "I served my country! I was there. That's a lot more than sitting behind a desk lying to kids."

BY APRIL it was only a matter of weeks before he would be discharged. Dan was getting out around the same time as Sami, and they came up with a brilliant idea. For a long time, Dan had wanted to move to New York, but he didn't have any family or know where to go in the city. Sami suggested that his brother-in-arms could live with him in his family's house. They could save money that way and then buy some real estate together, maybe with the Department of Veterans Affairs Home Loan program or something. His parents, he said, had been thinking of moving to Egypt anyway.

"No. You can't bring a stranger into our house, Sami," his mother told him on the phone. "That's going to change our way of life! I can't walk around in my nightgown anymore if he's going to be there. I can't be re-laxed in my own home!"

But thinking about life after active duty always left Sami nervous. Over the last four years, he had lost touch with all his high-school friends. Sure, there was Ana, but no one else, and with Dan around he would have at least one other person to be close to. Besides, this would be Sami's first time liv-ing in New York over the age of twenty-one, which meant he now had New York City's nightlife in front of him. Life was ready to be lived! But his par-ents weren't leaving anytime soon, and they put the brakes on Sami's idea.

He told Dan, who acted disappointed and angry, as if he thought Sami had canceled the idea on purpose.

"Ah, man," he lamented. "I even filled out my home address on my dis-charge papers with your address."

"Hey, man, I'm sorry," Sami said. He felt bad, but wasn't ready to go against the whims of his family.

A few days later, Sami was filling out some paperwork in the office for his discharge when a snag appeared. Dan was in the office with him. Sami started arguing with the clerk, a woman below Sami's rank who was han-dling the red tape around his discharge. With tones unbecoming, she in-sisted that she had already given Sami some missing discharge papers.

"Excuse me?" Sami said. "Do you know who you are talking to? There's still a rank structure here. And no, you didn't give me no paperwork."

Dan was listening to the whole thing. He coughed a "bullshit" into his fist.

Sami turned to him. "Yo, we're the same rank, and you're helping this fuckin' subordinate make me look stupid?"

She looked at Sami and, as if taking his side, said, "I know!"

That didn't help. The two soldiers began yelling at each other. "Let's go outside. Let's go outside," Dan menaced. Sami looked at him. "Whatever, man," he replied, walking away and shaking his head. The friendship was over, just like that, in a civilian heartbeat. They had gone through so many things together—boot camp, combat training, job school, two tours in Iraq—but it didn't matter. Ana later told him supportively that Dan always creeped her out anyway. But the fact that the friendship had ended, and over something so stupid, worried Sami. Now what could he expect when he went home? He started wondering if he was going to burn bridges with all the friends he would make in the future, too.

AROUND THIS TIME he decided on the tattoo he wanted to have, once he'd saved enough money. With his large, muscular bulk, he has acres of skin to plow ink into, but he never wanted to stamp himself with the regular bull-dog or the eagle, globe, and anchor symbol of the Marine Corps. If he was going to paint himself, he needed something that expressed who he is, something that really spoke to him. What he came up with was the New York City skyline as the tattoo's basis, but instead of the World Trade Center towers, two memorial beams of light will shine upward. The moon, vaguely imprinted with the marine emblem, will land high on his shoulder. The stars will spell out "N-Y-C." Underneath, and in Arabic, will be written the words "Always remembered, never forgotten." A little bit of everything—New York, Marine, Arab—to be put carefully together and marked indelibly.

Sami was honorably discharged on a Friday afternoon, and the day before, Ana flew in on a one-way ticket to San Diego. Sami had decided to ship his major belongings with the marines but to drive his Acura cross-country. On Friday morning he went for his send-off. This is a time when friends, associates, and superiors assemble to talk about the fondest memories they've made with their departing comrade and what they will miss most.

Perhaps demonstrating how he was already drifting from the marines, Sami showed up in civilian clothes instead of in uniform. The ceremony was somewhat poignant—and he thought, *Wow, I really am going to miss these people, even the ones I can't stand!*—but it was also quick and, frankly, a little underwhelming. Less than half an hour later, he was ready to depart. *Okay,* he thought. *Now it's time to get out of here.*

He climbed into his car with Ana, with everything packed up, and stopped off at the discharge office to grab his paperwork, which stated that he was now on "terminal vacation" (meaning that as soon as his vacation was over, he would be discharged). They got on the road, and Sami couldn't believe it. His four years had been leading up to this date. He'd been count-ing down from year one to this date. He kept on saying to Ana, "Hey! We're actually doing this! We're actually driving home! We're going home!"

And that's when the anxiousness and the panic set in. On Thursday night a stomach virus hit him. On Friday night they stayed in New Mexico and rested. But on Saturday morning, it was a straight shot. Sami drove all the way through. Ana kept asking him, "Are you gonna relax? Do you want to rest?" Hell no! he said. Nothing was stopping him now from getting home. Nothing. He ramped up on NoDoz and packs of Red Bull and drove at one point for twenty-two hours straight. They passed St. Louis and Chicago, and Sami thought, *Yeah, it would be nice to stop and see these places, but not now!* He just looked at his navigation system and saw END DESTINATION. He didn't see St. Louis. He didn't see Chicago. He saw Brooklyn, New York.

The last hours, when they hit Pennsylvania, were the hardest. Only three hours away, but the time dragged. They crossed the border into New Jersey going 120 miles an hour. Finally they drove through the Holland Tunnel into Manhattan, and Sami almost started to cry. He felt so happy and so complete. "I'm back," he said to Ana. "I'm back!" And he was think-ing, *I always felt that I'd never left Brooklyn, that I had never left, even though I've been gone for four years. My heart's still here. That's all I thought about, coming home, over these past four years, and now I feel like the journey is over. My mission was to get back home, to complete the four years, and I did it. It was an exciting experience, but now I just feel so proud of where I'm from.* He spoke to Ana again. "I mean, look babe, we're in the city! We're in my city. It's *my city* right now. This is my home!" He was alive. He knew who he was and where he was from. The future would be his.

And Ana said, "I know. You're home, babe. Welcome home."

YASMIN

If i can't do
what i want to do
then my job is to not
do what i don't want
to do.

—Nikki Giovanni, "Choices"

Yasmin's sisters wanted Taco Bell. Her parents were out, and the girls were screaming, so food duty fell to her, at nineteen, the oldest of the four girls. "Okay, fine, I'll go," she said, sighing, and finally shut them up. She would take the bus the whole way up Brooklyn's Fifth Avenue, buy all that greasy food, and cart it back. Whatever.

It was the summer of 2005, right after the London bus bombings, and Yasmin tied on her white *hijab* as she always does, before she walked outside and waited for the B63 bus. The street smelled like an oil spill in the summer heat. A few minutes later, she was stepping onto the bus's black stairs as the vehicle chugged and burped its way slowly into Sunset Park.

The bus was crowded in the front, so Yasmin stood in the back like a blade of grass in a forest of people, next to an elderly white couple holding on tightly to each other. As the bus continued down its route, people mounted and dismounted, and several blocks short of Taco Bell another Muslim woman boarded. Like Yasmin, she also wore a *hijab*, but she had a baby slung to her chest and a blanket covering her sleeping infant. People moved out of the way as the woman walked carefully up the crowded aisle. She stopped at an empty window seat halfway along the bus, and a man sitting in the aisle seat stood to let her in. She sat down quietly, and the bus engine droned on.

Yasmin is one of those people who finds it hard to hold her feelings in, and as the vehicle began moving, she could hear the couple beside her begin talking. "What do you think she's got under there?" the woman asked the man. "I don't know," he said. "We don't know what's under there." They continued to talk, and Yasmin turned to look at them. *Are they for real?* she thought. *What do they think she's got under there? A bomb?* She had to say something, so she broke into their conversation.

"It's a baby," she said in her signature monotone.

The couple turned their faces to her. Yasmin could feel the man look through her before he spoke. "Did you see it?" he asked.

"It's a *baby*," she repeated. *This can't be happening,* she thought.

"But did you see it?"

Oh, my God, I can't believe these people, she was thinking. She wanted to roll her eyes at the man. But before she could say anything, the couple had already pushed their way up to the driver, a young African-American man in a pressed polyester uniform. She could hear them command the driver to do something. "You've got to check what she has under there," the man told the driver.

Yasmin glanced into the driver's mirror and saw his face looking back indifferently into the bus. "It's a baby," he said.

"But did you *see* it?" the man insisted. "Did you *see* that it was a baby?" New passengers began boarding the bus at the stop, and they could hear the conversation rise in tension and volume between the driver and the couple. The words "terrorist" and "bomb" floated through the bus. "Look, it's your job to check!" the man yelled at the driver, his wife egging him on. "It's your job to check," he repeated. "Otherwise we're calling the police!"

Yasmin looked down the bus at the Muslim woman. Her heart crashed for her. But she also began feeling uneasy in her stomach.

After her it's me, she thought.

The driver sighed. Yasmin watched him in the mirror as he rolled his eyes and put the vehicle in park. He stood up, walked down the aisle, and stopped in front of the woman, looking at her without saying a thing. "It's a baby!" he yelled across the bus to the man.

"But did you see the baby?" the man yelled back. Everybody in the bus was watching. No one said anything.

The driver turned back to the woman, and she spoke before he had to. "Do you want to see him?" she asked quietly. She pulled back the blanket, revealing a little baby boy lost in the innocence of sleep.

The bus driver was shaking his head as he sat down again, but the couple didn't notice. Yasmin did. And she saw the couple move to two free seats at the very rear of the bus, where they sat down, pulled out their newspapers, and began reading like it was Sunday brunch. She was furious. How could they act as if nothing had happened? They'd just targeted a mother, she thought, and now they simply sat there, self-satisfied, bland, and all puffed up, like a plate of rice? She was sure the mother was hurt by the incident, because if it had been her, she would feel humiliated and upset. It wasn't right.

The Taco Bell flew by the window. Yasmin slammed the "Stop Requested" tape and got off the bus, angry with herself for not doing anything. As the bus pulled away from the curb, she stood there, frozen in a cloud of diesel exhaust. She grabbed for a pen and scrawled the bus's license plate on her hand.

"911. What's your emergency?"

"There's a white couple on a city bus. I think she has a bomb in her purse. It's a B63 bus, going up Fifth Avenue. The license plate is . . ."

She wanted to call. She really did, just to make a point, to make them feel the same way—singled out, powerless, discriminated against, a source of irrational fear. But she didn't call. In fact, she didn't do anything, and because of that she was annoyed with herself.

YASMIN IS A HEAVYWEIGHT FIGHTER stuffed into a tiny, ninety-five-pound frame. Like so many women who wear the *hijab* in the United States, she is far from the stereotype of the submissive and retreating female. According to popular perception, the *hijab* is the paramount sign of oppression, a small piece of cloth that holds the talismanic power to destroy Western civilization. It covers and silences, keeping women relegated to second-class status. Most people who believe this, however, have probably not encountered many of the women in the West who choose to wear the *hijab*. Far from seeking pity, they are instead often the strongest people in the room, and not by any divine decree. Because their headwear so often attracts attention, the women are frequently called upon to define and defend themselves in front of others.

It can take a certain amount of courage to sport a *hijab* in the United States today, courage that is not lacking in Yasmin. Nor is she a stranger to a good fight. As a high-school student, she found that her religious beliefs brought her into a long conflict with the school's establishment, a battle that began in September 2000 and ended only years later, thanks to a little help from Michelle Pfeiffer.

YASMIN WAS BORN IN BROOKLYN and attended two private Muslim girls' schools in New Jersey until the seventh grade. She has been covering her hair since she was five years old, when it was an optional part of her school uniform, and says she could never now imagine not doing so. "I would feel like I'm walking around naked," she says. She has always lived the life of a religious Muslim, praying five times a day, fasting during the month of Ramadan, and abstaining from dating, alcohol, and pork. (Once, when we were setting up a place to meet, she wrote me an e-mail suggesting we go to a midtown Manhattan eatery she frequents. It's owned by Moroccans, she explained, and the bacon they serve is made from turkey meat. "We can sit by the window munching down on what appears to be pork, lol!" she wrote.) Ismail, her father, is an Egyptian Muslim, who married Jeanette, a Filipina Catholic, after they met in the 1980s through a mutual friend in New York. Their union gives Yasmin her unique looks—a sandy complexion, puffy lips, and black currants for eyes. Her aunts on her mother's side have Bibles and crosses all over their houses, but her mother

converted to Islam when Yasmin was a little girl. Her parents are both professionals, and when their girls began growing up and the parents' jobs began swallowing too much time, they made a decision that one of them
would remain at home. Ismail, who had also been a teacher, said he would
stay, and he started up a small business that he could run from his house
while he looked after the welfare and schooling of his four daughters. Like
many immigrant parents, they believed that nothing is more important for
their children than a good education.

In private school Yasmin learned Arabic and the fundamentals of Islam
along with a basic curriculum, but her parents felt that the public schools
offered better-quality schooling at the junior-high and high-school levels.
Her father especially didn't want to disadvantage Yasmin's chances for
medical school, his dream for his daughter. He enrolled Yasmin at McKin-
ley Junior High School in Brooklyn, and two years later she entered Fort
Hamilton High School.

Fort Hamilton is in an august residential area of Bay Ridge, Brooklyn,
that sits high on a cliff overlooking New York Harbor. Immediately below
is Shore Parkway, a constantly busy stretch of highway curving around
South Brooklyn. But Fort Hamilton is perched high enough away from the
road that the traffic noise immediately below isn't a bother. The homes
here are large and Victorian, many more than a century old, and they continue for several tree-abundant blocks in all directions. In Fort Hamilton
everything is quiet and serene. People generally keep to themselves, waving
a hello when they pick up their morning mail. The area feels much less
gritty and metropolitan than most of Brooklyn and more like some densely
populated coastal town.

The high school in Fort Hamilton could pass for an expansive redbrick
antebellum mansion. It has a soaring tower topped with a cupola, unob-
structed harbor views in the front, a full-length swimming pool inside, a
well-maintained athletic field behind, and handball courts nearby. The
school is also close to a historic military installation that is still in use, the
actual Fort Hamilton, built in 1825 to protect the coast from invaders.
Now, in this newcomer neighborhood composed of large Greek, Arab, and

Italian populations, many of the residents' children and others from beyond the immediate area attend the high school, one of New York City's
largest.

In the beginning of her freshman year at Fort Hamilton, Yasmin tried
out for the swim team. To get to the swimming pool, she had to pass by a
room where two of her friends were always busy in some kind of group activity. Yasmin wondered what the room was, and she eventually discovered
that it was the classroom of the leadership program, which contained the
student-government offices. (Leadership was a required class for student
officers and an elective class for those interested in student government.)
Oh, that sounds kinda cool, she thought. *How do I become a part of it?* In the
spring the next round of student elections was announced on the school's
PA system, and Yasmin mulled it over. That voice in her head told her, *I
probably don't have a chance of winning, because no one is going to elect a girl
who covers her hair,* but she ignored her own misgivings, challenging herself
as she frequently does.

She picked up the application and looked over the documents. The
whole process was astonishingly bureaucratized, a lesson in institutional
democracy. You had to sign the application and get a parent's signature.
You needed to provide a host of things: a photocopy of your school ID, a
written recommendation from a teacher, a copy of your transcript, and
other supplementary items. You had to have earned an 80 percent or higher
grade average. You could not have failed a class or have had any type of
school infraction. And you needed a hundred signatures (in blue ink) from
your fellow students. All applications also had to be vetted and approved
by the Election Committee, so any irregularity risked voiding your elec-
toral dreams. And since Fort Hamilton was known for having a strong
leadership program—the school had previously sent a student to serve on
the New York City Board of Education—Yasmin expected that it would be
a tough and selective process. At other schools Leadership was just a class
where you went, sat, and ate, she told me. At Fort Hamilton, she said,
Leadership was "hard-core."

Next came deciding what to run for. The presidency was too high an aspi-

ration for a freshman, she judged, so instead she aimed for secretary. It was
a Goldilocks decision for her, "not too high and not too low, but just right,"
she said. She collected her documents and began thinking about her campaign speech. At the bottom of the application was a statement that read

> *I hereby certify that these signatures were obtained justly, honestly, and
> in a manner outlined by the Election Committee. To the best of my
> knowledge, all of the above signed are currently Fort Hamilton High
> School students. I understand that if it is found that these signatures
> were obtained in a dishonest manner, I will be disqualified from
> running in this or any other Student Organization election.*

She gathered the required signatures and had her father sign the form,
in blue ink.

ON THE DAY OF the campaign speeches, Yasmin's nerves were raw.
"I'm here to help *you*," she proclaimed, "I'm a really hard worker, and I
will stop at nothing to make our school the best *ever*." The address won't
go down in the annals of American political oratory, but it was honest and
heartfelt. She had to deliver the same speech to hundreds of kids over multiple periods in the auditorium, and as she did, she slowly became convinced that she would lose. Two people were running against her. One was
a guy who was popular and Greek, and ethnic politics enters government
at an early age in Brooklyn. The other was a pretty Russian girl, who was—
purposefully, it seemed to Yasmin—dressed in a miniskirt and a tight, revealing top. While sitting onstage, Yasmin stared as the girl's ambitious
chest rose and fell, and she thought, *I have no chance against these people.*
She looked to her left. *He's popular, but*—and she looked to her right—
*sometimes image sells. Here I am, the Muslim girl who really has no sense of
style, who just said, "I care. I'll help."* She sighed a sigh that if it could speak
would have said, "You're doomed!"
  Well, at least she was proud of her posters. Photocopies were forbidden,

so all campaign banners had to be hand-drawn, and Yasmin has a flair for sketching cartoons. She had already plastered the (regulated) campaign areas with her trademark look and delivered her speech. Now she just had to wait.

Voting was set for the next day, and to her surprise many of the Arab and Muslim students approached her, beaming. "We're proud of you," they told her. This was especially true of the other Muslim girls who covered their hair. "We think you're doing a good job," they said, after telling her she had their vote. And the next evening she received a call at home from the Coordinator of Student Affairs, or COSA. "Congratulations," he told her. She had been elected secretary by a landslide.

She put down the phone, shocked and elated.

RESPONSIBILITIES BEGAN RIGHT AWAY. The new student government handed out the caps and gowns before graduation, and the officers met regularly over the summer to learn their duties for the next year. Yasmin was taught how to file, how to write up minutes, and how to perform other required tasks. By September 2000, when the fall semester finally began, they started having regular Executive Board (E-Board) meetings. They were fun, and she solidified her friendships with all the people on the board. Since she was now on the E-Board, she was also enrolled automatically in the Leadership class (made up of the E-Board and other registered students), and she began spending all her free time in that classroom, called simply "Leadership" by the students. It became a second home to her.

One day, early in the semester, she walked into Leadership and Elona and Eriola, twin Albanian girls, were already sitting there. Although they were also Muslim, the two were entirely secular, and they began talking excitedly about the first school dance of the year. They asked Yasmin about it. "Oh, I'm not going," she said. Dances were an activity that a religious Muslim girl like Yasmin would automatically forgo. The twins stopped talking and looked at each other.

"What do you mean you're not going?" Elona said.

"I don't think we're allowed to go to dances."

They looked at each other again. "I think you better talk to the COSA," Elona said, since he oversaw Leadership-led events like dances.

"Why?"

"I think it's gonna be a problem."

"Why? Why's it gonna be a problem? If I can't go, it's no big deal."

"I'm pretty sure they're gonna have a problem with it."

FORT HAMILTON'S COORDINATOR of student affairs was a sharp, stout, and principled man. Tireless in his leadership, he was widely admired (and somewhat feared) by the students. He never ruled by edict; instead he always got his way through intelligent conversation by showing you *why* you were wrong. He would talk to the students at their own level and above it simultaneously. Despite this, many of the students were devoted to him.

Yasmin told him about her reservations. Her religious beliefs meant that she couldn't attend the dances, and she expected he would just nod and say okay. Instead he told her that it didn't work that way, that as an E-Board member she was required to attend all school functions, dances included. He indicated that this was part of the job description that she had signed on to, and that if she didn't want to attend the dance, she could sit in another room in the basement during the event. That was the only compromise he offered, and Yasmin didn't see how that would help her. During the conversation they both held fast to their beliefs, and Yasmin saw a gray cloud overtaking the room, a mist brewing from their clash of principles. She knew that it wasn't that the COSA was opposed to her as a person. It was more that he felt that everything had to be exactly the same for everybody and that *his* principle of equality was being violated. On the other hand, Yasmin believed that she wasn't asking for any special treatment, only fair accommodation for *her* principles. But then the COSA implied that Yasmin's troubles stemmed from an overly protective Arab father, and that bothered her.

He cut the conversation short, telling her that he would call her parents. Yasmin walked out of his office with his final words bouncing around in her head: "I don't think this is going to work if you can't go to the dances," he had said, setting her nerves on edge.

As she expected, the phone call between the COSA and her father resolved nothing. The two men agreed to meet instead. Yasmin had told her father about the COSA's idea of her sitting in another room during the dance, and her father sought advice on the idea. He called up Sheikh Ibrahim, a local African-American Muslim leader who, Ismail figured, had grown up in New York and so was familiar with both American ways and Muslim doctrines. Ismail asked him if his daughter could attend the dances, and, as expected, the sheikh said that she should not. Ismail then asked if she could go but sit in the basement. The sheikh's answer employed analogical reasoning. If you're in a drug house, he rationalized, and it's a three-bedroom house, and somebody is using drugs in one of the bedrooms, when the police come, you will still be arrested as being a part of that house. His answer was resolute and categorical. She could not attend the dances. Ismail agreed and asked the sheikh to accompany him to the meeting. Yasmin became jittery. Her name was already up in big letters in Leadership under "Student Organization Secretary." She already loved the E-Board. She just wanted the issue settled.

Meanwhile, word spread in Leadership that Yasmin couldn't attend the dances, and on Friday the E-Board held a meeting without her to discuss the issue. The COSA spoke up, reminding the E-Board that he had spelled out the duties of elected positions before the election to all those who ran. Jessica, the sophomore representative, said that she had spoken to Yasmin, who very much wanted to continue as secretary, but the E-Board unanimously agreed with the COSA that unless you attend the events, you must resign.

The meeting between the COSA and her father was held on Monday, during one of Yasmin's classes, and she ran to the COSA's office after her class finished. The COSA let her in, closed the door, and told her that her father was unwilling to budge. He then reiterated his position that as secretary she had to attend all the events, and if she didn't, he explained, she would have to resign her position. "But that's not fair!" Yasmin pleaded. "There must be something we can do!" Over the weekend she had tried to look up the issue on the Internet and had come across the Federal Equal Access Act. She quoted it back to him as well as she could remember. "We're all supposed to have equal access!" The COSA shook his head paternally and told her it wasn't going to work. She remembers him apologizing. "I'm sorry," he said. "I don't think your father is going to agree to our terms." He told her it would be best if she prepared a resignation letter, and Yasmin started to cry.

At home her father described to her what had happened at the meeting. The sheikh had told the COSA the reasons she couldn't attend the dances, and the talk naturally gravitated to the option of her sitting in the basement during the events. The sheikh ruled that out. Dances entailed listening to sexed-up secular music, the fraternization of girls and boys, and usually illicit drinking. He knew, he said. He had grown up in New York. The COSA pointed to the speakers in the wall. "What if music came through the speakers right now, while you're sitting here. Would that be wrong?" The sheikh responded by saying, "Well, if I'm sitting in here, you're imposing the music upon me, correct? Then the fault is not mine. Do you understand?" The COSA turned to Ismail. "With all due respect to your religion, sir, how long do you think you can control your daughter?"

This line burned Yasmin's father like acid. As he relayed details of the meeting, he told Yasmin how much he resented the comment. The meeting concluded with the COSA pronouncing either that Yasmin would attend all the events or she would be removed from her position. "It's better if you resign," her father told her, "than to have it show up on your record that you were removed from a position."

She felt powerless, defeated, and angry. She dragged herself to the computer and formatted a very official-looking resignation letter, complete with Approve/Disapprove checkboxes for the COSA and the principal. It also included this statement:

I was forced to submit my resignation due to the system's inability to understand my moral obligations. For example, my beliefs prevent me from having anything to do with drinking/dancing. When I was young, the system told me to stand up and fight for what I believe in. While now I am being told to do the exact opposite, instead I should give up what I believe in for some rules and regulations. Martin Luther King Jr. fought for what he believed in and gave up his life for it. I too am taking that same stand by giving up my position to defend what I believe in.

Much later Yasmin regretted the spurious comparison with Martin Luther King Jr. "I caved in, and he was killed for what he believed in. It was so wrong," she told me, laughing, but at the time, she said, she was traumatized for having to do something against her core principles. She felt as if she were committing a crime against herself, she said, as if she were signing herself off life support.

THE DAY SHE HANDED the resignation letter to the COSA, Yasmin went to Leadership and saw some papers in her mailbox. Somebody had carelessly deposited the minutes from the E-Board meeting at which her resignation had been discussed, presumably for her, the sitting secretary, to type up. She collapsed in a chair and pored over the handwritten notes, learning that the entire E-Board had had this discussion about her and had unanimously voted against her position. She had thought of the E-Board representatives as friends. They knew she wasn't a bad person, she thought, so on some level she expected they would fight for her, or at least work to make an exception for her. But they hadn't, and she swallowed the bitter taste of betrayal.

Meanwhile, the COSA and the principal accepted her resignation letter, and they appointed Alina, the pretty Russian girl and runner-up in the election, as her successor. During the next Leadership class, Alina hugged Yasmin warmly and comforted her while someone else was busy taking her name off the Student Organization list and taping Alina's on the glass. "Alina is a nice girl," Yasmin told me, "but I couldn't help feeling angry at the girl who had taken my place."

IN YASMIN'S BAY RIDGE HOUSE is a tiny room with a computer and a fax machine used by her father for his business. This became her war room. She just couldn't accept that in the United States a Muslim girl would have to choose between her religion and her elected responsibilities. Over the next few months, she would go online and read all she could about the law. She began printing everything out, organizing a file in a folder decorated with multicolored smiley faces, as well as studying the front matter of a planner given to her by her high school, especially the "Bill of Student Rights and Responsibilities," where she highlighted everything relevant to her situation (even correcting its grammar). She put yellow marker to the sentence "Students have a right to be in a safe and supportive learning environment, free from discrimination, harassment and bigotry," and she underlined "discrimination." A fire had been lit under her, and researching the law became first a task, then a hobby, and finally an obsession.

The planner was essential for Yasmin. It was where, she told me, she first grasped the concept of rights, and she would use the idea of students' rights in every conversation she could. She began sounding like *Black's Law Dictionary*, arguing with her friends in high-school legalese about her situation. She would rustle printed-out pages of legal Web sites under the COSA's nose. He would hear her out and then tell her that it wasn't going to work, that the decision had been made. She posted her story anonymously to a student-leadership Web site to gauge the reaction from strangers across the country. ("If your religion prohibits you from doing something, and if your opponent can participate, then logically your opponent will be selected over you," was a typical response.) Her parents suggested she forget the past and concentrate instead on her schoolwork. Rather than compelling her to study, the admonition caused her to hide most of her research. And at night she continued to cry over her resignation, unable to let it go. "I must have been an annoying person!" she says now.

But no one—not her friends, her parents, the students in Leadership—was listening to her, so she changed course in early 2001. She looked up the New York City Board of Education online and e-mailed a trustee her story, signed with only her first name and the first initial of her last name. A few days later, she received an e-mail response. "Your letter has been forwarded to the Board's legal office for investigation," it read. "We need some additional information in order to respond. Please identify what school and district you attend. Also, what events were you unable to attend and when were they held? Who instructed you to resign from your position, what position did you hold, and for what period? To whom did you explain that your religion prevented you from attending events? We share your concern that religious beliefs be respected. With the additional information I have requested, we should be able to investigate your complaint."

Yasmin wrote back immediately. "I have great concern for what happened to me, however, I do not wish to identify the school. If extremely necessary, maybe I'll give it to you, however, I do not wish to tar my school's good reputation. I love my school to death, but if really necessary I will reveal it. I attend a high school in Brooklyn, NY. I don't know the district. I most certainly could not attend dances, or rock shows. We have many dances on Fridays, which is by the way a holy day for me, almost like the Sabbath or church Sunday. . . . I just can't be there. For example, it's like people are selling drugs, and I'm just an innocent stander-by, I would get arrested even if I had nothing to do with it. This is just an example, no offense meant. That's what it's like, I can't go against my religion. . . . Even if you find out my school, please keep it confidential until I am notified. I take that much pride in my school."

E-mails traveled back and forth for a while, but ultimately Yasmin wasn't prepared to reveal her school, and so the communications trickled off and then stopped. Meanwhile, she kept confronting the COSA with her pseudolegal arguments, until one day he gave her the phone number of Dr.

Irizarry, the school's superintendent and the author of the "Students' Bill of Rights." She called him full of hope, but again she reached a dead end. Dr. Irizarry asked her if people thought it was unfair for her to be an exception.

"Yes," she said. "A few."

"Well, that's not a good atmosphere," he said, and she hung up the phone after ten minutes, having achieved nothing.

She was losing her fight, and she felt abandoned and alone. She began looking up inspirational sayings on the Internet for support. She wrote in her notebook, "Those who stand for nothing fall for everything."

If no one would help her, she reasoned, she would have to do it by herself. For months, she spent hours after school at the Brooklyn Public Library on Seventy-third Street, checking out law books and guides (*And Justice for All: The Legal Rights of Young People, The Rights of Students: The ACLU Handbook for Young Americans, Teens on Trial: Young People Who Challenged the Law—and Changed Your Life, Sue the Bastards!: Everything You Need to Go to—or Stay Out of—Court, Law for Dummies,* and others). She would bring them home and type up relevant portions, which is how she learned the basics of contracts and lawsuits and various legal concepts on religious accommodation and antidiscrimination. Whenever she felt she had a new argument, she would go talk again to the COSA after Leadership. As always, he listened to her carefully, never shutting her up or getting impatient with her, but he would always shoot her down, telling her that the point she had discovered didn't apply to her situation or that she was falsely extrapolating from the law. Then he would send her packing.

Meanwhile, the Leadership class was planning further school events for the year, which entailed rearranging the dance schedule twice, once when the dance landed on the night of a Jewish holiday, which would have prevented the religious Jewish students from attending, and again when the event fell on the same night as the sweet-sixteen party of one of the girls in Leadership. Steam poured out of Yasmin's ears at the double standard.

But what bothered her most was something she encountered in her own amateur legal education. It was called "the statute of limitations,"

which stipulated that in many cases you had only one year from an incident to file a lawsuit. So when the election cycle came around again in
April, Yasmin had an idea. She would push back. If her case threatened to
become moot after a year, then she would have to find a way to keep it
alive. She would run again, this time for vice president, and then when the
same issue arose, she would have another full year to make a case, now with
much more legal experience under her belt to fight for her rights. Actually
winning the election was a minor bump in her plan. The main thing was to
keep the issue burning.

As she had done a year earlier, Yasmin picked up the application
packets the day they were made available. But this time she was stunned to
find that a new clause had been added to the Declaration of Consent form
required to run. "I understand and acknowledge the responsibilities and
the commitments needed to hold a position on the Student Organization
of Fort Hamilton High School," it read. "If elected, I agree to attend all
Student Organization sponsored events." *All events?* Yasmin felt as if she
had just been punched in the stomach. The new contract was aimed
squarely at her. Moreover, the new form disqualified all people like her
from ever running for office. *Damn!* she thought. She'd believed that she
had outsmarted them, and now they'd trumped her by cutting her off in
the race before she even left the starting line. Round one in her new battle
plan had gone to the school.

But she had an idea. Stipulations! She had learned in one of her legal
books that if you are confronted with disagreeable provisions in a contract,
you should just cross them out and add acceptable language. Yasmin carefully filled out her application of intent to run for office. When she made it
down to the new, offending section, she crossed it all out and wrote a letter
on another page she marked as CONFIDENTIAL. "According to the Student
Government application of 2001–2002, I realized that a whole paragraph
was inserted into the application totally excluding me from running at all,"
she began.

I believe that moral obligations are a valid reason for one to be exempt from attending certain events. Otherwise we are preventing every religious person to run for office. An example is the current elections of 2000 in the United States. If Mr. Gore was elected president and Mr. Lieberman as Vice President, we acknowledge that he cannot perform his duties on Saturdays due to his religious beliefs. If Mr. Lieberman was able to be exempt from working on Saturdays while leading the whole nation due to his religious beliefs, why are we to be treated any differently? We are all equal in the eyes of the Constitution and the law. That's why I am puzzled as to why we are treated differently due to our beliefs.

This time she also offered a compromise: "I am willing to attend the events within the guidelines of my beliefs"—explaining that she would help in setting up and taking down the hall but not be present "during the events because some things conflict with my beliefs."

Her stipulations ended on a legal note: "I am willing to answer any questions that might help you to reach a reasonable decision regarding my situation. However, I reserve the right to appeal." Her father cosigned her letter, and she handed in the form, believing she had the force of law on her side.

Instead of securing her a place on the ballot, the letter got her a meeting with the principal.

EVERYONE USED TO JOKE about the pasted-on smile of the principal, and that's precisely what greeted Yasmin. When the door opened, she saw the stretched lips and white gleam of authority wielding its power politely. The principal invited her in, and she began by asking Yasmin about her current run for office. The COSA was also there, and Yasmin began her regular catalog of justifications for her legal right to run. Behind the principal's smile, Yasmin thought, was annoyance, and the principal told her that the school also had laws in place, laws that had to be respected, followed, and abided by. She mentioned that the way to resolve the conflict was not by complaining to the school district, implying that the principal was getting heat from the superintendent, but by talking to her father. Yasmin wrote down what she said: "It was your father's choice to have you resign, not ours. The answer lies in your father's hands, not ours." And that was that.

She went home defeated—for a while. Previously her father had mentioned a Muslim civil-liberties organization to her, and one day she looked them up on the Internet. She sent off an e-mail to the Council on American-Islamic Relations (CAIR), and when someone from CAIR's office wrote her, Yasmin sent back a longer e-mail describing the case. Their civil-rights coordinator promised to look into it.

Yasmin sighed with relief after bringing CAIR into the picture. She hoped she could now finally achieve change by calling in outside help. CAIR wrote a letter to the school's principal, arguing for Yasmin's right to run, but nothing happened. The school ignored the letter, and the elections proceeded without her name on the ballot. Another Muslim girl, Waffiyah, a Pakistani American, won the position of vice president. "I don't see what the big deal about going to the dances is," Waffiyah told her. "I just stay downstairs. Why can't you?" Yasmin growled at her, holding in her frustrations. *Doesn't anybody else understand what's at stake here?* she asked herself, the thought screaming in her head. Her principles were leading her to feel more isolated than ever, and she moped for most of the summer. One August afternoon she faxed a lengthy handwritten letter to CAIR. "For a long time I refused to take any real action against the school," she wrote.

I didn't want to hurt them or their reputation. I still feel bad about it, but then I realized that they didn't really care as much about me as I did the school. So for a while I didn't really complain—I just gave up. I still cry about it sometimes, even though it's been a yr. But it hurt so much. In fact—I think it's stupid to cry over such a little thing—but what hurt me most was that when I won secretary as a Freshman, I felt that I had achieved my dreams and broken a racial barrier that I thought would hold me back. I finally felt that as a Muslim that I was doing something and I could make a difference in the world. I believed people would have confidence in me because of what was in my heart and not prejudice against my outer appearance—I had hope that I could achieve my dreams—but when they took me out I felt different and segregated and it shattered everything I had hoped and dreamed of. Now all I feel is hurt, sadness, and I feel that as a Muslim I can never be something because America is prejudiced so much and will never let people like me succeed no matter how hard we try. I never told anyone that this is what really hurts me and makes me cry. My family doesn't even know that I still cry and that I am still hurt and think about it every day. I felt so bad, and knowing how that feels, I don't want to have anyone else go through what I went through, Muslim or non-Muslim.

It was a cry in the wilderness.

IN SEPTEMBER the school year began again, and just days later terrorists attacked the Pentagon and the World Trade Center. On that Tuesday morning, Yasmin was in Spanish class. One girl walked in late and told everyone what had happened, and confusion immediately reigned. Teachers were walking in and out of classrooms, and students were constantly on their cell phones, talking to their parents, many of whom worked in the Twin Towers. It was soon clear that order would not be restored to the school: Parents began showing up and taking their children home early. Classes were in shambles. By lunchtime Yasmin wandered in to Leadership. Even after being evicted from her position, she still loved the atmosphere in Leadership. Maturity was more valued here than in the rest of school, as was creativity, and the students in Leadership saw themselves as student citizens participating in the project of Fort Hamilton High School. Besides, it was where all her friends were.

In Leadership they had a radio on, and everyone was listening to the news. Waffiyah was there, and Yasmin and Waffiyah started talking to the other kids. If Muslims did this, they agreed, then they didn't do it because of Islam. Their faith would never condone such a thing. The other kids listened, and someone brought up the Oklahoma City bombings. A respectful and reasoned discussion followed, and the feeling in Leadership was actually one of solidarity. Everyone was coming together because everyone was scared and trying to understand what was going on, she told me.

Her parents were concerned that there might be a backlash against their *hijab*-wearing daughters. They decided to keep Yasmin home for a couple of days. But after nothing serious materialized, she returned to her classes—and her fight.

SHE KEPT UP her correspondence with CAIR, which, though it was now overwhelmed by the fallout from the September 11 attacks, still continued to advocate for Yasmin. CAIR sent another letter to the princiapl, enclosing one of its pamphlets, titled *An Educator's Guide to Islamic Religious Practices*. ("Thank you so much for helping me," she wrote in November 2001, "especially while your hands are full enough with everything that's happened.") She enrolled again in Leadership—it continued to be one of her favorite classes—and she would repeatedly confront the COSA with arguments as to why she should be able to run again in the elections. Still she got nowhere.

By the end of the fall semester, she was putting pressure on her younger sister, who had just entered the school, to run for freshman representative. The election cycle for freshman representative begins in January, and Yasmin thought Mariam should run out of principle. "I don't know," Mariam said. "Look at what happened to you!" But Yasmin was insistent. "Come on, Mariam. That's why you have to," she whined. "Then it's two against the world instead of just one!"

Mariam capitulated. She picked up the application form when it was made available, and, as expected, it contained the same language in the Declaration of Consent that had disqualified Yasmin from running. This time Yasmin instructed Mariam to write "as long as it doesn't conflict with our religious beliefs" at the end of the paragraph. Mariam initialed the addition and had her father stipulate and initial the form where it asked for his signature. She then handed in the documents. In return Mariam received a letter from the current Student Organization president. "We have received your signed declaration," it read. "However, we regret to inform you that we cannot accept this declaration with your stipulated conditions. It is impossible to know from your statement what terms you are willing to agree to. Therefore your name will not appear on the ballot for 2002 unless we have your declaration signed without any additional conditions, made by any persons and/or organizations other than the Student Organization of Fort Hamilton High School. For your convenience, enclosed is another declaration form. You may begin campaigning as soon as your form is signed unconditionally, and filed with the Student Organization."

Yasmin expected opposition from the school, but then her family started to turn against her. Her father sent an angry letter to the school, threatening legal action if they didn't alter their policies, but at home he was telling Yasmin to forget it. It was jeopardizing her medical-school future. He already couldn't believe that she had reenrolled in Leadership after all the problems she'd had. Nor could he fathom the amount of time Yasmin was spending on the issue. He would continue to walk into the computer room and find her sitting there with browsers open to legal Web sites and a guilty look on her face.

"Yasmin," he would say, sighing. "What are you doing?"

"Researching," she would answer, blushing.

Then he would yell. "Stop wasting time! Do your homework instead! This isn't leading anywhere!" He thought time would grow skin back over the wound, but she kept pulling at the scab.

One afternoon she was in the kitchen with her mother, and Mariam walked in to get some food from the refrigerator. Her father had again told her to forget her battle, so Yasmin posed the question to her mother. "What do you think? Should I keep fighting it? Is it worth it?"

Her mother looked at her kindly. "It *is* taking up a lot of your time," she said with soft eyes. "You could use that instead for your studying. Why waste your energy?"

Yasmin leaned on the fridge door while Mariam was rifling through the refrigerator for something to eat. "What do you think?" Yasmin asked her sister.

"Well," she said, stretching up. "I don't know." She shrugged. "They're not going to change their minds."

Mariam had long ago given up her notions of becoming freshman representative, and Yasmin walked away hurt. She had considered Mariam her comrade in arms, her last best hope. Now that Mariam had quit the struggle, she felt she was fighting not just the school but also her family, and it was a heavy burden.

Rather than deterring her, however, it hardened her resolve. She would try again this year to run, but this time for the presidency, regardless of how impossible that would be. She faxed the ACLU a five-page, single-spaced narrative of the events, hoping to enlist their help, but she heard nothing back from them. Meanwhile, CAIR's civil-rights coordinator called the school one day and spoke to the assistant principal, who told her that Yasmin and Mariam had "to decide what is more important to them, their religion or the student body" and if they wanted "to observe their religion, they should go to private school." The CAIR coordinator was insulted by the comments and their tone, and CAIR faxed a letter to the school again affirming the case and now demanding an apology for these remarks. They asked for a meeting with the principal and also offered to present an educational forum "on the Islamic way of life" to the school. As before, the letter went unheeded.

Then, in early 2002, there was a minor breakthrough. An attorney who worked with CAIR agreed to meet Yasmin and her father to discuss the case. She shook with excitement. Finally concrete legal help was coming to her aid. She compiled all the paperwork she had and waited anxiously for the meeting, having realized a long time before now that she was powerless to change her world on her own.

It was an early-evening meeting, and Yasmin and her father took the subway to midtown Manhattan after school. They exited the elevator and found the offices empty except for the attorney, who invited them in. Yasmin was impressed by the stately, reserved elegance of the place. *A Muslim lawyer,* she thought. *That's awesome!*

He sat them down in a boardroom with a big oak table and asked Yasmin to explain the story. She immediately launched in by describing the Equal Access Act and the basics of contract law.

"Just explain the story to me," he said patiently.

So she did. She took out her smiley-face folder and detailed how she had won the election, been forced to resign, lost her right to run again, and everything else that had happened. He took notes on a yellow legal pad as she spoke, interspersed with nodding his head or humming assent. Yasmin finished, and then he spoke, first offering the now seventeen-year-old some advice. Whenever anyone said something related to the case, he told her, she should note what was said, the speaker, and the date. Yasmin listened with open ears and canyon-wide eyes. That will be your evidence, he said, and Yasmin nodded. "So what should we do?" she asked, almost holding her breath. He thought they had a case, he said, and she began breathing again. He couldn't promise they would win, he said, but there was a case to be made here, one that the courts would decide. And then he started talking about money.

He told Yasmin and her father that a lower-court decision would require a six-thousand-dollar retainer. If it moved to a higher court, fees might reach ten to twelve thousand. And he kept walking up the litigation ladder with higher figures and higher courts while Yasmin nodded and her father said nothing. The meeting ended. "Think about it," he said as he showed them out. "You know how to contact me." For the first time, the thought hit Yasmin. *Wait. Is my dad going to pay for this?* He'd said it was worth it, she surmised, so he'd probably pay.

Outside, Yasmin was bubbling with excitement over the meeting. She turned to her father. "What do you think, *Baba?*"

They were walking to the subway, descending the stairs. "It's a good case, *habibti,*" her father said, "but I have four daughters. I have to put you all through college. I can't pay twelve to twenty thousand dollars to bring a case to court that might lose." They waited on the platform, and suddenly Yasmin felt her imminent victory sliding away. "But, *Baba,*" she pleaded. "It's for a good cause! It's for all the Muslims! If it becomes a good law, then it applies everywhere!" She had learned this from her legal research. The subway roared in, all rattling noise and clanging steel.

"Think of the money, Yasmin. It wouldn't be fair to your sisters. They have to go to school, too."

He paused, and the conductor announced, "Stand clear of the closing doors, please."

"We'll think about it," he said, which in Egyptian parentspeak, as Yasmin well knew, really means no.

In FEBRUARY, Yasmin took the lawyer's advice to heart. She was sitting in Leadership class when the COSA explained that since Greek Easter begins on a Friday, Greek students in Leadership would be excused from a bodybuilding event to be held on a weekend in May. (In addition to dances, Yasmin didn't attend the school's bodybuilding contests, which she described in an e-mail as "a show of half-naked contestants flexing their muscles, which I feel is inappropriate.") She scribbled a note on a piece of paper beginning with the date and time of the COSA's comment. "2-4-02, 12:41 pm. Greeks—Good Friday Greester—will be excused for religious obligations," and then she quoted the COSA, "'For religious obligations, I'm willing to make exceptions ONCE in a while.'" She recalled when the E-Board changed the date of a dance so it wouldn't conflict with one girl's private party and wrote underneath, "Sweet 16—not a religious holiday, duh! Make one exception—5 follow."

Later she found out that the E-Board had put her on a "maybe list" to get kicked out of Leadership.

YASMIN KNEW twenty thousand dollars was a lot of money, but she started to think about how she could raise it on her own. She racked her brain but came up with nothing. What a fantasy! she realized. She was seventeen years old—how was she going to get $20K? Instead she started paying close attention to those personal-injury lawyer advertisements on the subway that offer free consultations. At home she would flip through the Yellow Pages and call up attorneys in her spare time. They all promised a free first visit, but when she asked them over the phone how much the case would cost after the consultation, they all said the same thing to her: Come in and we'll talk about it. She knew it was a lost cause and stopped calling.

After a few weeks, her mother took the girls to the movies. It was a Saturday afternoon. The theater is next to the neighborhood mosque, so the conservatively dressed Muslims and belly-button-showing moviegoers frequently find themselves congregating on the same sidewalk after their respective communal events. Yasmin and her family checked out the movie posters advertising current attractions, and since everyone liked the young Dakota Fanning, they decided on *I Am Sam*. A few minutes later, the screen lit up with Sean Penn acting the part of Sam, a mentally challenged father whose child is taken away from him, and Yasmin felt a twinge of recognition. Here was Sam, battling a system that steamrolled right over him, needing legal help. In the movie he visits the office of Rita Harrison, a high-octane attorney played by Michelle Pfeiffer, only to be pushed out of Harrison's office. But he goes back, and Harrison is embarrassed in front of her colleagues by Sam's presence. In an effort to salvage a modicum of her humanity, Harrison sputters out an offer of pro bono legal representation. "My lawyer for free!" Sam screams, jumping around her office after she explains to him what "pro bono" means. In all her research, Yasmin had never hitched on to the term "pro bono," and she immediately raised an eyebrow in the dark. *Pro bono?* she thought. *That sounds like something I need to know.*

As soon as she got home, she powered up the computer and discovered the pro bono world of legal representation. Yasmin was stunned. There are lawyers who would take your case for free? It seemed like a godsend, an impossibility, a dream. She typed "pro bono" and "free" into Altavista, her search engine of choice in 2002, and page after page came up. She scoured her results and narrowed her search, until she finally landed on one Web site, Advocates for Children, a New York organization aimed at protecting the rights of children in public education. She couldn't believe it.

IMMEDIATELY SHE CALLED and faxed Advocates for Children her story, and a few days later Jimmy Yan, an attorney who was then on the staff of the organization, called her to set up a meeting. She told her father about the call, and he speculated that perhaps the legal services were free because the lawyers were recent graduates or were learning to practice their art (neither of which is the case—in fact, the American Bar Association urges attorneys to offer at least fifty hours of service a year pro bono publico, for the good of the people).

Once again Yasmin and her father took the subway to Manhattan, with Yasmin carrying the smiley-face file holding all her papers under her arm. This time it was an early-morning meeting. This place had the same professional allure as the other lawyer's office, but it was larger and full of cubicles and desks stacked high with papers and folders. Yasmin judged from the size of the office and the number of cubicles that a lot of work must be done in the organization. Yan invited them into the boardroom. Since no one else was in the office at that hour, they had his complete attention.

And once again Yasmin described the whole situation, pulling out her papers to prove her position, while an attorney took notes. She had amassed even more documentation since she had been advised to write everything down, but it was the difference in the applications that seemed to draw

Yan's interest most. He examined the first paragraph carefully and then moved on to the second. He riffled through more of the papers as Yasmin finished the story and waited expectantly for him to say something.

Finally he spoke. "This is absurd," he said. "Absolutely absurd. I can't believe they would do something like this." He pulled out a piece of paper. "Sign this," he said. "I won't even ask about your income. Just sign here, and I'll take care of it." Yasmin's jaw dropped. Someone was listening to her. And not only was he listening to her, he was listening to her pro bono publico, for the good of the people.

"CONTRARY TO WHAT a lot of people think," Jimmy Yan told me when I called him to discuss the case, "most of the racism in our society happens to the most vulnerable members in our public schools." Yan is now the general counsel to Manhattan Borough President Scott Stringer, but at the time he worked tirelessly at Advocates for Children in the generally neglected field of education law. Yasmin, he told me, "was remarkable in seeking resources to fight her battle, and I was happy to work with her."

Yan set to work by reviewing the constitutional issues in Yasmin's case. "Do Yasmin and Mariam have a claim for violation of their rights under the free exercise clause of the First Amendent?" he asked, in an internal legal memo drafted at Advocates for Children. "Yes," the memo answered. "The Fort Hamilton policy of requiring members of the student government to 'attend all Student Organization events' lacks neutrality because of its intent to restrict [Yasmin's and Mariam's] right to Free Exercise of religion and lacks general applicability because it was discriminatorily enforced." The memo cited years of legal precedent and noted that "when Yasmin first ran . . . the application contained no requirement that she attend all school functions. It was only when Yasmin intended to run for office during the next term that the application stated that attending school functions was a requirement."

Yan found the school's arguments unconvincing. "The one compromise the school offered was to allow Yasmin to remain in the basement during the dance. It is hard to understand how remaining in the basement, out of sight, would further the school's policy objectives [of fostering school spirit] any more than simply allowing Yasmin to participate only in activities prior to and after the dance." Moreoever, the memo noted, the school "has a history of making exceptions to the rule that undermine its stated intent. . . . Jewish students were exempted from attending a school dance for religious reasons and just this spring Greek students were exempted from another Student Organization activity because it conflicted with Orthodox Easter. . . . There is no reason why making exceptions in those cases would not hinder the school's objectives while an exception for Yasmin or Mariam would." The memo concluded, "The school's policy is neither neutral nor generally applicable and fails to meet the hurdle of strict scrutiny. The policy should be invalidated entirely."

Armed with the memo and legal precedent, Yan called the school and the district, arguing that the school was applying its policy unconstitutionally. He also explored a discrimination complaint through the internal discrimination procedures of the Department of Education. Resistant at first, the school finally yielded, and it redrafted its policy in line with the standards of reasonable accommodation. Yan's work was done.

What was a relatively quick case for him was the whole world for Yasmin.

ON APRIL 15, 2002, the election cycle was announced and applications were distributed to interested candidates. Yasmin picked up the packet and flipped to the back. She couldn't stop smiling because of what she read. There was another new paragraph, but the relevant section of this one read, "In the event that I am unable to fulfill all the responsibilities of the office for which I am running, as stated in the Student Organization Constitution, and I provide a reasonable justification for such an inability, a reasonable accommodation will be considered by the members of the Student Organization Executive Board, under the condition that the accommodation does not create an undue hardship and unduly compromise or jeopardize the principles vital to the existence of the Leadership Program and the Student Organization." She could see right through the dense legal language, and to her the paragraph read like Thomas Paine. It was the language of democracy. Now she—and everyone else like her—could run for office.

She faxed Yan the new paragraph and asked if she should sign it. He gave her the go-ahead, and she completed the application. She knew that the Election Committee would scrutinize her as if she were radioactive, so she was fastidious about the application. Instead of the required one hundred signatures in blue ink, Yasmin gathered five hundred, in the event that if the committee disqualified any, she would have more than enough replacements. (This turned out to be a good campaign strategy, getting her campaign noticed.) She made sure that everything else about the application was also perfect, leaving the committee no choice but to accept her in the race.

And they did. She was now officially on the ballot, running for the presidency against Andrew, a very popular Greek boy, the Bill Clinton of Fort Hamilton High. She knew it would be next to impossible to beat him. But even if she lost, she believed, she had won.

"What if I didn't see *I Am Sam*?" Yasmin asked me. She told me she still finds herself thinking about that very question. "I would have given up," she said. "I feel like I have been taught a lesson that just because something seems impossible, it doesn't really mean that it's impossible, and that you never really know what you're capable of or what you can accomplish if you don't keep fighting for it, no matter how bad things are."

SHE HAD TWO WEEKS to campaign for the presidency, and she began hearing from her friends how the partisans of Andrew were spreading the word that Yasmin would be a lousy president. They were saying things like, "Vote for Andrew. Yasmin can't do anything. She can't go to late-night events," and "You want somebody who can be there. Not somebody who can't! She can't do the job." She would lie awake at night worrying about the effects of all the gossip and suggestions and agonizing over her speech.

On Wednesday, May 29, she delivered her final campaign speech. "Before I begin, I would like to thank everyone who has always been there for me, supported me, and encouraged me to fight for what I believe in," she said. "Without them I wouldn't be here today. So thank you!" She proceeded to describe how she would be a "true leader who won't make false promises," like McDonald's franchises in the school. And then she turned to talk about students' rights. "Of all the elections I've seen, not one candidate ever mentioned defending students' rights. Why is that?" she asked. "Whether I win or not, I will always be here to defend your rights, no matter what obstacles lie ahead. Student government is meant to serve students, not themselves." She finished her speech and noticed that her hands were shaking. As she sat down, the audience clapped politely.

Andrew went next with a speech that was a frontal attack on Yasmin without mentioning her by name. He did, however, gesture frequently in her direction. His speech consisted essentially of the same material as the rumors she'd already heard, asking rhetorically if the students wanted a leader who could be there for the events or one who couldn't. Yasmin listened to it in shock. *Wow, he's really hating on me,* she thought.

She had to go through it six more times. By third period Yasmin had her speech down. The auditorium, now holding hundreds of students, was filled with many more of her friends and her classmates. Again she stood up and spoke, and again people clapped politely. She sat down and braced herself for Andrew's speech, all the while staring at her shoes in embarrassment. She couldn't look up and was waiting for him to finish. When he finally did, she heard the audience start to clap, low at first, before picking up in volume. But then, underneath the clapping, Yasmin heard it, a boo that spread across the auditorium and only increased in volume. Andrew went back to his seat looking confused. (Manal, a friend of both Andrew and Yasmin, told me, "People booed Andrew because his speech was all about 'my opponent this, my opponent that.' And Yasmin's so very tiny. She looked so innocent.")

Voting took place during third period the next day, and the official results were supposed to be announced the following morning. Yasmin went home to wait it out, and she surprised herself by crying. Maybe her fight was going to waste, she thought, convinced she had lost the race. What if they started excluding people like her in the future? she thought. If she had been elected, that would have proved that she could do the job, but if she lost, then maybe that only proved that they made an exception in this one race, and that was good enough for them. Besides, she really wanted to be president.

The next morning a friend on the Election Committee told Yasmin that the race was extremely close, that the committee had counted twice, and that Andrew had won both counts, but with different numbers and by a very small margin. She went to her Leadership class, and the COSA called her into his office.

He told her the same thing, that the race was skating along a razor's edge and that it was too close to call a victor. He explained the school's constitution to Yasmin. The Election Committee would perform another count, he told her, which they expected to be final. But, he said, she had the right according to the school's constitution to ask for an official recount, which would be public and which she would be officially invited to watch. What, he asked, would she do?

Yasmin was about to say no—she even felt the *n* on her teeth—but out of nowhere she said, "Yeah, I'll want a recount. And when you do the recount, I want to be there, and I want either my lawyer or my father there, too." She didn't know where these words came from, but the COSA looked at her with a smile on his lips. Okay, he said, but he didn't know about having her lawyer or father present. She dragged her feet home after school and was sitting around doing nothing when the phone rang. Immediately she recognized the COSA's voice.

"Hello, may I please speak to Yasmin?" he asked.

"She's not here right now," she joked. She was feeling playful in her depression. After all that the COSA and she had been through, they had developed this strange kind of friendship based on mutual respect. He laughed a little, and she said, "No, it's me," settling back into her monotone.

"Well, congratulations, Miss President."

In a heartbeat she understood. "No way!"

"Yes," he said. "We did another count, a proper count, and you won." He sounded happy.

"No way!" she said again. "Oh, my God! Oh, my God!" she screamed. She stopped to inhale. "For real? I won? You're not lying to me?"

"No, I'm not lying to you," he said. "You're president. Congratulations."

Later she discovered that she had won the election by seven votes.

IT TOOK SOME TIME, but Yasmin was able to win over the E-Board as well. She completed a successful term as her high school's president and was admired by teachers and students alike. When college-application time rolled around, she asked the COSA to write a letter of recommendation for her, and he gladly obliged. "Perhaps the most exceptional quality about Yasmin is her dedication to her cultural and religious beliefs," he wrote. "She has brought about an awareness of cultural diversity to our school, the likes of which we have not seen before. Yasmin is leading our school's transformation from a climate of mere tolerance to that of understanding and acceptance. Her commitment and willingness toward promoting intercultural harmony is most inspirational." To this day she and the COSA have remained friends.

Since finishing high school, Yasmin has burned through her undergraduate degree in three years and has begun a master's degree that she will soon finish. She has also challenged her father's wishes. After finishing college she told him that she would not become a doctor. She has other ideas now, plans that illustrate the growing assertiveness of young Arab and Muslim Americans to claim their rights through the system. Yasmin is going to law school.

AKRAM

In the dark
They could not see
Who had gained
The victory.

—LANGSTON HUGHES, "Peace"

A kram is a twenty-one-year-old Palestinian American with a Caesar haircut and silver wire-framed glasses that give him a serious, almost Roman, look. But Akram is no mirthless senator. He laughs easily and has impressive comic timing along with an equally striking work ethic. At his father's Brooklyn grocery, he labors for sixty-five hours a week during the school year, while also attending college full-time. In the summer he works a full ninety hours a week. When he's not at work or at school, he's usually flopped out at home, where he lives with his extended family, thirteen of them, in a narrow two-family house in Sunset Park. Exhausted from work and school, he's normally in his room watching television, where he gets absorbed to the point that he can't pull himself away from all the terror talk in the culture. For the last two seasons, his favorite show has been Fox's ticking-bomb terror drama *24,* and he never misses an episode. He likes rooting for the "wrong side" and loves to tell me that I'm the spitting image of one of last year's terrorists. He has his own pride in his heritage and his religion, but everywhere he turns—from television shows, movies, news reports, and the occasional customer—the culture is droning on that Islam is to be feared and that Arabs are a problem to be dealt with. Most of the time, he laughs with his friends at these cartoonish representations, but behind the humor is the ache of an identity under siege. And so Akram is looking for a way to redeem his own sense of himself.

This is not a front-page story of violence or rebellion, the responses that we have been programmed to expect by a culture mired in fear, sensationalism, and complacency. It's in fact a far more typical tale of quiet frustration, full of longings for escape and rebirth. Akram wants to be free of the drudgery of his work by moving up and beyond the store, but he also wants to be rid of all the stereotyping and misunderstanding that is floating around like a bad odor. This is his story, about race and class and opportunity, and about trying to figure your way in a world of progressive disenchantment. What do you do when everything and everyone—from teachers to TV—is screaming that you and your culture just don't belong? You have to come up with your own solutions, and Akram has found his answer. He's quitting the United States and heading to Dubai, a newfound land of opportunity, a global oasis of modern wealth done up Arabic style. Dubai. It's the latest Arab-American dream.

I'VE KNOWN AKRAM FOR several years, and when I visit him, it's not at his home but usually at his family's store off in East Flatbush. To get there you board the B17 bus and head south down Remsen Avenue. The subway doesn't serve outer Brooklyn neighborhoods well, so the bus is almost always full, and you will usually be forced to stand unsteadily and hold on to the aluminum balance bar while the bus pushes and wheezes asthmatically along its route. Peering out the window, you can play a counting game with yourself: There are seven churches and one Burger King before you get to your stop. If you see the Wendy's, you know you've gone too far.

East Flatbush is a mostly Caribbean neighborhood that has become a monotonous geography of faith and fast food. It's about eight miles and a world away from New York City's empire of luxury, where the apples are hand-polished and the buildings stretch out into sky. Skyscrapers colonize

air and land mountain-size shadows on the ground there, but in East Flatbush the buildings are low and simple, so the sun shines brightly on beaches
of concrete. It's a commercially desolate landscape, a neighborhood of
hardworking regular folk who depend heavily on the entrepreneurial immigrant's grocery store. From the bus window, you can see rows of single-
family houses, some with gravel yards instead of grass. Cars rush by and
kick up discarded plastic bags that float back down like leaves in autumn.
Running shoes hang like white fruit from the electrical wires. Finding fresh
vegetables or a secular bookstore poses a challenge.

Soon after I press the tape to get off the bus, I am standing in front of a
small gray strip mall with a storefront evangelical church (called Hebron),
a Chinese restaurant (called Fortune Cookie), and one of the two small
groceries that serve the neighborhood. Mike's Food Center is Akram's
family store, and it isn't big but it's clean and has a better selection and
cheaper prices than the Korean-owned grocery on the next block. A
NY LOTTO sign is glowing neon promises in the window. A metal bottle
opener is bolted to the outside doorframe. Inside, I can smell the lemon-
sour scent of supermarket antiseptic hanging in the air. Refrigerators hum,
frozen foods sunbathe in artificial light, and nickel candies tempt kids by
the register. In the summertime, an open box or two of yellow onions and
green plantains spills out onto the sidewalk. Sometimes they'll have a few
fresh avocados by the register that they ask you not to squeeze.

When I walk in and say hello, Akram and Kareem, his younger cousin,
will usually yell out a salaam or two until there's a lull in their commerce
and we have time to talk. Mike's Food Center is always busy, and almost
everyone in the store is black—Jamaican hipsters, Haitian city workers,
Barbadian mothers, African-American old-timers—except for the four
Arab men—Akram, Kareem, Abdel Salam (Akram's father) and his brother
Khalil (Akram's uncle)—working the register or stocking the shelves. If it's
Sunday afternoon, the store is packed with the after-church crowd, both
Caribbean and African-American, shopping while dressed sharply in fine
suits and fancy hats. ("You're looking good," Akram will sing while ringing
up the sale. "You just come from court?" And the customers will laugh

while pocketing the change.) They're often buying orange juice, diapers, and loaves of pure white bread. On Thursdays it's a different clientele. Thursdays are paydays, which means that the sales are mostly phone cards with special rates to the Caribbean, along with cashews, sweetened condensed milk, and single bottles of Guinness. On those days I'll have to push my way through the crowd at the door. The whole week long, customers stream in a constant flow from seven in the morning until eight at night (and six on Sundays), when the lights go out and Akram and his father pull down the metal grate in the day's final fit of exhaustion. Tomorrow it starts all over again.

Akram knows that Mike's Food Center is everything to his family. It puts meals on the table and structures their lives. But it also swallows their time. One Sunday night a friend called Akram while he, Kareem, and I were on our way to see the Palestinian film *Paradise Now,* the first movie they'd seen in a theater in over a year. (They loved it.) "Tell him you just sat down and are having dinner with your family," Kareem joked. Akram laughed and reported this to his friend in serious tones. "I don't know, all my white friends," he said, after he got off the phone, "whenever you call them, they always say they're having dinner with their family." He chuckled. "When was the last time you had dinner with your whole family?"

When business does slow down, Akram reads the newspapers that are delivered to the store. It's the *Daily News* during the week and the Sunday *New York Times* on the weekend, and he reads all the stories about the war in Iraq and the conflicts in the Occupied Territories until the last one is sold and his reading has to stop, even if he's in the middle of an article. Then he might pull out his PSP and play video games until a regular customer comes in and the conversations begin. Sometimes the talk is political, but it usually starts off as banter. The same conversations happen over and over, with Akram leading the way. Someone will walk in and ask, "What's up?"

"The cost of living."

"You're not ripping me off now, are you?" a customer will ask as Akram's fingers fly on the keys of the cash register.

"It's not the first time," he'll quip, "and it won't be the last."

A sidelong glance, a chuckle, and the customer moves on.

Other conversations appear almost scripted. One summer day when I was there, a pretty teenage girl walked into the store wearing short black shorts and a pink tank top. Akram shot Jerry, one of the regular Bajan customers, a look. "How are you?" asked Akram.

"I'm fine," she said flatly.

"Yes you are," Jerry said intensely.

Akram laughed. "Ah! Fifteen gets you twenty, my friend. Fifteen gets you twenty." He turned to his cousin. "You know that movie *Boyz n the Hood*?" he asked. "This is *Boyz from the* Quds," he said, using the Arabic word for "Jerusalem."

Unlike many of Brooklyn's Muslim youth, Akram didn't become more religious after the terrorist attacks of September 11. He doesn't regularly attend Friday prayers at the mosque. He's usually too busy at the store, and anyway the imam at the nearest mosque is constantly lecturing his mostly Yemeni store-owner congregation about the sins of selling alcohol and pork, ideas that Akram and his cousin find boring, repetitive, and unrealistic. On the other hand, owing to his interactions with his customers, he knows all the countries of the Caribbean, their politics, their foods, and their vernaculars. He'll joke with an older Grenadian woman that he went to school with Maurice Bishop's son. Just when she believes him, he'll smile the bad news to her that he's joking. He curses the Haitians in Jamaican patois and the Jamaicans in Haitian Creole, to everyone's surprise and amusement. He's a curious mix that isn't so strange in Brooklyn, equally at home with Arabs, African Americans, and West Indians. He's a twenty-first-century United States American, absorbing and refracting all the ethnicities and histories surrounding him. What he loves most about Brooklyn is this heady human geography. He likes Walt Whitman, and Walt would have liked him.

In many ways the store is what gives Akram this complexity. His gregarious personality comes alive there, endowing Mike's Food Center with a kind of familiarity between owner and customer that strikes me as quite unique. But the immigrant grocery store itself is not uncommon. If you've spent any time in New York City, you've probably been in one of them. These groceries are rungs of commerce for immigrant entrepreneurs that they can step on and hoist themselves up America's economic ladder. Arab-owned grocery stores in New York City number over two thousand, most with Palestinian and Yemeni proprietors, making them a central location of Arab-American life in Brooklyn. Sociologists call the entrepreneurs of these stores "middlemen minorities," ethnic businessmen and -women who function as intermediaries between inner-city clients and the conglomerates that want to sell them things but don't want to deal with them directly, and Arab Americans are among New York City's most numerous middlemen minorities.

The sociologist Edna Bonacich is one of the primary investigators of this phenomenon, and she reports that middlemen minorities tend to stick together, usually in families, to overcome hardships that often derive from hostility in the host society. She cites the Jews in Europe (labeling them "perhaps the epitome of the form"), the Chinese in Southeast Asia, the Syrians in West Africa, the Parsis in India." As they tend to be "pushed out of desirable occupations and forced to make a living in marginal lines," middleman minorities are often found concentrated in merchant professions, Bonacich explains, where "thrift" is valued and capital is easily moved or transferred. Since they are less involved in the "status hang-ups of the surrounding society," middlemen minorities are also "free to trade or deal with anyone," even with those typically ignored by elite society.

Palestinian store owners in Brooklyn are the latest manifestation of an old form, in which the work often pays off financially but requires long hours and intense dedication. Like every other middleman minority, Palestinians also exhibit a strong attachment to an ancestral homeland and a high degree of ethnic solidarity. With many middlemen minorities, the short-term hardship of such strenuous work is offset by the long-term goal of returning to their homeland. Many Yemeni store owners in Brooklyn, for example, save most of their income to pay for return trips to Yemen for months or even years at a time, while the store is overseen by a relative.

This option is obviously unavailable to Palestinians, as it once was to Jews, making them, to use Bonacich's term, "lasting middlemen minorities." And sometimes, as Bonacich also notes, the stores that middlemen minorities own can become the causes of conflict in the neighborhoods where they are based, even though the store owners, too, are often discriminated against by the culture at large.

We have become in some senses conditioned to this conflict through American cinema and culture. Remember the scene in Spike Lee's film *Do the Right Thing,* for example, when a mob is on a rampage after the police choke the life out of Radio Raheem. They lay their eyes on the Korean store in the neighborhood and are ready to burn it down as the Korean shopkeeper yells, "Me no white, me black!" and the people in the mob start to laugh, deciding to leave the Korean man and his store alone. (Koreans and Arabs are the two most common middlemen minorities in New York City today.) Thankfully, Mike's Food Center has never seen any riots, and the atmosphere there is often more like the one in *Barbershop* than *Do the Right Thing* or the nihilistic *Falling Down.* In fact, the relationships are even more complex than black/nonblack at Mike's Food Center and in East Flatbush, owing in large part to the triangulation in the store between African Americans, Caribbean Americans, and Palestinian Americans, a complicated mix of groups, all of whom have unique histories in the United States. But East Flatbush wasn't always this tricky.

IN 1982, Abdel Salam, Akram's father, bought Mike's Food Center, but he had already been in the country since 1971. When he departed his West Bank village of el-Bireh and landed in Brooklyn, he was seventeen years old. Having left his family's farming life and the ugliness of the Israeli occupation behind him, he arrived nearly penniless in the United States, holding little education and even less money. Bewildered by his new life, Abdel Salam did what every lost immigrant does: He sought out his own kind. In the hardscrabble days of the early seventies, he trundled his way out to the concrete sidewalks of Atlantic Avenue and began working in the same traditions that Arab immigrants to New York had followed since late Ottoman times in the United States. Abdel Salam peddled whatever he could get his hands on. He bought clothes and costume jewelry wholesale and sold them at retail prices around the neighborhood and all over the city. It was a hard, tenuous existence. Once, when he had nothing left to sell and only dust in his pocket, he picked up a stray cat and walked into a pizzeria in Brooklyn. With a smile and some sweet talk, he convinced the man behind the counter that the cat was a purebred Egyptian and worth two dollars and two pies. Maybe the Italian took pity on the poor Palestinian man, but it didn't matter. This was the best sale and the tastiest pizza of his life.

He left peddling behind, and over the next eleven years Abdel Salam worked in other Arab grocery stores around the city and saved every penny he earned. He shared an impossibly small studio apartment with six other men, where they lived one on top of the other, rotating occupancy between shifts of work. He sent money home and spent nothing superfluously, until he and his brother Khalil, who had followed him to Brooklyn the year after he arrived, had saved enough to make the move from worker to owner. The two brothers found out that another Palestinian friend from el-Bireh was selling his store in East Flatbush.

The store was still called Mike's Food Center from two owners earlier, and back when the original Mike ran it, East Flatbush was mostly Jewish. But the casts are never stable in New York's ethnic drama, and in the mid-1980s, Caribbean immigrants began moving into the neighborhood in large numbers, and the Jewish population moved out and up. (A very few old-timers—but really no more—still live in the neighborhood.) The two brothers watched the transformation from the stoop of their store. They began stocking plantain chips and ginseng potions and selling single bottles of Guinness. They hung a framed paper sign (that has since yellowed and crinkled with age) on the wall. TAWAKKALTU ALALLAH it says in calligraphic Arabic, which translates into "I place my trust in God." Much later, when he was old enough to work in the store, Akram taped a handwritten sign above the register. It has almost the same message but this time in a more

American idiom: "IN ALLAH WE TRUST. EVERYONE ELSE MUST PAY—*NO CREDIT.*" The customers laughed. From the moment they had started coming to the store, they had been calling Abdel Salam "Mike," and the name has stuck to the man ever since.

Eventually both men married women from the West Bank, and each had three daughters and two sons, all American born, "unfortunately," Akram now says with a sly shrug. The sons were important, because when they were old enough, they could help in the store. Daughters, on the other hand, were to stay at home and help their mothers. When they were about ten years old, the boys spent their Saturdays at the store, sweeping up and stocking the lower shelves that were within easy reach. By high school they had grown taller and stronger and worked every day after their classes. By the time they reached college, they did their homework during stolen moments of respite at the store. The two oldest sons finally moved on—one became a city worker, the other a car mechanic—and store duty fell to the younger sons. The boys split their time on the cash register. They learned how to charm customers while ringing up their sales, and they Americanized their names for the store. Akram reversed his and dropped a letter, becoming Mark. Kareem became Sal, and they began spending more time at the store than anywhere else.

Abdel Salam had come to this country with nothing, and a generation later he was sharing a successful store with his brother and their two sons. The store is now paying for Akram's education, and he will be the first in his immediate family to graduate with a college degree. In America's recurring immigrant saga, Abdel Salam's success with Mike's Food Center is not just an accomplishment of American proportions, it's textbook American dream. But it's no longer enough for Akram, nor does his life in the United States satisfy him any longer. He's looking for a way out. When he first told me of his plans to move abroad, I asked him why he didn't want to stay here anymore, and in answer he deliberately paraphrased a line from a Countee Cullen poem:

"What's America to me?" he said, raising an eyebrow.

———

AKRAM AND I talk regularly about these things, but I wanted to discover more pointedly where his feelings came from, so I asked him to meet me one night in February. I suggested a Dunkin' Donuts on Fourth Avenue in Sunset Park, which is open all night and usually quiet. "Oh, the Egyptian one," he said. "How about nine-thirty." This Dunkin' Donuts, in the middle of a primarily Hispanic neighborhood, is owned and run by Egyptians from Alexandria. The woman behind the counter in the candy-colored polyester uniform was wearing her company baseball cap over a pure white *hijab*. The place was empty except for two young Latina women in tight jeans, with pierced belly buttons and glittered fingernails. They sat with small coffees and laughed into their cell phones for hours. I ordered a large coffee and waited for Akram while a group of young Hispanic men walked in noisily. Akram followed shortly afterward and salaamed one of them before sitting down. "He's my cousin," Akram told me, a drag racer who had gotten into trouble for his driving exploits in the past. I thought he was Hispanic, I said, and we laughed, since Akram is always kidding around with me about how I look South Asian and he looks Jewish.

Arkam had told me in the past about his salad days during high school and how they'd been disrupted, especially by the terrorist attacks of September 11. He attended Brooklyn's Edward R. Murrow High School, a massive four-floor block of Brutalist architecture sitting atop an old New York City sanitation site in Brooklyn's Midwood neighborhood, a place where the restaurants serve kosher meats and Jewish and Muslim women, sometimes indistinguishable from one another, rub shoulders daily in the vegetable markets. Named after the famed newscaster, Murrow was established in the 1970s as an educational establishment to promote the arts to its 750 (now 4,000) students. It's one of New York City's specialty schools for gifted children. You have to earn your enrollment based on your prior excellence, and you can "major" in a program at Murrow by concentrating your few elective courses in different areas. Akram majored in English and social studies. He also told me how he joined the Third Floor Crew.

Murrow had its own political geography of race and ethnicity, divided by floor and by lockers. The second floor belonged to the Hispanics. The Asian kids hung out next to the library. The Goths squatted in the first-floor lobby and were eyed derisively down the long hall by the well-dressed Italian kids. The third floor was split in a détente between the Russians and the African Americans. When Akram was at Murrow, there weren't that many Arabs in the school, so they didn't have their own space. Anyway, being Arab, you could fit in with almost any nationality, he explained.

He opted for the third floor, which was the most multiethnic group in the school, including Russian kids, Hispanics, Bangladeshis, Filipinos, Pakistanis, Blacks, Arabs, and Jews. It was precisely this heterogeneity, the lack of identity politics, that drew Akram here from the beginning. Among the Third Floor Crew, he was known as the funny guy, always cracking jokes in class, never taking himself too seriously. In the currency of high school, comedy pays, and Akram was rich. His humor was rarely rude and often infectious. It riffed off the clichés and stupidities of what other people said. It was his way of getting along with students, teachers, deans, and security staff alike.

Still, ethnicity was a fact of life at Murrow, and Akram wore his Palestinian roots on his shoulders, most notably with his keffiyah (also called a *hatta*). For Palestinian kids in American high schools, their keffiyahs matter. Unlike other kids, they don't have a country to lay claim to so they hold tightly to their symbols. "Some people have do-rags," Akram said. "We have our *hattas*."

The *hatta* had elicited comments beforehand. Once, when he was a junior, one of his English teachers passed him in the stairwell while his *hatta* was on his shoulders. She stopped above him, peered down at the scarf, and spit out questions to him. "What does that mean?" she said. "You hate all Jews?" He was stupefied. "Nah. It's not like that," he said. "It's just traditional!" He resented the idea that the *hatta*—and by association his culture and ethnic origin—could be interpreted as hatred. He resented the fact that the teacher thought he hated anybody just because of that person's religion. He resented her. He later warned three of his friends—two African

Americans and one Latino—that the teacher was a racist. Toward the end of the semester, they came up to him and conferenced on the issue, agreeing with Akram. "When the white girls talk, she doesn't say anything," he remembers them saying. "But when we talk, she's all on top of us."

Akram is not the only person to report unsympathetic high-school teachers to me. In fact, this issue recurs again and again in my talks with Arab-American youth, and it was a situation that only got worse after the September 11 attacks. And like every other person in New York City, he remembers exactly where he was that day when he heard about the attacks.

He was beginning his senior year at Murrow in 2001. Summer break had just ended, and his classes weren't even in the swing of things yet. That terrible morning, when the world's eyes turned with shock to Manhattan, was a beautiful Tuesday day free of humidity and full of sunshine. He was already at school, in the halls between periods (called "bands" at Murrow). He was heading to one of his English classes when people in the hall started repeating the news that an airplane had crashed into the World Trade Center. The class he was going to was called Magical Realism.

It's a joke, he thought. But by the time he sat down in the classroom, he realized that the unbelievable was true. The teacher had pulled out a boom box and placed it on top of his desk. He had tuned it to 1010 WINS, and they all sat quietly in their places for the duration of the hour. The radio blared on and on, and nobody said anything, the horror rising with the monotonous repetition of the news. Finally, the band ended, and in the weird silence that had overtaken the school, Akram walked down the hall, dazed like the rest of his peers, to his next class. It was also an English class called Person-to-Person.

The students here were mostly sophomores and juniors, with only a few seniors like Akram in attendance. Since it was a new school year, he didn't yet know the other kids in this class, nor had he had a class with Mrs. Dachs, the middle-aged teacher. But Mrs. Dachs was in distress. She said she couldn't teach and pretend that everything was normal. Instead she wanted the students to talk out their reactions. "I want to hear your feelings about it," she said.

But what Akram heard began to scare and repel him. "We should go over there and bomb them," one boy said. Another suggested the same thing, with the variation of "kill them" instead of "bomb them." Where "there" was was never really clear, but this continued for a while, and Akram was stunned into silence. "I'm just sitting in my chair, you know," he said. "I'm the funny guy. I'm always happy. But just hearing what they said, I thought, wow, man! The people 'over there'—Afghanistan? the Middle East?—they had nothing to do with it!"

Akram had already traveled several times "over there." He had gone to the Palestinian territories six or seven times, always as a kid and with his mother, and he would stay for stretches that would last from weeks to the length of the long, hot Mediterranean summer. He started thinking about what the other students were saying and then about the kids in Palestine whom he'd met. "They are kids just like us. They might dress differently than us, but they still like to watch the same cartoons that we do," he said. The comments continued in this vein until, in the middle of the discussion in his Person-to-Person class, Akram could hold it back no longer. He started to cry.

"I'm a sensitive guy," he said in all seriousness. "I don't mind telling you."

The class stopped talking. Mrs. Dachs saw his tears, and nobody moved. She said nothing, just silently walked up to him and hugged him in front of the class. "Everyone's looking at me like, 'Why's he crying?'" he said. "And I told them, 'These people had nothing to do with it! Why are you saying these things?'"

It was a new school year in a new class full of new people. "They didn't know I was Arab," he said. "They did not know."

THE NEXT BAND was Council for Unity. This is a community-service organization that runs a course through Murrow to put high-school students into action through various charitable projects around the city. Later that year their accomplishments included painting a pool in Sunset Park, collecting toys for the needy, sending books to Alabama, and holding a car wash whose proceeds they contributed to the 9/11 Fund.

Akram sat down, waiting for the class to start. His head cleared a little after Mrs. Dachs's class, and the teacher for Council for Unity hadn't yet arrived in the classroom. One of the girls in the class, Marcy, walked into the room and announced—incorrectly as it turned out—that "they just confirmed that it was Hamas." For some reason, her words felt like a blow in his stomach. He sat there in frustration and confusion until he stood up, walked to the door, and punched the glass in the frame, cracking it like ice. He left the classroom and walked out into the hall.

"Young man. Where do you think you're going?" Mr. Perlowitz, the assistant principal of math, had spotted him down the corridor.

At the same time, Akram could hear his friend Ramir calling for him from the other side of the hall. "What's wrong, man? What's wrong?" Ramir cried out. Akram stopped, unsure of where to go, and Ramir came up to him. "What's wrong?" he asked again, in quieter tones.

"Just leave me alone right now," Akram said.

The teacher showed up a minute later and coaxed the two boys back to the classroom. She waved Mr. Perlowitz off, and Akram sat down and put his head on his desk. He started worrying about his mother, his aunt, and his sisters. Some of them wear *hijab*. He was a man, he thought. He could take care of himself. But what about them? And what about Palestine? He rolled his forehead on the desk, and it felt cool on his skin. *What's going to happen to us now?*, he kept thinking.

SCHOOL LET OUT EARLY that day. The buses weren't running, even in Brooklyn, so Akram met his cousin Kareem, and they walked to the store. It took them forty-five minutes, and Errol, also a student at Murrow and a regular customer at the store, spotted them part of the way there and went with them. They trekked out of the shaded Midwood trees and into the bleak East Flatbush landscape. When the boys walked into the store, Akram looked to his uncle and said in Arabic, "We did it." His uncle cursed America and its foreign policy and said that they didn't do anything.

The store was safe. Nothing terrible happened there. It wasn't like the newsstand in the Bronx, where the Yemeni owner was beaten with a bottle by three men who were yelling, "You Arabs get out of my neighborhood. We hate Arabs! This is war!" Nor was it like the candy store in upper Manhattan, where five teenagers attacked the elderly Arab owner, breaking his dentures in half. Nor was it like what happened at the convenience store owned by a Palestinian-American man in Missouri. That was torched. Or the one in Venice, Illinois, where three men attacked the Iraqi-American store owner. Or the one in Somerset, Massachusetts, where three teenagers firebombed an Indian American's grocery, later confessing to the police that they wanted to "get those Arabs for what they did to us." Or like what happened to the Palestinian-American store owner in Chattanooga, Tennessee, who was shot four times in the back and killed in front of his grocery store. Or like the tragedy that befell Adel Karas, the Egyptian Coptic owner for twenty years of the International Market in San Gabriel, California. On that same day, September 15, two young men burst through the doors of his store and shot him dead. Nor was it like what happened to Waqar Hassan, a Pakistani immigrant who ran a convenience store in Dallas, Texas. Also on September 15, Mark Anthony Stroman walked into his store, ordered two hamburgers, and then proceeded to shoot Hassan in the face, killing him. Expressing no remorse, Stroman later said, "I did it to retaliate on local Arab Americans or whatever you want to call them. I did what every American wanted to do but didn't." Stroman also killed Vasudev Patel in another hate crime two weeks later. He was then arrested, convicted of murder, and sentenced to death. Nor was it like what happened on September 29 to the fifty-one-year-old Yemeni immigrant Abdo Ali Ahmed. He was shot three times in the torso and died in his store in Reedley, California.

At Mike's Food Center, customers came in to ask if everything was fine. They offered help. Akram's father later told me that he believes that was because he's been in the neighborhood for so long, that most of the customers know him, that he has watched their children grow up, from buying candy at the register to visiting their families when they return from college. In reality, luck probably also played a role, since Adel Karas was also said to be a beloved store owner, and he became a victim of this random vigilante violence. But it certainly is true that Mike's Food Center is deeply and warmly embedded in the neighborhood. During the week of September 11, several people popped their heads in the door. "If you need anything, Mike," they would say without making a purchase, "just say the word."

In fact, everyone pulled together beautifully, and it meant a lot to the men in the store. Everyone but Walter. A regular customer, Walter is a portly, middle-aged, African-American man who holds a master's degree in urban planning and used to work for the city until he took early retirement. Then he began hanging around the area at all times, becoming the neighborhood's unofficial "mayor," a title conferred upon him by the rest of the community.

Right after 9/11, Walter got into an argument with Akram's father about how the Arabs had celebrated the attacks. It escalated into a screaming match, and Akram's father kicked him out. After that, Walter would walk right by the store and have lunch at the restaurant on the corner. Every day on his way to the restaurant, he would stop everyone whom he passed. "Don't shop at Mike's," he would say. "They support bin Laden. They support Hamas. Don't give them your money." He would stand next to the store bad-mouthing the family for their Palestinian roots. Few took him seriously, but his one-man campaign continued for over a year, until one day he simply lost his conviction.

Around the same time, Walter started shopping at the store again, choosing to hang around and argue with Akram and Kareem about politics and the failures of the Arab world while they rang up other customers. One June 6 he walked in while I was there and asked the boys if they knew what day it was. Akram and Kareem glanced at each other. They both wore a "What's this now?" kind of look. It was the anniversary of the three-day war, Walter said triumphantly. (He meant the Six Day War.) While standing off to the side of the register, he carried on about how the Israelis had rousted all of the timorous Arab armies. He said, "The Arabs can't fight. You know that, right?" The boys looked at each other, waiting for Walter to finish, but he never seemed to stop. "Do you want us to get you a chair?" Akram asked after a while. "Nah, I got to get going," Walter said, oblivious to the jab disguised in polite speech.

But Walter's actions were an obvious manifestation of something more subtle that was going on at Mike's Food Center and in some parts of the culture at large after September 11. "The West Indians are with us," Kareem told me one day while packing soda bottles onto a shelf. "The American blacks are another story." Watershed moments like September 11 tend to throw America's bedrock of racial stratification into flux. And despite the fact that African Americans continue nationally to be exceedingly critical of the Bush administration—a Harris Poll conducted in June 2007 found that 88 percent disapproved of Bush's handling of the "war on terror"—Walter and a few others at the store project themselves as real Americans protecting the nation against a pernicious, un-American threat. West Indians and Palestinians, on the other hand, share similar kinds of postcolonial sensibilities. Enduring affiliations to distant homelands, lived experiences connected to American foreign policy, and contemporary immigrant aspirations to thrive in places like Brooklyn all complicate their attachments to the United States.

Before the attacks the American popular imagination was essentially blind to Arabs and Muslims. If they were to be found anywhere, it was probably in the image of the middleman-minority Arab shopkeeper, who himself would perhaps have been conferred with a kind of "almost white" status along America's abiding axis of racial definitions. The commercial success of the middleman-minority store could easily have been scripted into the "model minority" story, yet Arabs and Muslims still remained largely out of view.

After the attacks, however, they have formally entered American discourse around race, and with a bang. But the primary question remains: To which racial category do they belong exactly? Are they white, brown, or black (all of these, actually), or are they their own novel category? With race being rescripted everywhere after the attacks, and with Walter asserting his Americanness against the Palestinian store owner, where does that leave people like Akram and Kareem? And what relationship does being Arab or Muslim in America have to blackness, to notions of American belonging and participation in American politics, and to social mobility and economic opportunity? In other words, have Arabs and Muslims today become less "white" and more "colored"—that is to say, have they in some sense become more "black" than blacks?

Arab Americans are not the only ones asking these questions. "Black New Yorkers joke among themselves about their own reprieve from racial profiling," explained a *New York Times* article from October 2001. "Even the language of racial grievance has shifted: Overnight, the cries about driving while black have become flying while brown—a phrase referring to reports of Muslim-Americans being asked to get off planes." The article continues, "Ever so slightly, the attacks on the trade center have tweaked the city's traditional racial divisions." These racial vacillations prompted African-American novelist Ishmael Reed to write that "within two weeks after the WTC and Pentagon bombings, my youngest daughter, Tennessee, was called a dirty Arab, twice." America's racial legacy, complete with such noteworthy accomplishments as the "one drop of blood rule," by which a single drop of African blood turned you black in the Jim Crow eyes of the law, now enables Reed, after September 11, to ask the question, "Is anyone with dark skin Arab-American?"

Suddenly "African American" meant "American," while Arab Americans, middlemen minorities, were falling down the ladder. Economically, the grocery store was and will do just fine, but the ladder here refers to other kinds of capital: social, political, and cultural. In fact, we can see the change coming in the distance if we take a longer view, examined through the myths that the movies tell us. Images of African Americans as American heroes have been widespread for several years, especially against an Arab threat or in contradistinction to Middle Easterners. In her discussion of the recent film *Crash*, the cultural studies scholar Sylvia Chan points out that Don Cheadle's character in that movie "is a type of black male protagonist who's very common these days: a proxy for the state, working against all the unruly elements of internal diversity and external threat. Think Denzel Washington in *The Siege,* Will Smith in *Men in Black* and *Independence Day,* Samuel L. Jackson in *Rules of Engagement,* Morgan Freeman as the president in *Deep Impact.* This is the type of narrative Hollywood needs to keep putting out there right now—the black man as the symbol for our nation, the guy who's going to provide order for not only the U.S., but for the world. And let's be real: this isn't happening in real life."

Of course, it's easy to substitute Hollywood for the world—precisely the caution that Chan warns us about—and what is happening in real life is not the elevation of African Americans in the culture at large or a new and constant tension between Arab Americans and American blacks. On the contrary, most Arab Americans and African Americans, Walter notwithstanding, can recognize what is going on, and they see familiar patterns, trends that don't portend the rise of African Americans as a group into positions of leadership and opportunity but rather the demotion of Arab and Muslim Americans into a new but lowly domestic racial category, as if they are sliding down a greased pole. Thayer, another cousin of Akram's, put it to me this way one night: "We're the new *abeed,*" he said. We're the new niggers.

EDWARD R. MURROW HIGH SCHOOL closed down for the rest of the week after September 11, and class resumed on Monday. That morning Akram was hanging out in the third-floor hallway when one of the English teachers, Mr. Ross, passed him and his crew. Just as the English teacher before had done, Ross stopped and glared at the boys. "Where are your scarves now?" he said, challenging the boys. "You're scared to wear them." Akram felt that the comments were directed to him. "The scarf isn't scary," he replied defensively. "It's a traditional garment."

That night he couldn't stop thinking about what Ross had said. His brain raced between school, the Middle East, Ground Zero, and back to school. He tossed and turned in his bed. By the next morning, before he left home, he had come up with a plan. He looked around his house and found five different *hattat*. Away from the eyes of his parents, he folded them up carefully and placed them in his school bag. When he got to school, he called his friends over and handed them out. His cousin took one. A Pakistani friend put one over his head. Two Yemeni friends draped them over their shoulders. They waited in the hallway for Ross while Akram practiced what he was going to say to the teacher. "Who's scared now? No one's scared here," he was whispering.

But before Ross showed up, Annie, a security guard at the school, spotted them, five boys wearing Arab headdresses in the hallway, and she blew up. "You know what's going on now!" she yelled at Akram. "Why are you doing this?" And they began arguing and screaming at one another in the hallway. Akram didn't know what had gotten into him, why the confrontations, the confusions, the anger, but he exploded.

"Really, I'm the funny guy," he said later. Annie continued to yell at him, and he yelled back, and the scene was getting bigger and more unmanageable. Panama, another security guard, and one whom Akram considered a friend, showed up and walked up to the boy. Panama placed his huge bulk in front of him and pushed him back.

"Relax, man," he said. "Relax."

But Akram couldn't. He started yelling "Bin Laden didn't do it! Bin Laden didn't do it!" Annie was yelling back at him the whole time, but his own voice was so loud in his ears that he couldn't hear a thing she was saying.

Panama grabbed Akram and took him downstairs to the dean's office, where he explained to the dean what had happened while Akram was silent. By now Akram wasn't yelling anymore. "Bin Laden didn't do it," he told the dean quietly when asked what was going on. The dean sensibly replied that they weren't there to discuss who did and who didn't do what. The whole room fell silent while the dean thumbed the *hatta* for a while.

Then he asked Akram, "Who told you to bring these in?"

"Speak to your staff about what they tell us," Akram spit back. He felt lonely and wounded and confused. He stayed in the dean's office for the rest of the band, until the dean was sure he had calmed down enough to be sent back to his classroom. Later that day Akram handed off the *hattat* to some of the girls in his crew, two Bangladeshis and a Filipina. They laughed while they put them on, and someone snapped a picture. That photo made it into the yearbook.

"I had just turned seventeen," Akram told me, laughing and sighing. The blender ground loudly in the coffee shop while he looked away with half a smile on his lips. "The funny thing is," he said, "before September 11, I had never even heard of Osama bin Laden."

By 2003, Akram had graduated high school and entered college. For years someone in his extended family always went to his grandparents' house in el-Bireh during the summer to help take care of the aging couple. This summer Akram's uncle was supposed to go, but his daughter, Akram's cousin, was getting married, and so Akram volunteered to go in his uncle's place. He wanted to get away for a while anyway and welcomed the opportunity to connect with his family in the West Bank. He convinced his parents of the idea. It was an impulse decision, and he bought his ticket and waited in line downtown to get his own passport in one day. Before, he had traveled on his mother's passport, but now, at eighteen years old, he was flying for the first time by himself. His father had come to America when he was seventeen, Akram was thinking, and here he was leaving America at the age of eighteen.

When he landed at Ben-Gurion International Airport, Israeli security checked him before he could pass through. A young Israeli woman with the Airports Authority met him. She thumbed his passport, rifled through his luggage, and checked his story. Akram stood off to the side and watched her. Before he left New York, his father had warned him not to make any trouble with the Israelis and please not to make any jokes. When she asked him why he was coming to Israel, he said, "To see my grandparents. They're sick. I'm going to stay with them over the summer, you know, enjoy their company." Then she asked him if he had any weapons. He chuckled at the absurdity of the question. "Yeah, I have a couple of grenades in my bag. What kind of question is that?" He laughed, but she didn't. It was just procedure, she said. She was doing her job. Akram looked into her brown eyes. She was pretty.

"Your English is very good," he said. "Like an American."

"I grew up in Buffalo."

"Wow," he joked, "you guys are getting deported, too?"

AKRAM CALLED THE TRIP "the most spectacular, the best time I ever had." He was on his own. He didn't have to work in the store or go to class. He would wander around the sleepy village of el-Bireh, then meander down the street for five minutes and walk into the more urban Ramallah. There he saw the Muqata'a, Arafat's compound that the Israelis had laid siege to in September 2002. Arafat's people kept it in a state of disrepair as a gesture of defiance and memory, and Akram strolled around the compound, his mouth agape at the destruction. Wrecked cars were strewn about. The walls were crumbling. You could still see where the tanks had fired shells into the walls.

Palestinian soldiers were patrolling the area, and he went up and talked to them. He told them in Arabic that he had come from America, and they asked him about American girls. One of the soldiers let him hold his Kalashnikov and snapped his photo. Akram asked to see Arafat, but they wouldn't let him in. He would have to get approval from a minister in the Palestinian Authority, whose office was in a different part of Ramallah, and then he would need another signature from this man and then from that minister and someone else. The explanation continued through a maze of bureaucracy. He gave up on the idea and left, looking again at the compound from a distance and at the neighboring buildings. *This is the way the Palestinians live,* he thought. "You can see people on top of the roofs waiting for an attack," he told me.

On a previous trip several years back, when he was still just a kid, he and

Kareem had gone to a well near his grandfather's property that had the sweetest water they had ever tasted, and so now, one morning while walking around, he decided to go searching for it. His family had told him not to go. The Israeli army had blocked access to the water, building an impromptu border between the aquifer and the town and digging up the earth around the well, surrounding it with piled-up dirt and broken cars. Impetuously Akram decided to try to find it anyway. One morning he grabbed a stick for the walk as a precaution against the scrappy stray dogs in the area. He passed the berm of dirt the Israeli army had set up, made his way down the hill, and proceeded to walk the good distance to the well. Not long after, a Humvee came chasing him.

Ah, crap, he thought. *Here they come.* His heart started beating hard. He didn't have his passport or any papers with him that morning. *Should I stay or should I go?* he asked himself, his fear rising. He stopped. The Humvee pulled over, three soldiers inside. One soldier got out and approached him. Another stayed in the vehicle talking on a phone. A third stood behind it and pointed a rifle directly at Akram.

The first soldier said something in Hebrew to Akram, who shook his head.

"Do you speak English?" Akram asked.

"What are you doing here?" the soldier demanded. He spoke English with a Hebrew accent.

"Nothing. I'm just here to get some water," Akram said, emphasizing his American intonation.

"What water?"

"There's a well over here."

"There's nothing here," the soldier said.

"There's a well just over there," he said. "It doesn't belong to you." He surprised himself, how he slid from one comment to the other. He could hear his heart thump in his ears, and he wondered what was going to happen. Would they take him in? He really wished that he had his papers with him.

"Where do you live?" the soldier asked, and Akram said that the family house was just over the hill.

"I'll make you guys some tea," he said, offering an invitation that he hoped they wouldn't accept. And he was right. They said nothing, and the soldier went back to the Humvee and started talking to the others. Akram took advantage of the situation. "All right. I gotta go now," he said loudly, and he walked away, first slowly and then as fast as he could, without looking as if he were running. It was a small moment of confrontation, but it stuck with him.

On his last Friday in the West Bank, he talked to his family about going to Jerusalem for the Friday prayer. "You'll never get in!" they told him, since the Israelis won't let any male under forty-five into the al-Aqsa compound. But he was determined to try. He took his passport and told them he'd be back by late afternoon. He shared a taxi to the drop-off point. In Jerusalem's old city, he worked his way through the crowds in the narrow alleys, looking for the entrance to the mosque. When he found it, a small metal door, a phalanx of soldiers stood in his path. He tried to walk through the line, but one of the soldiers began yelling at him.

"*Ya walad, ya walad!*" he shouted in Arabic. Hey, boy! Akram ignored him at first, surmising that since he was an American who spoke English, the soldier shouldn't assume that he could understand Arabic. Then the soldiers yelled with such ferocity that Akram thought it wise to pause.

A group of soldiers began crowding around him, asking him where he was going. An Israeli in regular clothes, who also spoke Arabic and English, led the questioning. Akram tried to talk his way through the soldiers, speaking only English and showing them his passport. He told them that he had come from America and only wanted to pray at the holy site. They asked him where he was staying. "With my grandparents. If you want, you're more than welcome to come by for some tea." (It had seemed to discourage them before.)

For fifteen minutes the man asked him a series of questions, and the soldiers continued to crowd around him like he was some kind of novelty. The questions were becoming increasingly idiotic.

"How did you get here, to Israel?" the man asked him.

"What do you mean, how did I get here? I swam!" Akram said. No one laughed.

"How would you get from Guatemala to Jerusalem?" the man asked.

"What are you talking about?" Akram asked back.

Finally the ordinary-looking man in the regular clothes motioned with his arm, and the soldiers cleared a way so that Akram could pass.

He prayed with his fellow Palestinians and afterward went looking for the checkpoint just outside the old city's walls to pick up a ride home. This is a place controlled by the Israeli army but where loads of vans and cars are normally waiting to transport Palestinians back to the West Bank. But now he couldn't find any cars. There was only an Israeli jeep there with a bunch of soldiers crouching behind the vehicle. A sole civilian white van was off in the distance. The space—now vacant and too quiet—was eerie. Someone in the van spotted Akram twisting around and looking lost. "*Yalla, Yalla, Imshee!*" the man from the van yelled. Hurry up! Hurry up! Run! And Akram ran and the Israeli soldiers yelled something to him that he didn't understand. He stumbled headfirst into the vehicle.

Inside the van were the driver and another man with his two young daughters. The mood was anxious and everyone was waiting for something terrible to happen. The Israeli soldiers had halted all cars, and the air was unbearably still. Then Akram heard a gunshot.

"And that's when it got real," he told me.

The van owner yelled, "Roll up the windows!"

Akram laughed in disbelief. *For what, buddy? They're not bulletproof!* he thought in English. But he did it anyway.

The father was yelling to the driver. "Let's go!"

The driver yelled back. "I can't go anywhere! They won't let me pass!"

The father got fed up. He opened the door and left the car with his two daughters, holding on to one and walking with the other. He stepped slowly but proudly up to the soldiers, showing them that he wasn't going to do anything and was holding only his children. They stared at him hard but let him walk through the area and beyond, and a taboo was for a moment broken. Akram and the driver watched it all from the car. Eventually the soldiers let the van pass, and the driver and Akram traveled down the road. Akram could now see the mosque from the van's window. "Jeez. Hoe-lee cow!" He whistled. About a hundred Palestinian kids were throwing rocks and bottles at the soldiers, who were sometimes firing back at the crowd with their rifles. *This isn't CNN anymore,* Akram thought.

Akram comments easily on how daily life for the Palestinians is really more difficult than what he experienced. But the Palestinian struggle affects him deeply and sometimes closely. Until the end of his life, Akram's grandfather, elderly and frail, was constantly frightened that Israeli troops were going to break down his door and force him out of his home. Other people in his family have been injured by the Israelis. "My cousin," Akram told me, "was shot in the hip for throwing rocks, and one of my in-laws had part of his face and skull blown off. He had to go to Abu Dhabi for reconstructive surgery. He lives here now, but he's so scared all the time. His whole soul is shattered."

Akram is thankful that he didn't have any more direct contacts with the Israeli occupation than he did, but the trip was important to him in all sorts of ways. It allowed him some independence. It gave him an adult taste for travel and for connecting directly with his roots. But it also underlined for him the importance of formal schooling with regard to his own political education. "It's good to see the struggle," Akram told me, "but it's generations now of fighting with nothing to show for it. And it hurts you." His solution is to fight back with reason and education. "You have to use your head," he loves to say. When he was at the store, he almost flew into a rage after the Danish cartoon controversy. A customer came into the store cursing the Prophet and saying that he, the customer, believed in only one thing, pulling a dollar bill in front of his face. Akram found it insulting in the extreme, but he was able to hold himself back after his uncle told him in Arabic to pity the man rather than fight him. "The older I get, the more I realize that the violence isn't going to do anything," he told me. "Education is important. Being educated about certain things. You have to do that instead of using violence."

———

AKRAM CAME BACK to Brooklyn before classes started in September and started working at the store again. He was still exhausted most of the time, but he poured his energy into school and managed to earn a place on the honor roll. The university held an afternoon ceremony for the students that spring, but his father was too busy with the store and his mother too busy with Akram's younger sister for either of them to attend. He looked forward to Monday nights, because *24* was on TV. He would still read the paper when business was slow, especially the news about Palestine and Iraq. Walter would still come by the store and annoy the boys. They continued to kill him with kindness.

Sundays were the best, because the store closed early. One winter night when I was with them, Akram, Kareem, and Akram's father pulled down the grate and climbed into their car to drive me home. ("Put your seat belt on, Moustafa," Kareem said. "Four Middle Eastern men in a black van. We don't need to give them a reason.") It was already dark as we inched out onto the street and began driving. The boys started talking about how easy Sundays felt. Those two hours really made a difference, Kareem said. Akram suggested that if only they opened two hours later, then they could even sleep in luxury. Kareem agreed with the dream of the proposition. That would mean that they would be in the store for eight hours. "I can't even imagine," Kareem said as they drove by a twenty-four-hour Yemeni store, its awning's colored lights constantly blinking like Christmas. Akram nodded. "Wow, man," he said, mostly to himself while looking out the window. "Eight hours a day. That'd be so easy. Like a regular American job."

One day in 2005, Akram struck up a conversation with a customer who was buying his groceries at the store. This man had served in military during the Korean War and had stayed in that peninsula country after the war for a few years to teach English. He told Akram about his experiences and about the opportunities available to English teachers who want to go abroad. This started Akram thinking, and he began looking up teaching English on the Internet. He found a program in Prague that certified teachers. He looked into the countries that were calling for English teachers. Japan was listed, along with several other countries in Asia. Eastern Europe and the republics of the former Soviet Union needed English teachers. Brazil captivated him for a moment, but one place stood out from all the others: Dubai.

Dubai is the new American dream for many Arab-American youth. It is a bizarre wonderland of glassy skyscrapers, forest green golf courses, and man-made islands, all built by foreign labor and springing Athena-like, full blown on the edges of the Arabian Desert. It's an unreal place, a clearinghouse of global capital deliberately projecting a flashy personality that is equal parts Disneyland and Las Vegas. The most American of all the Arab lands, Dubai also holds the attraction for Akram of being a place where he can get in touch with his Arab past, make a living, and learn about himself. This is also the case with his friends. Whenever they start discussing it, Akram and his friends speak glowingly of the emirate in near-mythic terms. They talk about how Dubai has built a ski resort in the middle of the scorching desert (a picture of it is the screen saver on Akram's computer) and erected a hotel, el Burj, that charges fourteen hundred dollars a night for its simplest room. "We were talking about it at the store," Akram explained. "One customer said that he'd just sleep outside the hotel for that kind of money. Yeah, but that's five hundred dollars!" Akram joked. "By this time next year, I'll be there. I'll be settled," he continued. *"Insha Allah."* God willing.

Dubai is an Arab city glittering with similar kinds of gleam and glory that America did for Arab immigrants a generation ago. After I asked him why Dubai, Akram told me, "It's important that it's an Arab place. I know the language, and now I want to learn the culture even more. I was thinking about going to Brazil, someplace exotic, but I'll get closer to the Middle East. I'll get closer to Islam. I want to learn how to read and write Arabic. I'm twenty-one years old, and I can't read Arabic. I'll have that time to learn, to pass it down."

For Palestinian Americans like Akram, it is even less surprising that Dubai has its enticements. Akram's friends go back to Lebanon, to Syria, to

Egypt routinely and for extended visits. His Yemeni friends return sometimes for years at a time. But in the West Bank, you are lucky if you get a
three-month tourist visa. You have to deal with constant border closures
and the insecurity of the situation. Residency is difficult, if not impossible.
Dubai, with its attraction to Palestinian Americans, is another footnote in
the continuing epic tragedy of Palestinian dispossession.

It's also a place that will gain from America's loss. Akram is a funny,
talented, and thoughtful young man who works incredibly hard. He's quick
and versatile, sensitive and empathetic, a global and local citizen of the
United States and the planet. The world is his oyster, really, and it's important to emphasize that leaving is his choice, not something forced onto
him. It is done with clear eyes and not a hint of self-pity. And when Akram
makes a decision, he follows through with it. His parents are familiar with
his resolute will, especially after he bought a motorcycle to cut down on
travel time between the store and school, and they have accepted his choice,
hoping that he will return before too long, which he very well might. "If
you're going to do this," his father said, "do this in the Middle East."

But the point is why he has opted to leave for Dubai, to reverse the
geography of his father's American dream. "I've been rereading Frank
McCourt's *Angela's Ashes*," he told me. "Without being so grand, they"—
the McCourt family—"were worse in America than they were in Ireland.
We're becoming like that. I find myself becoming like that, more and more
miserable, in a sense," he said. "I'm tired of it. I love the diversity of this
country, I really do, but the whole politics and the whole . . ." He paused,
looking for the right word. He settled on "everything!" He took an exasperated breath before continuing his thought, paraphrasing Langston Hughes
this time. "America's not America anymore to me."

ON THE FEW OCCASIONS when Akram goes out with his friends, he
can sometimes be found at one of the *shisha* cafés in Bay Ridge, even though
he doesn't enjoy smoking a water pipe. But his friends do, so on a cold and
drizzling Friday night in the spring we went together and were later joined

by four of his friends. The café, high up on Fourth Avenue and almost underneath the massive Verrazano-Narrows Bridge, is one basic room, with rickety chairs and plain tables. Unlike the Manhattan *shisha* cafés that have become fashionable with the mainstream, often done up with Oriental carpets on the walls and desert motifs throughout, this one is very simple. The sweet, perfumey smell of apple tobacco hits you in the face as soon as you open the door. A new flat-screen TV is the only hint of luxury. People constantly play backgammon and card games while sucking on the long tubes of their pipes. After New York mayor Michael Bloomberg outlawed smoking in bars and restaurants, a few establishments that were tobacco-related, including this one, were able to get special exemption licenses for the pipes. But cigarettes are not included in the exemptions, so No Smoking signs are taped without irony all over the café.

A lot of Brooklyn's young Arab-American men are fond of these cafés and of shops like Dunkin' Donuts. These social geographies, far away from all the din and jam of the outer world, are public spaces where it is comfortable to be Arab in America. For one thing the doughnut shops are often owned and run by other Muslims, who can advise the more religious patrons on what they can and cannot eat and drink. And both the *shisha* cafés and the doughnut shops are cheap, so the guys can spend hours hanging out with each other for just a few dollars. (Arab women can be found in the *shisha* cafés, but usually in far fewer numbers, along with what seems to be one constantly packed table of young Russian men and women in each café.) But mostly, with their overwhelmingly Arab male clientele, the spaces offer up a sense of social solidarity, an easy place to band together and share stories freely with one another.

Akram's cousin Thayer is here. He has the same haircut as Akram but also sports a thin beard. He speaks fast, and his eyes move with every word he says. Thayer also lives in Sunset Park, but he works in Queens for a bail-bonds company. "I hate it," he says when I ask him about his work, "but there's nothing out there now. Me and my friend, we had an idea of opening an arghile [another name for *shisha*] club in the city, you know, where you can charge like eight, nine dollars a pipe. But now I just got this."

With us was Mohammed, or Mo, as he likes to be called. Mo is also Palestinian. He's short, with sandy brown hair, also cut in a Caesar. An accounting student who works in New Jersey, he's convinced he's being taken advantage of in his office. He can speak, read, and write Arabic but hates going to the *bled*, the homeland. He can tell you to the dollar the manufacturer's suggested retail price on any car, make and model. Mo is the driver tonight, with his black Jetta that has electrical problems (the windows have a tendency to roll down at will, which poses a problem for parking). Later we are joined by Hussam, a serious Damascene who moved to New York in the third grade and who has just taken his citizenship exam. All but me are in their early twenties. Everyone but Akram has a tall *shisha* beside him and a mandatory cell phone sitting on the table in front of him. We are all drinking Snapple.

These young men work long hours, and it's a rare evening when they come together just to hang out. During the night, talk gravitates to two themes, their working life and the "war on terror."

"Al-Qaeda this. Al-Qaeda that. How am I supposed to live with that?" Thayer, out of frustration, asks no one in particular. He fiddles with his pipe while lodging complaints of being pushed downward in a culture that he feels is against him and his kind.

Eventually they turn to me and ask me about my story. I was born in Switzerland to Egyptian parents who were studying for their Ph.D.'s. We moved to Canada when I was young, and I moved to New York for my graduate education. I tell them this.

"So both your parents have Ph.D.'s?" Mo asks incredulously.

Yes, I respond.

"You're a strange kind of Arab," Hussam says gravely. "For us it's all grocery stores and this," he says, thumping the table.

"And even this is new," says Thayer.

Someone mentions Akram's dream of teaching English in Dubai, and they ask me if I have ever been there. No, I tell them, but Mo leans in and asks me if I think he could get a job there, too. Sure, I tell him. The Gulf is always looking for talent, especially from other Arabs. He leans back, lost in thought, while talk drifts to how they are going to save enough money to get married. They talk about dowries, ceremony costs, and other expenses. When they decide that ten thousand dollars is the absolute minimum amount needed, the Gulf starts to splash its appeal to them again.

Two hours later we are in Mo's car on the way home, and it has started to rain. The four of them are arguing about the best place to buy jeans as the car careens past Atlantic Avenue and turns onto Flatbush Avenue, passing a newly renovated shopping mall. The wipers clear the rain away in single strokes as the guys trade verbal jabs with each other. Akram suddenly changes the topic. "There's that new Arab store," he says to a car full of shopkeeper sons.

"Which one?" asks Thayer. Everyone stops talking and twists his head around, looking out the window.

"Target," says Akram.

And a moment later everyone is howling with laughter.

LINA

We are not survivors of a civil war

We survive our love
because we go on
loving

—JUNE JORDAN, "Grand Army Plaza"

There was no ice cream in Saddam's Iraq. This is not a metaphor about a black hole of happiness between the Tigris and the Euphrates. Dictatorships may make life miserable, but you can never truly legislate joy or enforce its absence. What had gone missing was the actual ice cream, that slow-churned deliciousness that can easily be taken for granted. It disappeared not because a dimpled scoop of pistachio dream was too luxuriously expensive or because, like the love of a good man or woman, it was hard to find. No. It was because ice cream in Iraq was more like expressing a political opinion—completely illegal. If you were an average Iraqi, savoring its sweet cold on your lips was tantamount to sedition. One lick could land you in trouble, and trouble under Saddam, as everyone knew, was something you worked very hard to avoid.

It was 1996, and Iraq was choking under sanctions. Lina was a cool seventeen years old and stuck in Ramadi, her second trip in the course of a year. This time her parents had sent her with a one-way ticket in hand. It was a punishment of sorts, a last-ditch effort on the part of a conservative mother and father to correct the wayward behavior of a teenage Arab girl gone astray in America. There had been a war at home. In Maryland, Lina had been skipping school, running away, and spending time with her American boyfriend. Nothing that Maisa or Haythem, her parents, were doing could rein in their girl, and they were at their wits' end. They talked it over and determined that what she needed was some time away in Iraq.

Iraq is a country now known to most Americans as a blur of bad news, a godforsaken geography of al-Qaeda terrorists and Shi'a death squads. But Iraq is also a real place steeped in centuries of history and peopled with families who have their own dreams and aspirations for themselves and their country. People live there; they don't just die there. But it is a country that has seen more than its share of suffering in its recent past, including wars with Iran and the United States, debilitating sanctions, and now military occupation. To many people, Iraq stands for the ravages of our contemporary world. But to Lina back in 1996, it was much simpler. She was just an Iraqi-American teenager, sent to live for a while in her homeland.

In July 1996, Lina left for Iraq with her mother and younger sister. They first flew to Jordan. From the airport in Amman, they took a taxi to the bus station, where they boarded a bus for Ramadi. It was a long ride across a dusty border to the capital of al-Anbar province. Long before they reached the border, Maisa carefully lectured her daughters never, ever to say anything about politics or against Saddam in Iraq. Finally, after two days of travel, the three women landed at Lina's aunt's house, and Lina saw the large and beautiful villa, with its marble floors and infinite bedrooms. But right outside the grounds, she saw an Iraq that looked like a massive landfill. Garbage was everywhere, part of the breakdown of social services that accompanied the sanctions. For the known future, this Iraq, Iraq under sanctions, would be Lina's world.

Lina knew the plan. Her mother and sister would spend the summer with her, and then they would return to the United States and leave her in Ramadi, and that's just what happened. The three of them spent two months constantly visiting relatives, handing out endless gifts purchased Stateside, and drinking bottomless cups of tea. As scheduled, her mother and sister returned home several weeks later. The day of their departure, Lina had a blowout fight with her mother at the taxi stand. She had seen her mother hand her aunt a bottle of her favorite perfume, Vivid by Liz Claiborne, and Lina was furious. "You're always giving stuff away to other people!" she yelled. "You never give stuff to me! You hate me!" Her mother shook her head in a rage, and that was their last exchange before she returned to Maryland. Now Lina was alone in Iraq and resentful. The weather was hot. The streets were dirty. And she wanted some ice cream.

But ice cream was a crime. The dairy infraction stemmed not from the caprice of a mad dictator but from the necessities brought about by living under sanctions. After Saddam's 1990 invasion of Kuwait, the international community, led by the United States and administered by the United Nations, erected the strictest and most draconian sanctions program the world has known, drastically limiting the importation of foods, medicines, and equipment into the country. Saddam's regime quickly realized that to maintain both the population and its terrifying grip on power, it would need to institute food rationing. Most families were sold monthly supplies of 180 pounds in total of flour, rice, sugar, cooking oil, beans, and tea along with sixteen bars of soap for about sixty cents. Under sanctions, however, medicines became scarce and child mortality and malnutrition skyrocketed, totaling at least half a million preventable childhood deaths, according to UNICEF. The country's entire physical infrastructure, maintained without any new equipment, sagged to the point of near collapse. Denis Halliday, the UN assistant secretary general who administered the program, stepped down in 1999 in protest. "I am resigning," he wrote in his departure letter, "because the policy of economic sanctions is . . . destroying an entire society. Five thousand children are dying every month. I don't want to administer a programme that satisfies the definition of genocide." Under sanctions, blackouts became frequent, since electricity was in short supply. Sugar imports also dropped. Considering the energy required to run freezers and the high sugar and milk content in the confection, ice cream became simply unsustainable. To ensure compliance, the regime banned the sweet dessert and criminalized its sale.

And so Lina became an American teenager surviving Iraq's twin terrors of Saddam and sanctions. She had been deposited for an indeterminate period with her Iraqi family and was living through a host of emotions. She was happy when spending time with her cousins, one of whom had lost her fiancé in the Iran-Iraq War. Her cousin was sweet, and they became close, but Lina could feel the aura of loss always burning a ring of blue around her. And Lina was sad because she could see firsthand how the sanctions were weakening all of Iraq, how living itself became a struggle. And she missed her American friends terribly, especially her boyfriend, Daniel.

She wrote Daniel long, expansive letters that she couldn't mail, so she carried them around with her like charms. Her family wouldn't allow her to go to the market unaccompanied, and even if she could send the letters, she had assimilated the paranoid mind-set necessary for surviving Saddam's rule. In a mix of teenage fright and political fear, she was convinced that the government censors, who read all the mail leaving the country, would pore over her correspondence and inform on her, revealing to her family not only that she was writing to Daniel but just what she said.

After a while she began getting sick of all the government cheese and blackouts and nothing to do. She became heartsick and homesick and depressed. Meanwhile, United Nations inspectors were busy scouring the country for weapons of mass destruction, hotfooting around the desert at the same time that Lina sat at home aching for all the things she knew while growing up in the United States. She craved certain foods. While the inspectors searched for banned computer chips, she pined for Doritos. They sought yellowcake uranium. She sought butter pecan.

Iraq sucked, at first.

I FIRST MET LINA in 2006. We made plans over the phone to meet in a Greek café in Bay Ridge one March afternoon. She texted me that she was running late, but after a few minutes there was suddenly this sirocco of a woman in front of me. She came crashing through the door with a friend and led us up to the second floor, where she grabbed a black plastic ashtray at the top of the stairs. Lina's reasons for meeting here were now apparent to me. "Do you mind if I smoke?" she asked as soon as we were seated. "All

Iraqis smoke," she proclaimed, laughing at her generalization while light-
ing up.

She is neither tall nor short, with dark brown hair and plump cheeks.
She looked at me through colorfully made-up eyes and flashed me bright,
friendly smiles as we talked. Energy swirled around her and enveloped the
room. I could feel the force of rebellion propelling her, but it soon became
clear that her struggles were private battles, more personal than political in
nature. For a long time, Lina had been fighting her immigrant parents for
her own independence. Hers is a story of class and generational divides that
pits parents aspiring to the comforts of suburban living against a daughter
who, until she discovers her own Arab and Iraqi dimensions, identifies
more with black and Latino culture. To listen to Lina tell the story is to hear
a woman describe a life signposted with her own romantic crushes and in-
fatuations, culminating in a grand romance, where, in spite of several failed
attempts at love and marriage, she finally prevails.

Lina's story is all over the place and has enough eccentric detail to make
it impossible to generalize to all Iraqi Americans. Yet at the same time politics will never leave you if you are Iraqi. It hangs around in corners and
stops you dead in the street. In the circus ride that is Lina's life, Iraqi politics has always trailed closely behind and occasionally overtakes it. Not
only did she move to Iraq under sanctions, but Saddam's invasion of Kuwait determined her own family's peregrinations. The two men, both Iraqi,
who would later define much of her life came from families that represented completely opposite sides of the Iraqi political spectrum, one affiliated with Saddam's regime, the other with the opposition, while Lina
floated somewhere in an apolitical middle until she eventually figured out
who and what she had to be. In the end Lina's story is about how the personal is political, and it's about how politics can get very personal, too.

LINA WAS BORN in Kuwait City, Kuwait, in 1979. Both her parents are
Iraqi professionals, and they were working at al-Sabah Hospital when she
was born, her father as a cardiologist and her mother as a pharmacist. In

1983, the year her sister was born, her father landed a grant from the Kuwaiti government to pursue a Ph.D. He was admitted to Georgetown University, and the family packed up their life in boxes and moved halfway across the world. Lina was four years old.

To supplement their meager family income, Maisa worked a clerical job at the Iraqi embassy in Washington, D.C., while Haythem studied. Attending embassy cocktail parties and official functions was part of her duties, and Haythem would come along. But all the necessary worship of Saddam at these events was like gargling with motor oil. It disgusted him, and he would find himself unable to hold in his feelings. He would carelessly speak ill of the great leader in front of a horrified embassy staff until it became too much for them to tolerate. Haythem's growing criticisms eventually led Maisa to lose her job in 1986, the same year his Kuwaiti grant ended. With their income stepping off a cliff, the family moved to Hyattsville, Maryland, when Lina was seven years old, where they lived in a working-class and largely African-American neighborhood.

In Hyattsville, Haythem and Maisa adopted the creed of immigrant parsimony by saving everything and spending next to nothing. While Haythem was at the university, Maisa went to work at a local thrift store and put aside all the newest old clothes she could find for her daughters. Lina recalls bright, plastic, new-looking shoes in particular. Maisa also took charge of the care of her daughters, providing for them as much as she could, helping them with their schoolwork, and instructing them on their behavior. But she ruled with a strict hand. A believer in tough love, she frequently scolded and sometimes slapped her girls for their misbehavior. She was a mighty and intense mother figure for Lina, who also remembers her parents bickering often with each other at this time. Meanwhile, Haythem completed his studies on the health effects of drug addiction and received an offer of work from the National Institute of Drug Abuse. The family hadn't yet decided if they would stay in the United States, but one month later Iraq invaded Kuwait, and whatever hopes they had had of returning to either country fizzed and evaporated like a drop of water on hot sand.

Haythem never considered applying for asylum in the United States. He was too proud to think of himself as a refugee, and he wanted his work credentials to speak for themselves, so the family moved briefly to Canada while he applied to adjust his immigration status through employment. A few months later, he received the proper visa, and the family came back to the United States. With a prestigious job, he could afford to hoist his family up America's class ladder. They took up residency in the much more suburban—and white—Elkridge, Maryland.

IT WAS A DREAM fulfilled for Lina's parents, the promise of upward mobility, the trusted normalcy of an American suburb, far away from an Iraq at war. But for Lina it was something different. In Hyattsville almost everyone had been black, and "you fit in everywhere because black people see past everything," she told me. To her, Hyattsville was a place where everyone was friendly, where all the kids played together, lived together, and were educated together. Her friends and neighbors "didn't look at you like you have a different skin color or different hair or skin tone or anything," she said. When her young Hyattsville friends discovered that she was Muslim, they would joke with her about eating bean pie. She had never seen, let alone tasted, a bean pie, but she knew they were making some kind of reference to Louis Farrakhan and the Nation of Islam, and the mythical bean pie made her feel like she belonged.

But in Elkridge everything was different. Maybe it had something to do with age, she admitted to me, because when she moved to Elkridge as a thirteen-year-old, all the judging started. You had to pick a group and stick with it. There were the white kids, the black kids, and the Spanish kids. There were the jocks, the Goths, and the brains. She could feel the tension among the groups, just as she could feel the stares of the white folk in town, a catalog of glares homing in on a skin's hue or the kink of one's hair. "It's not like I looked much different," she recollected, "but they see that your skin tone is not white, that it's like a yellowish color. And they just judge you right away." Elkridge was awkward.

———

WHEN SHE STARTED high school, Lina felt closest to the black kids, but she slalomed her way around the high-school political culture of cliques and clubs. Everyone liked her, and she was thrilled. She was put into several advanced classes, studying with juniors and seniors, so she successfully cracked the grade stratification of her school. Kids she didn't even know would greet her at her locker as they walked by. As a marker of how popular she was, she was even spared the traditional "beat up a freshman" day of her school, she bragged to me.

As were many high-school kids, Lina was looking around the whole time to find out who she was. She began wearing little tennis skirts with big hoop earrings to school. On other days it was oversize shirts and pants so baggy they could have been Turkish pantaloons fashioned from denim. She looked fly, but her mother wasn't happy with her choices. One day she fixed her eyes on Lina with the kind of composed stare that can devastate a person. "*Inti,*" she said, "you're turning into a black person!" She glared at Lina, waiting for her words to sink in. "You're dressing like them! You're talking like them! You're shaking your head like them!"

And so Lina meandered down the balance beam between her home life and school life until she fell off and began her full-blown rebellion. First she picked up smoking. Next came makeup, never applied at home but on the bus. Foundation, eyeliner, eye shadow, and lipstick were all carefully painted on with the help of a mini-compact on a bumpy ride. The trip home was taken up with wiping the various shades off her face. Then she would walk into her house and her mother would ask her why she smelled like cigarettes. "My friends were smoking at the bus stop," she would lie. But her mother always outsmarted her. "Let me smell your fingers," she would demand.

Other days her mother would ask her if she'd been wearing makeup. "No," she would say, playing as if she were horrified. But her mother would call her on her deception, bringing out a dry Kleenex and rubbing it against the side of her nose, because, as Lina told me, "no matter how much a woman washes her face off, she always has some sort of makeup there, by the nose. And she knew that . . . I don't know how. How does this woman know? Can she really feel me this much?" Lina paused. "There was no way I could get past this woman."

This scrutiny went on for a long time, and her relationship with her mother kept deteriorating. She had to come home directly after school. Phone calls were monitored, homework was mandated, and television was limited to wholesome material like *The Cosby Show, Family Matters,* and Disney movies. Meanwhile, the slapping and yelling and hitting became more frequent. For Lina, school was freedom. Home felt like prison.

DURING HER SOPHOMORE YEAR, Lina wanted more than anything else to go to the homecoming dance. All her friends were routinely going roller-skating or to the movies at night, or they spent time hanging around at the mall, but her mother never allowed her to do these things. She had to come home right after school, and she was losing her friends because of it. Going to the homecoming dance, however, would deputize her with the badge of normalcy, a validation of her as typically American, but first she had to get past her mother. She wasn't expecting much when she asked permission.

"Absolutely not!" her mother said, but this time Lina fought back. They had another loud argument, and a frustrated Maisa ended the row by spitting out, "Go ask your father," confident that that would be the end of it. Lina sidled up to her father with her voice dripping honey and innocence. *"Baba,"* she said, "I want to go to the homecoming dance with my friends." She explained how important it was for her while her mother pointed out that there would be boys there.

"That doesn't matter," her father said. "We trust her."

A weird silence enveloped the room.

"Fine," Maisa said calmly. "She can go."

Lina was floored.

And after that conversation, Maisa didn't only relent, she took charge.

Before the dance she bundled Lina into her car to take her to get Lina's hair and nails done. She helped her daughter pick out a dress, modest but pretty, and turned her into a beautiful teenage girl. Lina became so excited. Her mother set just one rule, that she had to drive Lina to and from the dance, and Lina quickly agreed. She didn't mind. She was going to the dance.

The evening of homecoming, Lina carefully put on her makeup, slipped on her dress, stepped into her shoes, and climbed into her mother's car. As they approached the school, Maisa told Lina to wait for her out front at the end of the dance. Lina nodded, kissed her mother, and closed the car door. She high-heeled it into the auditorium, catching up with her friends, and they all admired one another's dresses and hair and started dancing in a group. Lina felt free and normal, but after about half an hour one of Lina's friends turned to her. "Isn't that your mom over there?" she asked.

"What?! Where?"

"There. In the corner."

Lina was mortified. There sat a lone woman quietly spying on Lina and her group of girls. *How did they let her in?* Lina thought. *Why can't she just wait outside for me? Why would she do this to me in front of my friends?*

She never approached her mother during the dance, but she watched her. And her mother returned her gaze and watched her back. When the dance finished, Lina simply walked up to her mother. Without exchanging a word, the two of them turned and left the building. They climbed back into the car and drove wordlessly home. For Lina the entire purpose of the dance, marking some version of her own independence, had been killed.

SHE STARTED SKIPPING CLASSES. If freedom couldn't be found after school, it had to be stolen during the day. This was the only way to spend time with her school friends. At first they loitered around the Burger King, a common hangout for many of the high-school kids, but the police started showing up, chasing away the students during school hours. They had to change their scene, so after first period they would hike through the woods behind the school. The paths eventually let out behind a 7-Eleven, where they would pick cigarette butts off the asphalt of the parking lot or, if anyone had any money, actually buy a pack from the store. Then they would hike back into the woods and sit on a little footbridge, smoking their lousy butts with their legs dangling over a tiny creek while they traded gossip and talked about how much they hated their parents. Lina would go right home after school let out.

Her grades suffered. The school noticed her absences and informed her parents, whose frustrations with her increased. Something had to be done, her father said. Her parents talked it over and decided to send Lina with her mother and sister to Iraq for forty days that summer. It would be Lina's first trip since a forgotten visit when she was six years old. But it couldn't be a family trip, since her father would not accompany them. Not only had his criticisms of the regime years earlier put him in danger, but Saddam had also banned any physician from leaving the country. If he were to cross the border, he would never be able to leave.

LINA WAS ACTUALLY excited to go. Though she had talked to her Iraqi family regularly on the phone and in Arabic, she had no real image of them. And ever since she was a little girl, she had been listening to her mother constantly narrate the beauty of Iraq and the grand houses she'd grown up in. Lina imagined a country full of castles. What she found was an Iraq in shambles.

But in Ramadi her mother's iron grip on her relaxed. Lina could go out everywhere with her relatives, and they entertained their young American cousin in their homes and at the cafés of Ramadi. She felt pampered and special, and in a bizarre and ironic intersection of teenage life with political history, Lina found freedom in Saddam's Iraq. Finally she felt as if she belonged somewhere.

———

IT WAS A SHORT TRIP. Back in Maryland she began experimenting with herself and her identity again. She wore a *hijab* to school for a while, donning the scarf "for style," she said, "to stand out and be different, and not for religious reasons," but that didn't last long. Instead she began falling into her old ways again, and her parents had their backs up.

Then she met Daniel. He was in her class. Half Puerto Rican and half black, Daniel was patient, kind, and great-looking, with long, curly eyelashes and a wide, gentle smile. One day he came right out and proclaimed to Lina that he had a crush on her. She loved the attention but didn't want to lie to him. She explained the conservative mores of her mother and father, bracing herself for rejection. To her surprise, he told her he didn't care about her parents. He cared about her. She fell hard for him and his understanding nature, and soon they started skipping classes together. It was the only way they could spend time with each other.

Lina found it crazy and fun. Sometimes she wouldn't even go to her classes. She would meet Daniel in the morning at school, and they would take off for the day, and she would go home when school let out. They would hang out at a friend's house or walk in the woods. And he was always sweet and dependable with Lina and never tried to sleep with her. He just wanted to be with her. In the evenings he would call her at home, and soon her parents began suspecting that she had a boyfriend.

That left her with only one option: running away from home.

At first she would leave for a few days and stay at a girlfriend's house. Her parents would become frantic in their search for her, but she always came back eventually. Then her parents put locks on her windows at home, but Lina discovered a way to pick them and climb out her bedroom window. One night she had crawled out the window, down the side of house, and onto the street before her parents, hearing her, realized what was happening. From the street she glanced behind her and saw her parents yelling at her, screaming for her to stop, to come home. She ran. Looking over her shoulder, she saw her mother trip on her nightdress and fall on her knees, crying out in pain. Lina winced. She felt terrible. But she kept running.

SHE WOULD ALWAYS return home. And every time she did, her father would force her to undergo a drug test and visit a gynecologist to make sure she was still a virgin.

SHE RAN AWAY AGAIN, this time for almost two weeks. It was late spring, and school, which she'd been avoiding, had almost finished for the year. One afternoon she and Daniel were curled up on the couch in a friend's basement watching a movie. They heard the gate upstairs open and could see two pairs of legs walk into the house as if it were their own. Lina's heart jumped into her throat when she saw both of her parents rushing down the stairs. Her father ordered her up from the couch and demanded she come home. She was petrified.

But, astonishingly, when they arrived back at their house, Lina's parents told her that they would let her see Daniel. She looked at them with a question mark over her head. "We want to meet him," her mother said, and she asked her to invite him over. Days later, Daniel was on their doorstep, dressed up and full of polite speech, and they all had a nice time together. Lina was shocked, confused, and thrilled, believing that her parents were ready to accept Daniel in her life, but when he left, they told her that they had decided to send her again to Iraq later that summer. In the meantime she was to spend the remaining two weeks with some family friends in Virginia, other Iraqis whom Lina's father knew from back in his Kuwaiti days.

LOOMA WAS HER parents' friend's daughter. She was twenty-two and glamorous. She took Lina to the beach, where they lay on the sand and tanned like movie stars. She gave her wine coolers to drink. At restaurants she offered Lina her mixed drinks to taste. For Lina it was fabulous. She was now seventeen and, for a few days anyway, living the beach life of a twenty-two-year-old. Looma was gorgeous, and Lina was in awe of her. Here she was, hanging out with this pretty girl and all her cool friends. It almost made up for the forced separation from her boyfriend.

But she didn't stop thinking about Daniel. She wanted to see him and would needle Looma to take her. Looma resisted, and then one day Lina's father called and told her he'd read that Daniel had been arrested. He had carjacked a woman at the Columbia Mall, her father claimed, and, using a toy weapon, had forced her to drive to the nearest ATM, after which he stole her money and her car. Lina scoffed. Daniel had never done anything hinting of criminal activity before. She thought her father was lying to her, trying to get her to turn against her Daniel.

But it was true. She found the article in the local paper, a small item about a local crime. Lina read and reread the paragraph, and eventually she cajoled Looma to take her to the prison to visit Daniel. Looma waited for her while Lina emptied her pockets, was searched, and went into the visiting room to see him. He looked dejected, ashen, frightened and out of his element, and it devastated her to see him there and like that.

Lina went back to her newly adopted home, and Looma told her not to worry. She was scheduled to leave for Iraq within a few days now anyway, and she should just move on. Forget about Daniel, Looma advised. Lina confessed to Looma that she had this strange feeling that her parents were sending her off on a one-way ticket. Looma laughed. "Don't be insane. Your father would never do that to you." A few days later, Lina was at the airport, where she saw the ticket for the first time. "*Baba*," she asked, "why is there no return date here?" He rationalized it away for her. Since the three of them would be staying for a little more than three months, he said, and since they didn't know the exact date of their return, an open ticket was more reasonable.

SO LINA WENT TO RAMADI with her mother and sister and was later left there alone. She held on to the idea of Daniel for as long as she could.

She thought only of him for what felt like ages, but in the end he was like an ocean sunset. He hung around in her head, big and blazing and seemingly suspended above the earth for several months, until one day he just fell away from her like the sun dropping below the face of the earth.

In the meantime Lina was feeling a combination of liberty and boredom. With her mother back in the United States, Lina felt free. On the other hand, there was nothing to do. The majority of the day, the electricity was cut off, so she couldn't watch television. She couldn't do anything, really, but eat, sleep, and talk in her aunt's cavernous home. She had grown accustomed to her cousins, as they had to her, and their interactions had become routine. Her family felt her unhappiness, and they even tried to get her some ice cream. They scoured some underground connections, risking arrest for the treat, and brought it to Lina, who ate it with pure joy.

It was a sweet gesture, consoling but ultimately not healing, and eventually Lina broke down. It happened one night during Ramadan, when she was alone in her bedroom. Tears of loneliness starting pouring down her cheeks. She felt she had no one to talk to in Iraq—no close friends, no sisters—and that she couldn't entirely trust her family, who would inform her parents what she was thinking. She felt, at the center of her being, that the only one listening to her, the only who could understand her, was God, and that it was God who had found her.

Her family in Ramadi was not exceptionally religious, but one of the consequences of the deprivations that accompanied the sanctions was that the city became more staunchly devout. At first her aunts and uncles were pleased with Lina's transformation, which was not done with half measures. Every time she heard the *adhan,* the call for prayer, she would wait exactly five minutes and then begin her prostrations. But they started looking at her askance when she donned the entire regalia of a religious woman, *hijab* on her head, flowing *jilbab* covering her body, and even black gloves and thick socks. Lina would also be one of the few women to attend *salat al Isha,* the night prayer at the local mosque, and during Ramadan she would stay for *taraweeh,* the long, supplementary prayers performed through half the night. She had all the required patience for prayer and devotion, and she felt content, as if she had finally found some sort of guidance. But deep down she knew that it wasn't really a direction for her life. She wasn't studying and still hadn't finished high school. She wasn't really going anywhere. But at least she felt so much closer to God, absorbed by His presence, as if her own ego were disappearing.

Eid celebrations came after Ramadan concluded. The first morning of the celebration, Lina's aunt handed her a present, telling her that before she left, her mother had earmarked it for her daughter as an Eid present. It was the bottle of Vivid by Liz Claiborne, and Lina felt her heart crack and bleed into her chest.

HER MOTHER WAS COMING to fetch her. After more than a year in Iraq, it was time for her to come back to the United States and finish high school. Her uncles were about to go pick her mother up from the bus station, and Lina went nuts. She wanted to go with them. After a year she was excited to see her mother again. They explained that women weren't very welcome in that area, but she threw a big tantrum, until they finally relented. She covered herself up and drove with her uncles to the station.

From the first moment she spotted her mother stepping off the bus, Lina was overjoyed, but as soon as she saw her mother look at her, she felt a wall rise up immediately between them. Maisa, who never covered her hair, was shocked to see Lina draped from head to toe. When they arrived home, her mother ordered her to take off her coverings. She tried to reason with her daughter. "You don't have to go parading around in hijab to show your *iman*," your faith, Maisa told her. "*Iman* starts first in your heart."

On her mother's command, Lina stopped dressing the part of a conservative Muslim woman. She wasn't angry. She was sad, because she thought she had once again disappointed her mother. *Is there nothing I can do that is right for her?* Lina thought.

———

SHE CAME BACK to the United States engaged to her cousin Ahsain. A month before her mother arrived, her family in Iraq had floated the idea to her. They thought it would be an opportune match, and Lina didn't fight it. Ahsain was pious and respectful, and since he was six years older than Lina, he was a good match by age as well. Maisa, on the other hand, initially opposed the marriage. She had thought Lina should marry only after she'd finished college and begun a career, as she and most of the women in the family had done. But even Maisa gradually warmed to the idea.

In Ramadi the engagement ceremony was delayed three weekends in a row. The first weekend Ahsain injured his hand and had to have it stitched. The second week the cake, scheduled to arrive from al-'Annab, a famous Baghdadi bakery, was never delivered, due to a blackout and a generator failure. By the third week, Lina's older uncle voiced opposition to the union, but eventually he, too, was silenced. Two days before Lina and her mother left the country, the engagement was finally formalized with a party.

MUCH HAD HAPPENED in the United States since Lina had left, including her father's having changed jobs. He was now working for the Federal Bureau of Prisons in Colorado, so almost as soon as she arrived back in Maryland, the family headed west. They moved to Canyon City, and within days Lina and her mother were driving to Denver to visit bridal shops. It was a time of coming together. They looked at wedding dresses, and Lina tried some on and twirled in front of the mirrors. Their foreheads touched as they bent over the bridal magazines they consulted for tips on how to decorate the hall. The plan was for a summer wedding in Ramadi, after which Lina would remain in Iraq for a year or two while they worked on getting her new husband papers for the United States.

But Lina didn't like their new town in Colorado. It was "pure trailer-park trash," she told me. "They didn't have a mall there or anything. They had a Wal-Mart. Everyone hung out on Main Street, and that was two blocks long." To Lina, Canyon City was claustrophobic and small-minded. They had a Christian bookstore and a Christian bowling alley, and people were always asking about the origins of her parents' accents. But at least her home life was better now. She saw her parents getting along in new ways. Gone was the bickering from the past, and her mother and father seemed like a couple now. They would sit up together and watch the news while eating peanuts and sipping tea. Her sister, too, was thrilled to have Lina home. Over the last fourteen months, she had videotaped all the important college basketball games and collected her favorite music videos to catch Lina up on what she'd missed. With tea, peanuts, and bad television, Lina thought they felt like a family.

But tragedy struck suddenly when Maisa died two months later. It was the second day of the Eid. Haythem was away on the East Coast for professional training, and Maisa woke one morning with a blistering fever. She told Lina not to worry and go to school, but when Lina arrived home after classes, Maisa looked wretched and asked her daughter to take her to the hospital. The doctor told Lina that he'd found a lump on her breast and that Maisa ought to have a mammogram. He reduced her fever with medication and released her, but a day later the fever returned and kept climbing and Maisa died from a Strep A infection.

Haythem returned to Canyon City the next morning. He was incredulous, angry, and destroyed, walking around in circles in a shattered state of utter disbelief. He had to make arrangements for her funeral, and within two days they had buried Maisa in a quiet ceremony at the Muslim cemetery in Denver.

They all had their own ways of coping with the loss of Maisa. Lina felt her family pull closer and move apart simultaneously. They depended more on each other but retreated into their own silences. Lina found herself missing her mother terribly and feeling abandoned.

She called Ahsain, her fiancé, and broke off her engagement. "Things have changed," she explained over thousands of miles of telephone wire. "And I've changed, and I can't do this anymore." She worked hard to finish out her last semester of high school, believing that it would have made her mother proud, and in June she graduated. Her father came to the ceremony, and he cried at her success. He was proud of his daughter but was sad that Maisa wasn't there to witness her accomplishment. Lina thought he looked so small and melancholy in his suit.

That summer she stumbled. She started drinking hard and smoking a lot of weed. Her father, who had withdrawn into depression, soon lost all control of her. He tried moving the family to a neighboring city, but that didn't help. The two fought constantly, until one day when Lina was riding with two of her school friends in their car, she asked a question. "Hey, guys," she said, "can you take me to Denver?" They did, and she didn't come back.

LINA HAD ONE telephone number in Denver. She called Farida, a Moroccan woman who worked in the Arabic restaurant where Lina's family had happened to stop in after her mother's funeral. "This is my situation," Lina explained, not exactly telling Farida the truth. "I'm looking to go to college here, and I just need a place to stay for a few months. I'll pay my way. I'll get a job." Farida took her in and helped her land a spot as a cashier at the Jerusalem Restaurant, a popular eatery with students, close to the University of Denver. At the restaurant Lina worked the night shift with Ghizlan, also Moroccan, another young and attractive woman who dated only Persian Gulf guys. Ghizlan introduced Lina to Denver's Arab scene, and Lina soon had a new circle of friends, most of them international students. From then on she hung out mostly with other Arabs. One day she accompanied a Kuwaiti friend as he was registering for summer courses at the community college, and she decided to apply as well. She was astonished to be accepted on the spot, but she couldn't afford the tuition. The school told her about financial aid, and she discovered that she qualified for a diversity grant. She immediately enrolled for the summer session.

By now Farida knew Lina's real story and was always pushing her to call her father. "*Haram,*" she would say scoldingly, using the Arabic word for "forbidden." "He's your dad!" Instead Lina moved out of Farida's house and in with Ghizlan. But after a few weeks, she finally did call her father. "I'm in Denver," she admitted, "working and going to college." She thought he would yell at her, show his disapproval at her running away to a new life—and restaurant work was not exactly a respectable job for a girl, according to her father's standards—but he was quiet on the phone, and when he came to Denver to visit her, he seemed impressed by her independence. She was pleasantly surprised that he didn't demand she return home. Instead he offered to pay for her next semester of school and help her with her rent. She moved again, this time to an apartment in a preacher's house she found through an ad in the local paper.

At college she had a large group of Arab friends. There was also Lola, a beautiful Chechen girl with chestnut hair and a round, moonlike face who was in her Arabic class. Zaki was Lola's friend. A Palestinian from Lebanon, Zaki often flirted with Lina, and eventually they began a relationship. Zaki took her everywhere in his beat-up Toyota Corolla—to the food court in the mall, to Canyon City to visit her father and sister, to her mother's gravesite in Denver. After a trip back home to Beirut that summer, he returned to Denver bearing gifts from his family for Lina—jewelry from his mother and a shirt from his fourteen-year-old sister. It was hideous, Lina thought, and she never wore it, but she loved the gesture. On her birthday Zaki bought her a bracelet from Zales with an engraving on the inside. Lina thought it was too expensive. But she also thought it was really sweet.

Everything was working for her now, but for some reason she grew scared of her happiness. She called her dad frequently and began pushing him to get a transfer back to the East Coast, telling him she would go with him. She felt she wanted to go back to where her mother had raised her, believing she would feel more connected to her mother if they moved back to Maryland. Haythem welcomed the opportunity to reunite his family, so he put in for the transfer. But instead of landing a job in Maryland, he was assigned to Brooklyn, New York.

IN BROOKLYN everything was smaller. The stores were smaller, the apartments were smaller, the cars were smaller, even the shopping carts were smaller. Lina, her sister, and their dad moved into a drab concrete building in Bay Ridge peopled with other federal corrections staff. Even though she'd pushed for the move, Lina had wanted to go to Maryland. She knew no one in Brooklyn, and soon after the move she discovered that Zaki was cheating on her. She took a bus across the country to confront him with his infidelity, and their relationship ended abruptly, like a car slamming into a wall.

In the fall she enrolled in Kingsborough Community College and took mostly science classes to please her father (math was always her strongest subject), but she didn't like Kingsborough very much. Back in Denver she'd had a big social circle made up mostly of other Arabs. At Kingsborough she would wander around the campus between classes without talking to anybody.

The Internet became her haven. She would go online in the evenings and troll around various Web sites and chat rooms looking to meet people. One night she was logged on to ArabChat on AOL and started a conversation with Mohammad, another Iraqi. He was younger than Lina but, like a godsend, also lived in Brooklyn. Lina got excited and grabbed her sister. "Let go meet him!" she suggested. Mohammad suggested a Greek café in Bay Ridge, the same one where I first met her, and they sat upstairs smoking and drinking muddy coffee while they traded stories. He told them about his family. His father was a senior Iraqi diplomat, working at the United Nations as a liaison with the weapons-inspections program. The youngest in the family, Mohammad also had two brothers, Ra'ed and

Wisam, and a sister, Rana, who was a few years older than Lina. Mohammad thought Lina and Rana would hit it off.

But Lina thought Rana was stuck up. Iraq's class hierarchy was deeply
embedded in Rana, and as a diplomat's daughter she would smugly and re-
gally request Lina to drive her around the city for errands. Lina began to
resent her. Rana warmed to Lina only after she found out that her mother
and Lina's paternal aunt were actually close friends in Baghdad. Lina
pushed her off at first, but eventually the two overcame their differences,
and Rana introduced Lina to her next infatuation, her brother Wisam.

Lina immediately developed a crush like a landslide on the young man.
He was attractive, funny, and about a year older than Lina. Naturally, Lina
thought about how perfect the fit was, and for a while they were inseparable. He would call her in the morning, and they would go for walks by the
Sixty-ninth Street pier, standing beside the Mexican fishermen and looking
at the barges on the bay, endless New Jersey off in the distance. Afternoons
they would meet at the Greek café. In the evenings they would ride the
subway into lower Manhattan and spend time roaming around Battery
Park, walking oblivious to the Chinese caricature artists hawking their portraits and the lines of tourists herded like cattle to see the lady holding a
torch. They would talk to each other on the phone until dawn. The two became very close, and even though Lina fell hard for Wisam, she never pursued it as a romance. She loved their friendship too much, she said.

IN THE SUMMER OF 2001, Lina's father announced to his daughters
that he was considering remarriage. A Virginian friend was helping an Iraqi
widow with two young children who was looking for a husband, and Haythem was driving down to meet her. The introductions went well. The
woman came from a well-placed dissident family (Saddam had murdered
four of her uncles) who had turned on the regime and fled Iraq for Syria
years earlier in a five-day walk across Iraqi Kurdistan. Her father had been
part of Iraq's exiled opposition movement, and the entire family had immigrated to the United States in 1998 as political refugees. Her prior hus-

band had recently passed away of natural causes, and she wanted to marry immediately to give her children a father. Haythem agreed and quickly put his plans into action. In a mad rush of two weeks, arrangements were made for the wedding. The pace of things confused Lina, but she traveled down to Virginia for the ceremony and to meet her new family. Her stepmother was very young—only half a dozen years older than Lina—and Lina was skeptical at first. The woman also had brothers, and soon everyone began remarking—half as a joke but half for real—that Lina should marry one of her in-laws.

Laith is the oldest brother in the family, and when Lina first met him, she was unimpressed. He walked with a swagger, wore a flashy suit, talked loudly about being a manager at the Marriott, and his favorite movie was *Scarface*. Who was this Mr. Big Shot? Lina wondered.

But soon she saw a soft side to him. The bridal shower was held at the family's house just before the wedding. At one point Lina was sitting by herself, lost in sadness, when Laith spotted her. He came down the stairs and sat next to her, asking her quietly what she was thinking. She told him that the wedding was freaking her out. It wasn't that she resented her stepmother-to-be, but the whole thing was so confusing. All she could think about was how much she missed her own mother, how no one could take her place, and how she wasn't going to gain anything from the marriage. Laith listened to her quietly. She finished speaking and looked at him, and there was something tender behind his eyes. She thought about how she hadn't noticed that before.

At the wedding the next day, though, she still couldn't stop crying. The actual ceremony was tiny, held in a local restaurant, and during the reception Lina went outside to call Wisam. She wanted to talk to him because she missed him, but mostly because she kept missing her mother and thought he would understand this best. She felt better after she got off the phone, but when she returned to the reception, she started crying again. People began asking her what was wrong, and they crowded around her. She felt she couldn't explain her feelings. Instead she demanded that they bring her a CD by the Egyptian pop star Amr Diab. His music reminded her of Wisam, and it felt like the only thing that would comfort her and stop her from crying. They did, it did, and she did, too.

AFTER THE WEDDING, Lina's family suddenly expanded. They all lived in Brooklyn, and Lina and her stepmother started fighting. Meanwhile, she began corresponding with Laith, who wanted to get engaged to Lina immediately. She demurred. Wisam, on the other hand, slowly began disappearing from her life. He had met a young Iranian woman on the subway one day and was spending all his spare time now with her. Lina missed their relationship, but she grew closer to Rana, who got her a job at Pick-A-Bagel. Rana worked there as a cashier, and Lina, who had always been strong with numbers, did the accounting. They would arrive together and leave together, and Rana became like an older sister to Lina, telling her frequently that she wished she would marry Wisam so that they could become a family. The more Lina argued with her stepmother, the closer she grew to Rana.

OVER THE COURSE of the next year, Lina decided that she would like to be engaged to Laith, and the two had a torturous long-distance courtship. Laith was also involved with another American girl at the time, and it drove Lina crazy. She was miserable, unable to figure out what to do with her life. She felt totally lost, and one day in October 2002 she stopped at the army recruiting table on her campus. The salesmen in drab green uniforms sweet-talked the young lady into joining the army reserves. It would pay for school, she figured, and give her some discipline, which she knew she needed. She joined, believing she would be an operating-room specialist and be stationed at a hospital near Walter Reed, close to Laith in Virginia. She signed the forms and told her father later.

He was livid. How could she throw her life away like that? Didn't she know what the army means? He talked to his neighbors who also worked in the federal prison system, many of whom had served in the military, and after hearing their positive reports he began to think that the idea might not be as crazy as it sounded. But objections to her military decision didn't end with her father. Rana opposed it with a passion. The rhetoric between Saddam and Bush was ratcheting up in late 2002, and with her diplomat father Rana had direct ties to the Iraqi regime. She didn't want Lina to be associated with anything that could be construed as anti-Iraqi. Suddenly Lina felt an enormous distance grow between them. One night she asked Rana straight out, "Are you upset with me for joining?" Rana sighed. "No, I'm not mad at you." But Lina could feel her disappointment. The two women began talking far less often with each other.

The army reserves was also a way for Lina to get out of the house, a place where she and her stepmother didn't get along. Lina took advantage of the situation to move down to Virginia for a couple of months before reporting for basic training. While in Virginia, she spent more time with Laith. Lina began feeling more focused, more confident in her own decision making. She didn't need the military anymore. She asked her father how she could get out of the reserves, and he again asked his colleagues. Before her report date had arrived, Lina left the reserves on an uncharacterized discharge (and now believes this was one of the best decisions she has made in her life, especially considering the current war in Iraq).

Relations with Rana suddenly improved. Rana traveled down to Virginia once in December to visit Lina, Lina and Laith picked her up at the train station, and they all spent the weekend together, eating, laughing, and enjoying Washington, D.C. On Sunday they put Rana back on the train. Although Lina didn't know it then, it would be the last time she would see Rana.

BY EARLY 2003, Lina was back living in Brooklyn. One Friday afternoon, she heard a knock at her door. The men flashed badges and identified themselves as special agents from the FBI. They said they had come to talk to Lina about Rana's brothers, Wisam and Ra'ed. They were exceedingly polite.

Lina let them in, where they sat on the couch and began asking her a litany of questions: How long had she known the brothers? What did she know about them? Why had she backed out of going into the army reserves? She responded with small, honest answers, confused by the whole visit. Then they started explaining and talking about spies. *What is this, a movie?* she thought. *This stuff doesn't happen in real life.*

They told her that Ra'ed had been working as an operative for Saddam Hussein and that a friend of Ra'ed's, who'd been in her father's house, was a known assassin. He was code-named "The Scorpion," and he had visited them with the eventual intention to kill a member of their extended household, namely someone in her stepmother's dissident family.

Lina couldn't believe it.

This wasn't just Ra'ed they were talking about, it was also Wisam. Wisam. The one person she'd called, crying, when her father had remarried. Wisam. Sweet Wisam, who had been her closest friend and so much more. And now these men in suits were telling her that Wisam was helping assassins trespass into their midst? Unbelievable.

But later, when she talked to her father, she discovered that the FBI had also interviewed him at his workplace, where they pulled out a file and showed him photographs, pictures of Ra'ed and "The Scorpion" entering and exiting her father's building, and she saw how her father didn't consider the whole thing far-fetched. She was working hard to understand the whole situation, and slowly, as it started to seem credible, her confusion hardened into anger. She had trusted Ra'ed and Wisam and their whole family, and now they were responsible for bringing someone to their house who endangered her and her family? She focused her acrimony on Ra'ed, but the anger quickly morphed into vulnerability. After her mother died, Lina had worked hard to develop a toughness about her, but now the feelings of insecurity were back. Was Wisam really a spy? She felt used and betrayed.

RANA AND HER YOUNGER BROTHER were also picked up by the authorities. It was right around the time that the war in Iraq had begun. Both of them were arrested, held briefly on immigration charges, and then

allowed to leave the country easily and quickly, so quickly that Lina never
saw either of them again. Wisam and Ra'ed were not so lucky. Lina couldn't
help but soften her attitude toward Wisam, and she started worrying about
him while continuing to resent and curse Ra'ed. Suddenly everything the
older brother had done seemed untrustworthy to her. He worked at a dry
cleaner in Manhattan, but he had a love of electronics. Where did he get all
the money to buy the miniature cameras, the latest mobile devices? she
wondered. He had shoes up the wazoo. What was he, a Ba'athist Imelda
Marcos? His extravagant sense of style had now transformed into a costume of suspicion.

SHE THOUGHT BACK to a few days before the FBI visit. That evening
Ra'ed had asked her for a ride to an apartment where a friend of his was
staying. He wanted to drop something off, and she waited in the car with
her sister. A few minutes later, he was back, and as he sank into his seat, a
New York Police Department van, light flashing cherry red, pulled up
quickly behind them. The police ordered them out and kept each of them
separately on various sides of the car, asking them how they knew one another and taking their identification. For twenty minutes they couldn't talk
to one another until the police finally returned their IDs and told them to
leave. They got back into the car and drove away. "That was weird," Lina
said, the other two nodding. Now that episode didn't seem so strange.

And she remembered the time Ra'ed brought this "Scorpion" to their
house. It was back in early 2002. Late one night, around 11:00 P.M., Ra'ed
had called up her father because, he said, his friend had a rash on his ear
and wanted some medical advice before he left the country the next morning. Lina's father brushed them off at first. It was late, and Lina's stepmother had just returned home from some minor surgery that day. But
Ra'ed was insistent. "Please, *Amu*," he said, calling Haythem uncle. "We
won't be late. We won't stay long." Half an hour later, the two men were at
their door. Ra'ed's friend was built like a retaining wall, rough and imposing. When he was at the house, he even asked Lina's father if his daughter,

Lina's younger sister, was single and interested in marriage. Haythem ignored the question, offering the man some simple medical advice instead and politely urging the two to leave. At the time the visit seemed stupid, a tactless intrusion into their night. It did not seem like the spy mission she was beginning to believe it was.

THE INDICTMENT SAID it in legal language. "In or about December 2001 or January 2002," it read, Ra'ed "facilitated a meeting between an officer of the Iraqi Intelligence Service [IIS] and the family of an Iraqi dissident now living in the United States." The fourth count of the indictment charged that Wisam had "unlawfully, willfully, and knowingly falsified, concealed, and covered up by trick, scheme, and device material facts, and made materially false, fictitious, and fraudulent statements and representations" to the FBI, namely that he "falsely informed agents of the Federal Bureau of Investigation that he had not told IIS officers of the location in the United States of an Iraqi expatriate, the son of a former Iraqi diplomat." Both brothers were charged with acting as agents of the IIS and were arraigned in front of Judge Michael B. Mukasey. Several months earlier, in June 2002, the man known as "The Scorpion"—Abdul Rahman Saad, according to the *New York Daily News*—had been declared persona non grata by the U.S. government and ordered out of the country.

The brothers' attorney told the press that the charges were ludicrous and nothing short of vindictive. He claimed they had in fact been working with the FBI, giving the Bureau the names of Iraqi intelligence agents in the country. (Supporting his claim, the indictment admitted this fact.) Moreover, he said, the FBI had long pressured their father to defect to the United States in the belief that he might know where Iraq's weapons of mass destruction were hidden. The father left the country three years earlier, but days after the war began in March 2003, the brothers were arrested and charged.

The government also claimed that Ra'ed was tasked by the IIS to pur-

chase a miniature camera and a voice recorder but was then told by the IIS
to return the recorder to the store because its eighty-dollar price tag was
too high. In July 2003 a federal judge rejected that part of the government's
allegations. "It is difficult for the court to believe that an Iraqi intelligence
agent in New York could not obtain a slim-profile camera, if actually
needed for intelligence work, without enlisting help," Judge Alan Vomacka
wrote, adding that "it is also difficult to believe that a voice recorder for use
in intelligence work would be rejected because the $80 cost was excessive."
He then determined that the brothers posed no threat to national security,
but still the case went forward.

EVERYTHING CRASHED around Lina. Her relationship with Laith had
turned rocky. Wisam was in prison. School was going nowhere, and she
had stopped working at the bagel shop. Her menstrual cycle was disrupted
by the stress, and she found herself bleeding for a solid three months. She
went to see a doctor, who wanted to perform surgery on her uterus. "Does
that mean I will lose my virginity?" she asked him. She refused the surgery,
and in July 2003 she moved to Virginia instead. The relocation was calming. Within days her bleeding stopped.

She got another restaurant job, this time waitressing at T.G.I. Friday's,
and she enrolled at Northern Virginia Community College. She worked on
her relationship with Laith and wrote letters to Wisam while he was in
prison. She settled into a routine of work and school. Laith's sister-in-law
was pregnant, and Lina helped the couple with their newborn. Over time
in Virginia, her connection to Laith grew more solid and turned into real
love, with all its ups and downs. It helped her own mental health. Finally
she had the romance she'd been looking for. "Ever since I was a little girl,"
she explained, "I've always dreamed of living one big love story." Now she
had found it, and she felt as if she were acting a part "in an Abdul Halim
movie," she told me with a glow, referring to the black-and-white classics
from a bygone era in Egyptian cinema.

————

THEN ONE DAY, one of Ra'ed's friends called her out of the blue. Anne was a strong-willed woman and his devoted confidante. She was furious about Ra'ed's arrest, and whenever Lina went to Brooklyn to visit her father, she would go with Anne to the Metropolitan Detention Center to see Wisam while Anne visited Ra'ed. For the second time in her life, she found herself going to prison to see an incarcerated friend.

By December 2004, things had again turned rocky in her relationship with Laith, and Lina decided to leave Virginia and move back in with her father in New York. In Brooklyn she responded to a help-wanted ad placed by a local Arab-American newspaper and got the job. She worked on the business end of the publication and liked the challenge. She was particularly drawn to the idea of community journalism, and within a few months she and an editor at the paper decided to begin publishing their own broadsheet. They produced their first issue of the *Key* in August 2005. Now she had somewhere to put her energies. The *Key* was meant to be educational. Lina felt there was so much she hadn't known in her own life. She didn't know the first thing about applying for college financial aid, for example, and she wanted the newspaper to be a vehicle to spread this kind of information to the large new immigrant community in Bay Ridge and especially to other young Arab Americans. "I wanted there to be something for people my age," she told me, "to let them know that it's okay. I wish there had been something for me, to help me adjust." They put out about a dozen issues of the newspaper, but it was ultimately too much work with too many debts for the two founders, and the enterprise folded after about nine months. Still, the *Key* marked a change in her outlook, when she began looking outside herself and off into the future.

In January, Ra'ed and Wisam pleaded guilty to making false statements to the FBI and were handed terms of six months, far less than the two years they had already spent in prison or the fifteen years they faced if convicted. The main charge against them—that they conspired to act as agents of Saddam Hussein's government—was dropped with their guilty pleas. They were sentenced to time served and were moved to Passaic County Jail, where they sat out their deportation orders while waiting for a country to accept them. (Jordan eventually would.)

Lina continued to visit them. She went with Anne each time, but it was never easy. Wisam would never look her in the eye, and both brothers seemed deflated to Lina, as if they were lost in detention. It hurt her to see them this way, but she persisted. In total, she visited them almost a dozen times and wrote Wisam letters to keep his mood up. But in all the visits, she could never muster the courage to ask him if the two brothers were really guilty.

One day, on the ride back from Passaic County, Anne finally broached the topic of their guilt with Lina. "What do you really think?" she asked as they drove through the Battery Tunnel to Brooklyn.

Lina paused, then asked carefully, "Anne, you want the honest truth?" She nodded.

"Honestly," Lina said, "my heart tells me that they did it." She suspected they had been working both the Iraqi government and the United States as "double agents," and thought she could see guilt etched in the vacant, sheepish glances Wisam gave her with each visit.

"You're crazy," Anne blurted out, sounding hurt. After a pause she asked, "How come you still see them?"

"Because it's not in my hands. You know, God's the one that's going to judge them. I'm not. What I do as a human being is to be there for them, no matter how much they wronged me."

They emerged from the tunnel.

"You're a stronger person than I am," Anne said.

AND IN JULY 2006, Lina finally achieved what she'd wanted for so very long. In a simple, tiny ceremony held in an imam's cramped office in Bay Ridge, and with the constant whoosh of cars rushing along Fourth Avenue in the background, Laith married Lina. They signed the contract, kissed, and pledged their lives to each other. Following the wedding, Lina moved to Virginia with Laith, who was now managing an upscale Italian restaurant. They settled into a row house just off a highway.

I WENT TO VISIT them in March 2007, and what I found was that marriage seemed to center Lina, giving her something to hold on to. It was also a source of cultural accomplishment to her. "I feel proud I married an Iraqi," she told me. "I feel at least I succeeded with that. We both found each other. And I feel like there is a God after all this," she said, referring to the labyrinth of desires and choices she's navigated in her life. She had quit smoking and now moved more slowly. She was also pregnant, expecting a baby girl, and had a predictable glow about her.

The highway by their house is checkered with motor inns, Mexican roadside diners, and a Denny's managed by Laith's brother Hani. We used the restaurant as a surrogate office, meeting there often and talking through the evenings after Lina got off from her new job, as administrative assistant at an employment agency. Laith also took me out one night and we met up with his brothers and friends at an Arabic restaurant—called 1001 Nights, of course, located forty miles away and in a nondescript strip mall that could be anywhere. On weekend nights the restaurant transforms into a club with a live Arabic band. This night it was packed with young Arabs and South Asians who danced in groups and one table of middle-aged white women looking around expectantly. I sat with Laith at a table of drinking Iraqis, one with a cell-phone screen saver that was a picture of Saddam just before his hanging, and we cheered loudly when the singer yelled out his love of Iraq. A diaspora disco.

We left the club around 2:00 A.M., and Laith and I went back to the Denny's, now full of half-drunk college kids loudly snapping digital pictures of themselves—and the rest of the world. There was the Palestinian motel owner from down the street; the pretty Filipina night manager who talked about her real estate investments; the African-American security guard, built like a door, who explained the gun-control laws of Washington, D.C., to us; the Russian waitress who comped us our coffee; and of course Laith, whom everyone knew and liked. (He had worked there before.) This is another America, away from the dull, monochromatic life of suburbia and found in those places where immigrants, exiles, and native-born Americans live, eat, and laugh in a babel of languages and nationalities.

BUT EXILE is usually characterized as the terrible longing to return home, "an unhealable rift forced between a human being and a native place," in Edward Said's words. Yet this isn't true for Lina. Since I have known her, I have always been struck by how proud Lina is of her Iraqi roots but also by how she also talks about Iraq the country mostly in the past tense. Yet is it really any surprise? Lina simply no longer recognizes the nation she sees on television. Iraq's sectarian strife in particular overwhelms her. Before the war, she explained to me, "there was no such thing as Shi'a and Sunni in Iraq." Two of her uncles, both Sunni, are married to Shi'a women. Her father's sister is Sunni, and her husband is Shi'a. "So there was none of that before," she said, as we sat in Denny's rear dining room. "We never differentiated," she said, shaking her head. "Even in Lebanon, Shi'a and Sunni are separated much more than we ever were." She paused, then sighed. "It's *haram*."

She told me that in Iraq her family's businesses had nosedived since the American invasion and through the continuing war and carnage, but also that hardship is nothing new to the Iraqi people. "My whole family has been through the Iran-Iraq War, they've been through the Gulf War, they've been through the sanctions, and they're still alive," she explained. Nevertheless, the war has left its imprint. She told me about one of her uncles who had been shot in the leg by American forces and another who took a rubber bullet in the face at Abu Ghraib.

Despite these current traumas, it's pre-invasion Iraq that permeates her memory. "For me what hurt more was the sanctions," she said. "Now it's easy. People are just dying. You get shot and you're dead. But it was the sanctions that killed more because all the *sha'ab*"—the people—"were weakened due to them. It was a slow and painful death." Then she admitted, "I don't really feel the war, because I'm not there anymore."

Neither is her extended family. Except for two old aunts and an elderly uncle who have refused to move, both sides of her family have now fled the country and sought refuge elsewhere. (At least 2 million other Iraqis have also left the country and more than 2 million are internally displaced.) Lina's family is currently divided almost evenly between Syria and Jordan. For so many, Iraq is increasingly becoming at best an abstract idea. At worst it's a memory.

What happens when your homeland is in the process of disintegrating in front of your eyes? What do you do, especially when Iraq's turmoil has always hovered in the background of your life? Perhaps you do what immigrants to the United States and their children have done for generations. You build your own destiny from your American home while keeping one eye open to that which has been lost. And while your American life largely takes over, you still live somewhere between geographies, as you have for most of your life. It's just that the in-between has become harder than ever to locate.

I thought this was true for Lina. It seemed especially so when I listened to her and Laith talk about their soon-to-be family. That Lina will become a mother to her own daughter could be a daunting prospect, considering her own turbulent family life. "We're sending her back home when she's twelve," Lina proclaimed, laughing before continuing. "Seriously. I don't want her growing up here. I know what it's like!" Considering the challenges she faced in her own past, the comment perhaps made a certain amount of sense, but Iraq has plunged into a civil war with no end in sight. Who knows what it will be like after a decade? "You'll send her to Iraq?" I asked. "Syria," she replied, explaining that Laith has a sister there. When Laith joined us later, he expressed the same idea about saving his daughter from the temptations of the United States, and he also labeled Syria as home. "It's funny," I said. "You both call Syria 'back home.' Not Iraq."

In response, both of them spoke the same words at almost precisely the same time, an answer that explained living as an Iraqi abroad perhaps better than any other. "Iraq?" they both said. "What Iraq? There is no Iraq anymore."

OMAR

This is not a season for lovers
These staccato days of heat

—FRED JOHNSON, from "Arabesque"

I t's 2006, and twenty-two-year-old Omar spends his days pounding his head into his keyboard. Strange behavior for a guy with a disposition so sunny that you could get a tan by standing beside him, but Omar has been looking for a career in news media, and the job hunt is burning him out. His efforts are unremitting. Most of the time he is drafting cover letters, sending out applications, or following up yesterday's batch with those embarrassing phone calls. ("Hi, I sent in my résumé, and I'm wondering if you've had a chance to . . .") Yet close to a thousand résumés later, the only offers coming are for lousy sales positions pouring in from shady online marketers. It's not that Omar is unqualified. He may be young, but he has noteworthy experience in his chosen field. His references include internationally renowned professionals willing to stake their reputations on his work ethic. And he's tried everything from industry connections to Internet job sites. But still his phone doesn't ring, and frankly it's demoralizing.

Everyone wants a job, but Omar has his reasons for needing a career. Her name is Nadine. They were both students at Hunter College, the same place where his parents—both refugees fleeing political persecution—met a generation earlier, and Omar immediately tripped, stumbled, and fell in love with her. Sweet Nadine has straight black waterfall hair and deep button eyes. She's everything Omar could wish for: smart, pretty, fun, Palestinian, and she cares about the world (and about him). He knows he wants to marry her in a raucous and friendly Palestinian wedding, where the food piles up high on long tables and the dancing goes late into the night. He wants it to be the kind of wedding where people collapse into chairs after sweating through their best clothes, where they won't leave until well past 4:00 A.M., and where all the guests are complaining the next day about how much their feet hurt.

Before the wedding comes the engagement, and Omar wants to do that strictly according to custom as well. As he gets older, he is placing more importance on his Palestinian roots, especially since he lives in a country where, he says, people routinely forget where they come from. And so the fact that Nadine is Palestinian is important for Omar. "Since we literally have no country," Omar explained to me, "the only thing we have is our identity, and it's important for me, as the oldest son, to preserve that identity." The whole engagement plays out in his head like a movie. He narrated it one October evening as we were driving in his parents' car to a *shisha* café in Bay Ridge, Brooklyn:

The scene begins with his grandfather, the patriarch of the clan, calling Nadine's family on the phone and exchanging pleasantries in Arabic. He'll inquire as to everyone's health before gently raising a polite request to her father, on Omar's behalf, for the young lady's hand. Her father will defer the question for a while, maybe a week, as the bride-to-be's family researches Omar's family. Then his family's phone will ring again. Nadine's father will extend an invitation to Omar's grandfather and father, to Omar himself, and all three men will wear starchy white shirts with neckties and drive to her house carrying a tray of syrupy sweets. It will be afternoon, and they will be received with strong tea or coffee before polite conversation ensues. Negotiations will begin over details (dowries, living arrangements, and the like). All the while Nadine will be out of sight until called, but then she'll walk down the stairs like an old-time movie star. Omar will be sitting in his chair, an expectant young man, and they will shyly avert their glances from each other. Another date will be set for the public recitation of the Fatiha, the first chapter of the Qur'an, symbolizing their engagement. "I've been to some of them before," Omar said breathily. "It's pretty sexy."

But without a good job, the movie jams and the celluloid burns in the projector. Omar knows that a career is what her family will require from him. It's the necessary condition to connect the fate of the two families, and he's worried that his time is running away from him. Family pressures may soon bear down on Nadine to marry someone else, a cousin perhaps, as is common among Palestinians. Omar is a young man in a hurry.

Nine months ago everything was different. It was spring, and Omar felt he had it all locked up. He had just graduated with a bachelor's degree in communications. He'd been popular at school and had earned a decent GPA. And, most important, he had interned with one of the most recognizable media organizations in the world, the Arabic news network Al Jazeera. After this experience he thought landing a job would be a cakewalk. But nothing has happened, and since then a question has been increasingly gnawing at him. Could it be that American media organizations won't hire him because they find an Arab-American with Al Jazeera credentials too problematical? Rather than launching him toward the major media, Al Jazeera's reputation might be holding him down. Omar's spring of hope has turned into a winter of discontent.

THERE IS OF COURSE another possible explanation. Maybe it's just hard to find a job in media, and Omar's difficulties have nothing to do with his work at Al Jazeera or with his Arab ethnicity. He's not sure, and at any given time Omar will travel uneasily between explanations. One day he told me he'd read on the Internet that it takes, on average, two years for a college graduate to find a career job, while on other days he'll lash out at Al Jazeera for not hiring him full-time and for ruining his chances at finding a career in the media. He just doesn't know. But Omar's worries over employment discrimination in the age of terror are hardly unique. I hear the anxiety echoing everywhere around the young people I encounter, and some of their stories are cautionary tales.

Consider Sade (the young man who appeared in the preface and a friend of Omar's). He's twenty-five now, but when he was eighteen, he began working as a point clerk at the commodities exchange. (He was one of the guys on the trading floor who you see screaming orders and reading that bizarre sign language traders speak.) The exchange where he worked dealt mostly in cocoa, sugar, coffee, cotton, and dollars, and Sade worked primarily in cotton. In the beginning he clerked for four traders until he mastered his skills. Soon eleven people depended on him. He was eager and hardworking, and he also got his brother a job there. His brother worked in sugar.

But the traders at the exchange used to harass Sade constantly. "They're very racist there," he told me repeatedly. They would crumple paper into balls (as if they were stones) and throw them at him. "Go back to Palestine!" they'd yell, and laugh. When he wouldn't laugh back, they'd retort with, "Hey, we do it because we love you." But Sade didn't buy it. On other occasions they would scream, "Don't blow yourself up!" to him. On quiet days someone would run right up to him and bang chests, yelling, "Ba-BOOM!" Then the other traders would fall over in hysterics. Sade soaked it all up and pushed it aside, focusing instead on his own desire to become a trader.

After September 11 the exchange moved to a backup facility in Long Island City, and the harassment got even worse. A year later they moved back to lower Manhattan, but nothing changed for Sade. On the day the Iraq War began, in March 2003, trading was slow and all the televisions were tuned to the news. When the Baghdad sky lit up orange with explosions, the whole floor celebrated. "Kill those bastards! Kill those Arabs!" they cheered. Sade was silent.

Then one day shortly afterward, the bosses asked Sade's brother to bring in his passport. They wanted to check something on his application, they said. He's an American citizen, but they paid close attention to his Jerusalem birthplace. Days later the director called Sade into her office (it was 10:30 A.M., in the middle of the trading day) to tell him that he had to go. "We've hired four extra people," she said, even though Sade had been there for more than three years, and as if that were a sufficient reason for his being fired. "Impossible," Sade said. He shook his head but was suddenly out of a job. Two hours later his brother was also let go. Security took their identification badges and escorted them outside.

To this day Sade is convinced that the termination order came from on high, a cleansing of Arabs from New York's fragile cathedrals of international commerce. "I got sick for one year after that," he told me. "I couldn't sleep at night." He talked to a lawyer, exploring his options to sue for his job back. But the lawyer told him he didn't have enough evidence. "My mistake was that I didn't get it in writing. I was *jahil*," he told me, using the Arabic word for "ignorant." "I was young. I didn't expect it."

SADE'S TALE and Omar's anxiety led me to examine the status of employment discrimination against Arabs and Muslims in the United States. Immediately following September 11, employment complaints filed by Arabs and Muslims rocketed upward. In the first eight months after the attacks, the Equal Employment Opportunity Commission (EEOC), the federal agency that monitors employment discrimination, received 488 complaints from Arabs and Muslims, including 301 cases claiming unfair firings. Within a year the American Arab Anti-Discrimination Committee had cataloged over 800 grievances, a 400 percent increase over the past year. According to a report aired on December 15, 2006, on NPR, one-fifth of the complaints reviewed by the EEOC since 2001 have been from Muslims and Arabs, a number that is wildly out of proportion to their numbers in the United States.

Some cases dated to immediately following the terrorist attacks, while others continue to this day. An earlier case involved twelve Muslim, Arab, and South Asian workers who filed a claim with the EEOC against the "severe and pervasive harassment" that they underwent at the Plaza Hotel months after the terrorist attacks. According to the suit, managers wrote "Osama," "Binladin," "Alkada," and "Taliban" instead of the employees' actual names when handing out key holders with room keys. The employees were repeatedly called "terrorist," "Osama," "Al Queda [sic]," "Taliban," and "Dumb Muslim." They were accused of destroying the World Trade Center and cursed at for ruining the country. In 2003 the luxury hotel chain agreed to a $525,000 settlement and increased sensitivity training for its staff.

Labor-market discrimination continues. A 2004 study performed by the California-based Discrimination Research Center revealed the impact of first and last names on hiring in the Golden State. They sent out six thousand fictitious résumés to employment firms throughout California, with each candidate similarly qualified, but the names—"test-marketed" beforehand—could be identified as white, Latino, African-American, Asian-American, Arab-American, or South Asian. "Heidi McKenzie" garnered the highest response, at 36.7 percent. The lowest, at 23 percent, was the identifiably Muslim name, Abdul-Aziz Mansour.

Another study published in the *Journal of Population Economics* in 2005 discovered that "Middle Eastern Arab men and Afghan, Iranian, and Pakistani men experienced a significant earnings decline relative to non-Hispanic whites between 2000 and 2002." The reason? "The unanticipated events of September 11th, 2001 negatively affected the labor-market income of the groups most closely associated with the ethnicity of the terrorists." Likewise, Columbia University's Neeraj Kaushal and two other social scientists sought to quantify any decline through 2005. Their painstakingly detailed study, published in the Spring 2007 issue of the *Journal of Human Resources,* found that earnings fell 9 to 11 percent for Arab and Muslim men's real wages and weekly earnings. Kaushal and her colleagues developed a formula to test their hypothesis that looks like this:

$$Y_{ix} = \alpha_0 + \alpha_1 Sept_2 + \alpha_2 Tr_{in} + \alpha_3 (Sept_1 * Tr_{in}) + X_{in}\Gamma + (X_{in} * Tr_{ix})\tilde{\Gamma} + Z_{iz}\Lambda +$$
$$(Z_{12} * Tr_{iz})\tilde{\Lambda} + \delta, + \tau_m + (\tilde{\tau}_m * Tr_{in}) + \gamma, + (\tilde{\gamma}, Tr_{ix}) + \mu_{in}$$

Omar has a formula, too. His involves listening to a phone that won't ring.

I FIRST MET OMAR at a gathering at Hunter College's Arab Club in the spring of 2006. He was the tall guy dressed like a banker, in his navy blue suit and black shoes. Weeks shy of graduation, he had begun his job hunt and had landed an interview with a finance firm earlier that afternoon. "Honestly? I'd rather work in media," he told me, "but I need a job." We stood around in a small room with a bunch of other students, all eating baklava off plastic plates and talking about the latest Arabic pop stars. He began telling me about his time at Al Jazeera and how he now wanted to work for an American network. At the American networks, the pay is better and you can really make a difference, he said. He had sent CBS, NBC, ABC, and even Fox his résumé and had followed up with phone calls. Now he was waiting.

He also told me about his mixed background (Omar's mother is Chilean, his father Palestinian) and about how he had lived in Chile for five years. He explained how he's 100 percent fluent in Spanish and 46 percent fluent in Arabic (his estimates), but nevertheless it is his Arab side that has grown in importance for him, especially since September 11. "My father's a mental-health expert for the city of New York," he said, cracking a smile. "He's diagnosed me with post–9/11 syndrome." We both laughed.

His mother's Chilean roots are expressed in his looks. If you passed him on the street, you would never peg Omar as an Arab. In his high-school class, there were two Omars, one from Syria and himself. Everyone called the first boy Soori-O and called him White-Boy-O. He has a pinkish complexion and hazel eyes. His hair is the color of a coconut, but becomes curlier and darker when product is swimming in it. He's usually dressed in an oversize sweatshirt and baggy jeans, and although he walks with a typical Brooklyn-tough-guy gait, he honestly more closely resembles a big teddy bear.

Even other Arab Americans rarely recognize Omar as an Arab when they see him. One September night we were at Meena House, a local *shisha* café in Bay Ridge, Brooklyn. We walked in and were hit with the fruity smells of Middle Eastern tobacco, the pungent aromas of fried liver and grilled shish kebabs, and the sound of loud Arabic pop music. (Beside an Alexandrian fish store and in the heart of Bay Ridge's Arab-American corner, Meena House is a slightly more upscale *shisha* café than the one where Akram and his friends go.) As we sat down, Omar greeted his cousin, who was sitting with a group of men at the table next to ours. Eventually his cousin left, and the two of us drifted back to our own conversation. Later, as we got up to leave, Omar salaamed a good-bye to the other young men beside us.

"You're Arab?" one asked, his eyebrows arched.

"Palestinian," Omar said, a little defensively.

"You're Palestinian?" the man said again, in the same tone of incredulity.

"Palestinian," Omar repeated.

"You don't look like an Arab," the man said, and we walked away.

Omar shrugged the comment off. "I get that all the time," he said, but I thought he looked disappointed.

In a strange way, the disappointment is the irony of Omar's predicament. If discrimination is holding him back, it doesn't emanate from the paint of his skin. Instead, as Omar understands it, it must be ideologically driven, the fear and loathing of an upstart global Arabic news channel whose work was once lovingly described by Secretary of State Donald Rumsfeld as "vicious, inaccurate, and inexcusable." Al Jazeera is unpopular in Washington's circles of power—the United States bombed its offices in Kabul and Baghdad—and its disfavor seems to extend to American media as well. Former ABC News correspondent Dave Marash has been pilloried repeatedly in the media for joining Al Jazeera's new English-language channel, Al Jazeera English.

But this is also one reason Omar loved working at Al Jazeera. In many ways it was a perfect place for him, confirming his Arab side and giving him street credentials among his Arab-American peers. It was an Arabic news channel where he could put into practice his media-studies education, and it fully ensconced him in the complex world of foreign affairs. And this is a world that isn't alien to the young man. With his own refugee parents finding love at Hunter College in the early 1980s—their first date was at an international-solidarity event for the Palestinian people—Omar's family itself is an international affair.

OMAR'S INTRODUCTION to news media began in early 2003, during the buildup to the war in Iraq. While attending Hunter College, he had some part-time work with Metrovision, a production company, for whom he was delivering video equipment around the city to outfits like MTV. One day his father ran into Eman, a family friend who is also Palestinian American and who was looking for volunteers. She was helping organize the massive February 15, 2003, demonstration against the looming war. (With protests in eight hundred cities around the world, this was the largest antiwar rally the planet has ever seen.) Omar thought it might be interesting. He took his father's advice and met up with Eman, and soon they were sending out press releases to all the major networks about the Arab-American contingent from Brooklyn that would be marching.

Eman had been volunteering at Downtown Community Television (DCTV), a local progressive filmmaking and media organization, and she told Omar that at DCTV he could get real media experience with the same equipment he'd been delivering. So he went down there one day and looked into an internship. DCTV is located in an old firehouse in lower Manhattan. It has a fireman's pole in the back that no one is allowed to use. The building is four stories of creaky wooden floors and never-ending construction. *Democracy Now!* broadcasts from the ground floor. At DCTV, Omar met the director John Alpert.

Alpert is something of a legend in progressive media circles. He has won a dozen Emmy Awards, including for his 2006 HBO documentary *Baghdad ER*. He is generous and quick-witted, and he immediately took the young Omar under his wing. Alpert sat Omar down at one of DCTV's long tables and armed him with a computer and a phone. Omar worked on preproduction research for a documentary on intergenerational conflict in the United States that was supposed to be screened eventually on HBO. He spent long days combing through the LexisNexis database, looking for news accounts of various types of "honor crimes" from different traditions. He was frequently on the phone with the FBI, asking for more information on stories picked from newspapers around the country. He also used the time to learn more about filmmaking and video production. As an intern at DCTV, he was able to attend classes for free. "I took advantage of the whole thing," he said. "And it was actually much more tiring and consuming than I thought. You'd have to work eleven, twelve hour days." But he was bitten by the media bug.

Preproduction ended five months later when the money for the documentary petered out. But already a childhood job fantasy of working as a war correspondent had floated back to him, especially when he found out how Alpert had covered the First Gulf War. Alpert had been a stringer for NBC News, and he flew to Iraq, where he reported firsthand on the civilian devastation wrought by American "smart bombs." In a 1996 documentary called *Fear and Favor in the Newsroom*, Alpert described what he saw this way:

> *Right away on the road, you began to see evidence of destruction from the war, the vehicles that had been hit. Every city that we went to had no electricity, had no telephones, had no running water. We saw evidence of very, very accurate pinpoint bombing. And then we saw evidences of what appeared to be extreme inaccuracy. For example, in Basra, we saw residential neighborhoods that were just wiped out.*

With Mary Andolino, Alpert filmed it all and produced the first segment for U.S. audiences on the civilian toll of the First Gulf War. Alpert had gotten past the Iraqi censors, but not the official American narrative of the war, a story then endorsed by the major media. While the footage was damning, Alpert was damned. He was fired from NBC and ostracized from the fourth estate.

"He's a mentor to me," Omar told me about Alpert. "Not only because of the career path I chose but because of what he's done for journalism," Omar said. "Keeping it objective and being persecuted for it. Not something you see on American news, you know?"

POLITICAL FIGHTS for justice were things Omar had seen before. In fact, they are the very marrow of Omar's family. Ali, his father, is from the West Bank town of Beit Iksa, and Omar boasts easily about how his father spent most of his teenage years in defiance against the Israeli occupation, frequently landing in jail. The family eventually sought out a more stable life. Omar's paternal grandfather and great-uncle had married two sisters from the same town, and they immigrated to the United States in the early 1970s. Ali followed shortly thereafter. He was seventeen when he first arrived, and all the men in the family worked their new environment of New York City hard. They sold watches on the street and ran a gas station on Long Island. The family kept on growing (Omar's extended family in New York now numbers more than thirty people), and everyone had a duty to work and an obligation to save. Eventually they had saved enough money to buy a building in Park Slope, on a quiet street with thick trees, long before it went the way of the yuppie. Property bought stability.

Meanwhile, one September 11, several years earlier and thousands of miles away, General Augusto Pinochet Ugarte overthrew Salvador Allende's democratically elected government in Chile in a United States–backed and –orchestrated coup. It was 1973, and Pinochet's rule would ultimately lead to over three thousand deaths and close to thirty thousand detained or tortured. Working in the Chilean National Health Service at the time of the coup was Dr. Roberto Belmar, a physician who had friendly contacts with a few people in the Chilean military. They whispered to the doctor that, like Allende, he was also on an assassination list. Dr. Belmar took the information seriously, and within hours he had gathered some belongings, called his wife, and—with the help of two academics, Victor and Ruth Sidel, and the American Friends Service Committee, a Quaker action group that works for global peace and justice—boarded a plane for New York City. An hour after his departure, the Chilean military broke into the family's Santiago ranch house.

Without Dr. Belmar the house was made up of eight women, and all of them were forced to the floor, guns to their heads, while soldiers ransacked the place in search of the good doctor. The soldiers broke everything. They looked for evidence that the doctor might be hiding in the home, and when they found nothing, they barked a warning to the terrified women. The next day the rest of the family hurriedly followed Dr. Belmar to New York, eternal city of émigrés and refugees.

Inara and Albina, Dr. Belmar's daughters, became active in Jóvenes Chilenos, a youth group dedicated to restoring democracy in Chile. Seven years after arriving in New York, Inara enrolled in Hunter College, where she met Ali, Omar's father. It was 1980, and they had a lot of politics to talk about. In 1983 they married, and a year later Omar—the name is as Chilean as it is Palestinian—was born in Brooklyn.

AS A CHILD, Omar was exposed to more things Chilean than Palestinian. By 1990 the military dictatorship was over, Pinochet was out of power, and democracy had finally been restored. Dr. Belmar was back in his native land, and Ali moved his family there. Omar was eight years old. Ali had been working at the Long Island gas station when he was shot one day in a botched robbery. He wasn't seriously injured, but the incident frightened him. He resolved to finish his studies toward a master's degree in public health and seriously considered moving to Chile for good. First he sent his family without him.

Omar stayed in Chile from 1992 until 1997 and in those five years he learned Spanish, played soccer, went to a Chilean school, and lived under his grandfather's strict but doting ways. Within a few months, his father had graduated with a double master's and rejoined his family in Santiago. They expected to make their lives there, and Ali sought contact with the large Palestinian-descendant population in Chile. They have been there for decades, at least since the 1920s, and they are well organized and influential. In Chile, power emanates from the soccer clubs, and Club Palestina is one of the most prominent. But Ali quickly discovered that ethnicity is about all they share. Chile's Palestinians are mostly a merchant class. They are wealthy, and many were strong supporters of Pinochet. Ali, on the other hand, would slam on his brakes to stop for a wounded pigeon rather than run it over to make a business meeting.

The day before Omar turned twelve, the family moved back to Park Slope, Brooklyn. The change was difficult for Omar. He spoke broken English. His favorite sport was soccer, but all the American kids around him followed basketball. He wasn't making friends. He was depressed.

His parents decided that it was time to shake things up for their son, so in the summer of 1998, when Omar was fourteen, they sent him and his brother to the West Bank for three months. Beit Iksa was like nothing he had seen before. Underdeveloped and poor, it was a shock to the young teenager. Even the ghetto parts of Chile had paved roads, he thought. Here they spoke a language he didn't understand. Everything was alien to him. Even the food was different. And yet, despite being jumped by some local boys on his first day there, he could feel his Palestinian side growing.

By the time he got back to Brooklyn, Omar took to his Arab identity. He recognized his choices, Chilean and Christian or Palestinian and Muslim, and he chose the latter. He came back speaking more Arabic, and in high school he hung out with the rest of the Brooklyn Arab kids, doing the things Brooklyn high-school boys do—cutting classes, going to the gym, picking up girls, and looking for a fight, often with HDD, Hoodlums Doin' Damage, a Bensonhurst crew of young Italian-American kids. ("They were sadder than us," Omar told me, chuckling.) At weddings in Brooklyn and New Jersey, he learned how to do the *debke*, a Levantine line dance, and he began to crave those festivals. "Weddings are crazy amounts of fun," he said, and he felt as if he lived from wedding to wedding. He learned the little things—how to treat an elder with respect, how to pray—and all the proper customs associated with being Palestinian. He discovered how tight village life was, even in New York City, where Palestinians still often associate with those from their hometowns in the West Bank. It makes life richer, he felt, and he embraced it. "Sicilians have a very similar way," he explained to me, "where it's all about family honor and respect. Me and my cousins see it as a mafia." He laughed.

ON SEPTEMBER 11, 2001, Omar was going to his Bay Ridge High School looking fresh. The day before, he had cut his hair, and now he was heading out to a 9 A.M. class with his new look. But all his coiffed anticipation quickly ended when his teacher, a photographer, walked into class late and told the students that he'd been on the roof of the school taking pictures. A plane had hit the World Trade Center, he explained, but no one believed him at first. Soon the entire school was plunged into shock and dismay. Omar immediately called his parents on his cell phone, and after the school closed down early, he collected his younger brother and sister. They all walked home together.

The winds were blowing toward Brooklyn that day, and everything was covered in a thin blanket of white ash. Once he arrived home, Omar began to worry about his Aunt Leila, who lived directly beneath them. She worked on the seventeenth floor of Tower One, and he went and knocked on her apartment door, but no one answered. He went home and called his grandparents. They hadn't heard from her either. He climbed to the roof of his building and stared out for a while, over the tops of the trees in Park Slope and across the East River to wounded Manhattan. He went back down to the street, waiting to see her.

And finally she appeared. She was walking incredibly slowly. When she finally reached the house, Omar could see that she was completely covered in white powder. "Oh, my God, are you all right?" he asked her.

Aunt Leila smiled lightly and described how she was getting herself a cup of coffee from the Starbucks across the street from her office that morning. As soon as she stepped out of the building, she heard a roar and a crash. The plane had hit. After the initial mayhem, the police appeared and told everyone to leave. She explained how she trudged across the Brooklyn Bridge with thousands of other people, like refugees leaving a war zone. And she told Omar the story with remarkably little emotion. "Thank God for that cup of coffee," she said, and the two of them laughed a little. Then they turned and went quietly inside, and Omar shut the door.

FALLOUT FROM SEPTEMBER 11 led to increased vigilance among the Arab kids at Omar's high school. They watched one another's backs, and some parents didn't let their kids go to school for a while. Trouble never got beyond name-calling and few scrappy fights, but Omar took care to walk his elderly grandmother, who wears a *hijab,* from grocery store to grocery store whenever she left home.

There were more internal effects, though. For Omar, September 11 accelerated a process he'd already begun, his identification with his Arab ethnicity. He began attending a regular discussion circle in a Bay Ridge mosque, led by an imam who was popular with the young people. The youth liked this imam because he talked to them as if they were real people and addressed actual life issues, not just empty rituals or repetitive warnings about the hereafter, as too many others often do. The imam repeatedly told the youth about the importance of media, how the Muslims today suffer from a public-relations problem and how too many of them study engineering or medicine while not enough of them consider journalism or the arts. "We need to represent ourselves," he argued, "and not always be represented." The lecture sounded familiar. Omar's father had expressed similar thoughts. So when his father came home one day and suggested Omar help in organizing the Brooklyn contingent for the antiwar march, and when Eman then suggested he look into DCTV, Omar thought very carefully about the good work he would be doing.

TO GET TO THE PRESS offices at the United Nations, you have to go to One UN Plaza in Manhattan. You will enter a tent, walk through a metal detector, and move through a set of large swinging glass doors that open into a huge lobby. A series of portraits and sculptures that changes every month will greet you, along with a uniformed guard, who, unlike the art, seems very permanent. He will point you to another large hallway in the right wing of the building, and you'll push your way beyond one more set of swinging glass doors. An escalator will carry you up two long flights, and you will be deposited in front of a door with panels of dark frosted glass. Push it, and on the other side you'll find a long river of a hallway with small offices for tributaries, each with an inscribed name on its door. You'll notice the *New York Times,* and then you'll recognize the names of all the Spanish newspapers that, if you have a Chilean mother, you see lying around at home. At the very end of the hall, directly in your line of sight and in plain English text, is Al Jazeera.

Omar made this journey in February 2005. An uncle who works at the UN had secured an interview for him at the network as an intern production assistant. It was morning, and he walked into the interview proud that he hadn't betrayed his nerves. The office was full of activity. Abderrahim Foukara, Al Jazeera's UN correspondent, greeted him and sat him down. Omar was beside himself. His family and his friends spoke so highly about Foukara, and now he was sitting across from the man. A Moroccan who had studied at Oxford and worked for the BBC before coming to Al Jazeera, Foukara was trilingual, razor sharp, and very impressive to the younger man. Foukara made Omar feel immediately at ease, as they sat with Randa, another producer, and Glenn, their American cameraman, a CNN alumnus who'd defected to work with Al Jazeera.

Omar looked around the office. It was tiny, with two computers on two desks, and a view of the East River. The main room opened up into an interview space that looked like a walk-in closet, with a stool, a blue-screen background hanging on the wall, and blinking video-editing equipment. Three televisions were always on, tuned to CNN, UN-TV, and MSNBC. On one of the desks sat a gag roll of toilet paper printed with various "Bushisms." ("We encourage an energy bill that encourages consumption," is one example.)

Foukara began first by asking Omar straightforward questions about his education, but soon he was asking Omar why he wanted to be part of their news organization. Omar still recalls his answer. "I believe in news media that are objective," Omar said. "And that's very scarce in the world. News controls the world nowadays. Whatever people see, they believe. If you have companies such as Fox and NBC controlling the media, the attention of the people, then it's only going to lead to disaster. Then the people have no other option, no other source for information, unless they're extremely educated, which you hardly see, unless they read the *Independent*, the *Nation*, or something like that."

He stopped and looked around the table. Everyone was smiling.

By the time Omar reached home, his father told him that Al Jazeera had called and was offering him a four-month internship with pocket money. "I was really proud," Omar said, "to work with a news outlet that most of the world believes in." Only his father, who began wearing an Al Jazeera pin and boasting to everyone where his son was working, was prouder.

Omar threw himself into the work. He would spend his days at the UN and run to his college classes at night. Once he made his way up to Al Jazeera's office, he would begin researching stories, helping Glenn set up the camera and video equipment, or composing the talking points and memos for Foukara. The Darfur crisis and the Oil-for-Food scandal were the big topics of the day, and he began reading up on the events. He listened carefully to whatever Randa, the other young producer, would say. She was slow and patient with the young Omar, but the rest of the time her masses of energy seemed to bubble right through to the tips of her crazily curly hair.

One day Foukara sent Omar to take notes during one of the UN's daily press conferences, what are called the "noon briefings." The topic that day was the Oil-for-Food scandal, and the briefing lasted forty-five minutes. Omar sat down and listened intently. He furiously wrote down every word that was spoken, and by the end he had filled an entire notepad. He went back to the office and proudly showed Foukara his work. Foukara chuckled and moved the notepad aside. "Let me teach you something," he said. "Seventy-five percent of what they say is useless. You have to think of what's important. You have to think of the audience and what's being said to them. You have to learn how to take key words and learn how to refer back to them. Otherwise all you're doing is making your hands tired." Omar nodded and listened carefully. He went home and practiced his note-taking skills while watching TV in his room.

Later Foukara sent Omar to cover a press conference by Human Rights Advocates, a nongovernmental organization based in Berkeley, California. Omar arrived a few minutes early, and only the HRA members were there yet. They came up to Omar, who was wearing his Al Jazeera press pass, and mistook him for a correspondent. They started asking Omar a series of interested questions about the network, and he had to confess that he was only an intern. What he didn't tell them was how thrilled he was that they had identified him as the network's representative.

Foukara then handed off responsibility to Omar to co-produce a twenty-five-minute documentary on the decline of international student enrollment in the United States since September 11. Omar began researching the segment and was surprised to discover just how large the foreign students' contribution to the economy was (about $13 billion a year, according to the *New York Times*). Since 2001, however, the United States had become a far less welcoming place, with new immigration reporting requirements and an increased nativism, all of which have led to steady declines in international student enrollments. (This is especially true for students from the Middle East.) Total enrollments were down almost 20,000 students since their pre–September 11 highs. The opportunity to exchange American culture with international students and their societies was threatened by such declines. Omar also found that the United States' losses were the gains of countries like Canada and Australia, where international student enrollments had risen. He put it all in the memos and talking points.

Omar got on the phone and arranged interviews with various university administrators and with several international students on different campuses. He and Foukara traveled to Princeton and set up their equipment in a headmaster's office, where Omar suited the man up with his microphone and Foukara proceeded to do an interview based on Omar's research. To get extra sound bites from students, Omar brought Foukara to Hunter College, where he talked to a couple of Indian students who'd had trouble getting their visas. These small interviews finished quickly, and then Omar had an idea. He'd take Foukara to the Arab Club.

It was a moment of triumph. He walked through the doors with one of the Arab world's most recognizable media personalities, and Foukara, with his champagne charm and noble grace, shook hands as Omar introduced him around. Omar was beaming. "I felt like a big shot," he told me later.

Foukara was Omar's introduction to the wider world. Everywhere they went, Omar saw the elevated esteem in which people held the Al Jazeera man. He was a very popular figure especially, noted Omar, with Moroccan women. One afternoon Kofi Annan came out of the Security Council when Foukara and Omar were walking down the hall. The men stopped, and Foukara and Annan conversed in French for a while, until Foukara turned to Omar and introduced him to the elegant Annan. Omar shook the secretary general's hand and thought that Foukara was success personified.

A quick four months later, the internship came to its scheduled end. Omar was already regretting its rapid conclusion when Foukara sat him down and told him that he had been the best production intern assistant they'd had. Omar felt himself almost shatter with pride. "Every day was an adventure for me there," he told me. "I just took it in all at once. It was overwhelming."

OMAR DIDN'T WORK for several months after his internship, focusing instead on finishing his bachelor's degree and on his family obligations. When a *New York Times* reporter began hanging around Brooklyn's Arab-American community for stories, she enlisted the help of Ali, Omar's father, since he was a community leader. Ali directed Omar to show her around, and the two developed a pleasant and productive working relationship, to the point where she would volunteer later on to be listed as a reference for Omar during his job search. By the end of the summer, Omar was feeling tapped out, needing some coin clinking in his pocket, and again he began looking for a part-time job. Another family acquaintance was seeking help in her nonprofit housing-development organization. It wasn't in media, but it was a job. Omar went for an interview.

Landing the job, he thought, was a no-brainer due to the family connection, but soon there were indications that his time at Al Jazeera could become a personal liability. Susan, his new boss, had known Omar's paternal grandfather for years, and Omar thought he had impressed her at his interview. When she called him to talk more about the job, he was happy to go.

At the office Susan sat Omar down across from her. "Congratulations, Omar," she said. "You've got the job." She listed his duties as a database manager and described to him how the office worked. She then began leafing through his résumé, job application, and background report. Since this was a City of New York job, Omar had had to go through a background check.

"But look, Omar," she said. "I'm a friend of your family. And just for the future, I'd like to warn you." She paused. "This," she said, pointing to the line on his résumé that Omar was most proud of, his work at Al Jazeera, "this could work against you in the future. Especially if you want to get work with people who feel threatened by the whole Arab thing."

At the time Omar paid little attention to her comment. It passed over him like a breeze, but it never fully disappeared from the file cabinet of his memory.

But before too long, hints began appearing that Susan could be right. At lunch one day, the staff of the organization sat around a big table in the kitchen. Somewhere between sandwiches and coffee, the conversation slid into politics, and a crash was in the offing. Omar stayed quiet through most of it, until Brian—a twenty-something Brooklynite like Omar—brought up Al Jazeera.

"That's a terrorist channel," he said, chewing.

At this point only Susan knew about Omar's prior work experience. He hadn't mentioned it to anyone else, not out of shame or embarrassment but simply because it wasn't relevant to his work at this organization. But

Brian's comment suddenly forced him to defend the channel and his former coworkers.

"I used to work for Al Jazeera," Omar said. "And it's actually one of the best news organizations in the world today."

Brian was unconvinced. "How can you support something that promotes beheadings? That promotes terrorism?" he said blandly.

Suddenly Omar felt the blood rush to his face. He scoffed. "First of all, can you speak Arabic?"

Brian admitted that he indeed could not speak Arabic.

"Then how do you know what they're saying? How do you know if they're trying to be objective or not trying to be objective?"

"Because Fox tells me," Brian said.

"But it's in Fox's interest, as their competitor, to show them in a negative light," Omar tried to explain. He felt himself blinking.

"Well, that's what I see. That's what I hear."

This went on for a while, and Omar was afraid he wasn't convincing anyone as his face continued to flush red. Brian, who had trained him in his new job, was his supervisor, so Omar held back from really exploding the way he wanted to. But it bothered him that he didn't get all his emotions and ideas across. He thought he had failed to prove his point to everyone in the room and, more important, felt he'd let Foukara down. He scanned the faces around the table and saw agreement in some, but the majority, including an Ecuadorian woman who used to date an Egyptian, seemed unimpressed. She jokingly referred to her ex-lover as her "terrorist boyfriend" while taking Brian's side. When Omar asked her why she didn't agree with him, she shrugged her shoulders and told him that she got her news from her church. Omar was exasperated. "It seemed like a lost cause," he said to me afterward, his voice sounding like a tire deflating.

A few weeks later, and with graduation looming, he started applying for a career job. And he watched his chances slowly sinking. The lack of interest was frustrating beyond belief. One night he began thinking about the whole search and about his résumé. He pulled up the document on his computer screen and stared at it for a while. Then he selected the name

"Al Jazeera" and hit Delete. He started typing. Now his work experience innocuously listed a stint as a "United Nations Production Assistant/ Intern."

ONE UNSEASONABLY WARM October night, I went with Omar to Meena House. We sat and talked about the world, his job dilemmas, and Nadine while eating a dinner of perfectly cooked beef liver and salty french fries. After a while a young man walked in and sat down at the table beside us. He wore a black T-shirt with white letters that read, MY NAME CAUSES NATIONAL SECURITY ALERTS. WHAT DOES YOURS DO? Omar salaamed him, and they talked about an off-the-hook wedding they'd both attended over the weekend. Omar introduced us to each other. His name was Ahmed, and I laughed admiringly at his T-shirt and asked him where he got it.

"Off the Internet," he said, "Hijabman.com."

He sat with a group of four other young men, and soon their conversation shifted to the FBI, and our interest turned to their conversation. Louay, another of Omar's cousins, was with them, and he started talking about how the FBI had come to his high school last year, when he was a student at al-Noor, New York's largest private Muslim academy. I was surprised to hear this.

"The FBI came to al-Noor?" I asked.

"Yeah," he said matter-of-factly.

"Why?" I asked, wondering if it had been part of some misguided investigation.

"They came to give a pitch to become an FBI agent," he said, emphasizing the word "pitch." He described the recruiting event. Two agents, a woman and a man, boasting about the work of the FBI. "They showed off their shields, nice big shields," he said.

I asked him how the students responded.

"We asked them a lot of questions," Louay said. "Our principal, he asked them a lot of questions, a lot of tough questions. Some of them they couldn't even answer. The questions they didn't want to answer, they said,

'FBI information. We can't give it out.'" He smiled. "We actually have a page in the yearbook from the day they came: 'FBI Visits al-Noor school.'" He chuckled.

Louay explained why the high-school pitch wasn't very successful. "Most of the kids were too young to get what was going on," he said. Al-Noor's students, after all, begin attending in elementary school, and a memory flashed in my brain of when the police used to visit my elementary school in Canada as a public-relations exercise. We kids would invariably ask to see the officer's gun, and he would always refuse to take it out. Instead the burly officer would handcuff our young female teacher, to our great preteen delight. At the time such a practice was common to all the schools in my district, but how many schools does the FBI regularly visit to promote its service? Their recruiting campaign at al-Noor seemed calculated to solicit something else to me.

What law enforcement is seeking most of all is Arabic speakers, and if doors to jobs are closing in the private sector, they are opening in law enforcement for Arabs during the "war on terror." I knew this in part from a breakfast meeting I had attended at Gracie Mansion as a kick-off to New York's Annual Arab Heritage Week. The morning ensemble was hosted by Mayor Michael Bloomberg, who bragged in his opening remarks that the NYPD has more Arabic translators on its payroll than does the entire Department of Homeland Security. He elaborated about how proud the city of New York is when it loans out its native speakers to the feds for their investigations. It seemed a strange way to ingratiate his administration to the city's Arab-American population, which generally sees federal law enforcement as overzealous and driven more by politics than antiterrorism.

But the facts Bloomberg stated were true. The *Washington Post* reported that out of the entire FBI staff of 12,000 agents, only 33 have even a limited command of Arabic. (As a point of comparison, nearly 900 speak Spanish.) It's not just the FBI either. The State Department, for example, lists 279 Arabic speakers on its staff. But when a bipartisan advisory panel investigated this figure in 2004, it discovered that only 54 of them could be considered fluent. And of the 54, only 6 were fluent enough to appear on Arabic television. The Iraq Study Group pointed out that the American embassy in Iraq, staffed with over 1,000 employees, also has only 6 fluent Arabic speakers.

Meanwhile, many Arabs in law enforcement feel that they are treated as second-class citizens in their places of employment. Several have filed lawsuits against their agencies. Special Agent Bassem Youssef, the FBI's highest-ranking Arabic speaker, is suing the Bureau because he believes he was shut out of work when his expertise was most needed and because, he says, he was subjected to retaliation after he complained. There is also the lawsuit filed by an Egyptian-born police officer, decorated for heroism after the World Trade Center attacks, who alleges a hostile work environment while working in the New York City Police Department's antiterrorism cyber unit. On an almost daily basis and for three and a half years, the officer says, he was subject to hundreds of e-mails, replete with anti-Arab and anti-Muslim invectives, sent out by a former CIA official who was working as a consultant for the department. (The e-mails reportedly said things like, "Has the U.S. threatened to vaporize Mecca? Excellent idea, if true," and "Burning the hate-filled Koran should be viewed as a public service at the least.") It wasn't only e-mail harassment either. Others in his unit would remark that Muslims ought to be out driving hot-dog carts, while a high-ranking officer offered the assessment that "all Arabs are animals." Gainful employment for talented Arab Americans in the greater "war on terror" seemed to be less about finding a fulfilling career and more about being in a job where you would be used and then abused or discarded.

But I didn't say any of this to the young men. Instead I offered a simple supposition as to why the FBI would come to al-Noor. "They're desperate for Arabic speakers," I said.

Omar joined the conversation. "You have to be twenty-three to join the FBI," he explained to the rest of them. Omar was slightly older than the others there, and his voice was rich with the authority of an older brother, as if it were dressed in a suit. "You have to major in criminal justice, accounting, or something like that." He turned back to me. "I applied to the

FBI, too," he said, which surprised me, considering the political bent of his family and his past work experience. Finding a job was increasingly a fishing expedition for the young man. "And the DEA," he said, referring to the Drug Enforcement Agency. "The DEA wants to take me, wants to take me right away, after I told them that I speak Spanish and Arabic. Then I asked them, 'What do you want me to do?' They said, 'We're liable to send you to Afghanistan.'"

He explained how he had attended a hiring seminar held by the DEA in New York City. "The starting salary is like sixty K, and it goes up to one hundred K within three years," Omar said. (He has mastered the impressive skill of telling you the starting salary of any job on today's market.) "You need a minimum 3.0 GPA, it's a rigorous interview process, and you have to interview in front of a board of about twenty people and tell them why you want to become a DEA agent. You have to take these physical and mental tests, and then you train army-combat style."

He described how his family had eventually turned him against the idea, but the title of special agent was tempting. "I could be a double-O." He grinned. "But then a couple of things made me not want to do it. First, the moving. You have to move to wherever you're assigned, like Colombia. But when they found out I spoke Spanish," Omar said, pausing to take a drag from his water pipe, "they told me, 'We could use you. We could really use you.'"

I had a confused expression on my face. "Why would you want to join the FBI?" I asked all the guys, "after everything they've done to the community?"

"Why not?" Ahmed said. He sounded confrontational, as if I were making trouble. He looked directly at me and waited for an answer.

"Well, how many people did they arrest after 9/11?" I asked.

"Thousands," one of them said.

"And how many of them were terrorists?"

"None," someone else said.

"Right," I said, thinking I'd made my point.

"But if you haven't done anything wrong, you don't have anything to worry about," Ahmed stated flatly. His own T-shirt seemed to be arguing with him.

I tried again. "Let me ask you this," I said to all of them. "Do you think that Arabs or Muslims have equal rights in this country?"

"No," they all answered quickly.

"Right," I said again.

"Look. It's like this," Eyad, a portly young Egyptian, explained to me. He leaned in to the table and put his weight behind his words. "Before, they went after the Jews, the Italians, the Irish. And now it's our turn. Everybody gets their turn. Now it's just the Muslims." He leaned back.

To my ears these young men were living uneasily in an unresolved contradiction. They acknowledged that the rights of Muslims were being unfairly trampled on, but they were seduced by the lure of owning a marketable skill (the Arabic language) that was currently in high demand. What they didn't voice was the idea that the culture of the FBI would be changed by their contributions to the Bureau or that civic participation was calling them to serve. They saw an open avenue, wide and empty of traffic, to a job, a profession, a career. It was as if the grinding pressure on their generation to succeed at any cost was taking precedence over everything else.

Louay then declared his qualified admiration for the United States: "I love this country, I really do," he said. "The opportunity. You can make money. I only hate its foreign policy." To this there was wide and loud agreement all around. Talk then drifted to the ethics of suicide bombing, with the unanimous opinion that killing civilians was totally un-Islamic. That conversation then devolved into an esoteric debate over whether killing oneself in battle contradicts the Islamic dictate against suicide.

Omar turned back to me and told me that he was thinking of taking the policeman's exam, much to the dismay of his father. He'd heard about their excellent benefits package. But he'd also heard all the stories, as had I, that the NYPD was pulling young Arabic-speaking cadets out of the academy before they'd finished their training. The department, the story goes, sets you up with big salaries—the stories agree on eighty thousand dollars a year—and your only duty is to sit in the coffee shops and eavesdrop on conversations. Whether true or not, the stories are prevalent enough that many people are now generally suspicious when they encounter someone with endless amounts of time to sit and do nothing. Spying on his own community is something he won't do, Omar said. Yes, he needs a job, but the young man has his limits. When I suggested that the hierarchical structure of the police force could mean that he wouldn't be given a choice, Omar just looked at the air.

A COUPLE OF WEEKS LATER, Omar picked me up and we drove again to Meena House. Omar was telling me about the first time he saw Nadine, back in 2003. It was at the Arab Club. A group of young women were sitting around a table playing Hand, a card game popular in the Arab world. Amani, Omar's cousin, was there, and so was Nadine. After he salaamed his way to Amani, she introduced him to Nadine, and Omar was immediately smitten.

Nadine was always careful to hang around the girls in college and to avoid, as Omar puts it, "spending time in the club conversating with boys." Omar paid close attention to her, to the way she laughed and to her personality. "I remember thinking, she's different," he said. "She is the one I can see myself with. I was one hundred percent sure." They would see each other at the club until he started working at Al Jazeera and taking night classes. Then, he said, he always kept her in his mind.

He had Amani put in the good word and heard from her that Nadine thought he was nice. The next hurdle was his father, who thought the young Omar ought to wait until he was thirty years old to marry. But the elder could see the enthusiasm, the commitment, and the joy in his son, and they agreed in the end that when he found a full-time job, he could proceed. Omar told me he is convinced that Nadine will agree to the proposal. He was smiling broadly, and I could see that there is something sweet in the way Omar talks about Nadine and his plans. He has already invited Foukara to the wedding.

A few minutes into the conversation, we were talking again, as always, about his employment search. Everything was about work for Omar, and I asked him why he thinks he's not finding a job, especially a career in media.

"I honestly don't know," he said. "I can speak Arabic, I can speak Spanish. I can speak English. I have all those great references. I have all those great experiences. I thought I'd get a callback from Fox, from CBS, from NBC. But I didn't get a callback from none of these guys."

Then I asked him if he thinks the problem is one of discrimination.

"I think so. I definitely think so," he said, but then he backed up. "I mean, to be honest, I have friends who have graduated who have jobs. So I'm not going to just go ahead and say that it is something targeted ethnically against us. I think it's just the fact that I worked for a company that is looked down heavily upon by the wealthier class, the people who hire, the hirers, you know. I mean, I'm applying. I was always told that working at Al Jazeera would be a positive thing for me and for the community. My father, the people at the mosque, Eman—they told me it would be positive, because we need people to get in there," he said, referring to the media. "The community needs a trustworthy person that has connections. I don't want to be blaming it on the fact that I'm Arab and on the fact that I worked for Al Jazeera," he said. "But I don't know. I think it's just . . ." He paused. "It's strange."

He talked about his cousins. "Fadi works for Royal Jordanian Airlines. My cousin Eyad works for the New York City Construction Authority. I have friends who work in banking, who work on Wall Street. And they all have much more Arabic-sounding names than I do. Amr Abdul Aziz or something like that! So I don't know. It's a hard philosophy to build on."

He looked around the café before continuing. "The only reason John Alpert found out that he was blacklisted, I'm guessing, is that he had so many friends in the media industry. High producers in NBC who told him you can't work for us. Because it was obvious. But for me it's different. I would never know until I see the papers. I don't have any kind of pull. It's this emotional bump."

I could see Omar figuring it all out, vacillating between different poles of responsibility.

"My father says it's actually not true, that I'm being psychotic."

"What reason does your father give?"

"The recession," he said right away. "That's something I also kind of believe. The bad economy." Then he talked about a career in media again. "However, I spoke to Eman about it. Eman told me what Al Jazeera means to the outside world." He paused again. "Now," he said, suddenly smiling, "I think Al Jazeera's kind of responsible for getting me a job. To tell you the truth."

And that's where Omar is now. In a place shared with many others like him, a place where you just don't know how much power to attribute to contemporary prejudice. You know it's out there, but that doesn't mean that it has landed on you. And then you start thinking that maybe you have become paranoid. What is maddening is the not knowing. It's like lying in your bed at night and hearing a mosquito buzzing in your ear. You swat at it in the dark, convinced that you've hit the tiny beast. But just when you believe it's gone, the buzzing starts again. After a while you no longer know if the sound is real or if it's just stuck in your memory. So you lie there, awake and blinking into the night, knowing that either way you've lost sleep.

RAMI

Ah, Allah,
that thou hast not forsaken me
is proven by the light
playing around the plastic slats
of half-shut venetian blinds
rattling in this room on time
in this hemisphere on fire.

—AL YOUNG, "The Dancer"

It's past 10:00 P.M. on a thick summer night in Brooklyn in July 2006. Far away in the Middle East, Israel and Lebanon are at war, but here things are quiet. Sun became moon hours ago, yet the humidity still hasn't broken. The heat is strong, slow dancing on skin, but inside, where I have been for an hour now, the environment is controlled, the air artificially chilled, and the lights garishly bright. I am at another twenty-four-hour Dunkin' Donuts, this one in Bay Ridge, where posters for smoothies and Coolattas drop temptation from the ceiling. Sitting with me is Rami and his friend Ezzat. We are listening to Rami.

He is an earnest nineteen-year-old college student with a compact and muscular build and prematurely thinning hair. He has a bookish air about him, though he smiles softly and often. Whenever he wants to express a point, he opens his brown eyes boyishly wide. Ezzat, on the other hand, is two years older, garrulous, and fiercely intelligent. Built like a nightclub bouncer, he is massive and imposing. He barely fits on the doughnut shop's small, dimpled plastic seat.

We've been talking about Islam, and Rami is about to recite to us one of his favorite verses from the Qur'an, from Sura at-Tawbah (Repentance), and just before he begins, a V arches its way into his brow. Since these are God's words and since he's reciting from memory, he wants to make sure he has them exactly right. People are constantly moving in and out of the doughnut shop behind us. Ezzat leans forward in his seat. This is what Rami says, in translation:

> Say: If it be that your fathers, your sons, your brothers, your mates, or your kin; the wealth that you have gained; the commerce in which you fear a decline; or the dwellings in which you delight—are dearer to you than God, or His Messenger, or the striving in His cause; then wait until God brings about His decision; And God guides not the rebellious.

He relaxes with that soft smile. The words reassure him.

Ezzat nods in acknowledgment. Like Rami, he is also very religious. (Rami once described Ezzat approvingly to me as "all Islam, all the time.") Also like Rami, Ezzat lives without his father. His parents divorced a year ago, and his father returned to his native Lebanon while his mother moved to Florida. Ezzat and his younger brother decided to stay in New York to finish their schooling.

Rami's father is sitting in a detention center in New Jersey. On Mondays, Rami rides a train and then a bus to visit him. It takes almost two hours to get there, and then they speak for thirty minutes through a telephone connected to a Plexiglas partition.

Rami's recitation didn't come out of nowhere. Just before, Ezzat had been telling us a story about an old confrontation he'd had with his secular father. At home one night, he was reading the Qur'an when the time for evening prayer descended. He prepared for his prostrations and, as he often did, asked his father to join him. His father usually demurred, but for some reason he agreed this time. But who would lead the prayer? The father said that with his son's superior knowledge of Qur'an, he should lead. Aloud, Ezzat read from the ninth sura, which includes this key verse: "O you who believe! Take not for protectors your fathers and your brothers if they love infidelity above faith. If any of you do so, they do wrong." The men finished their prayers, and Ezzat's father silently turned his head to each of his shoulders. Then he exploded. "Are you saying I'm a *kaffir* [a nonbeliever]?" he yelled at Ezzat, who defensively replied that he was just reciting the Qur'an.

When Ezzat tells us the story, he laughs loudly, prompting Rami to remember how much he admires the very next verse from the ninth sura. I ask if they believe that their generation is more pious than the last, and Ezzat looks at Rami and then at me. His expression tells me he thinks I have asked a stupid question. Of course, he replies, but not because of the faith of individuals. He takes a breath. This is a historical trend, he explains. Each generation for the last fifty years has been getting more religious, he says, but still they aren't religious enough. Satellite television provides him with his evidence. "Look at all those Egyptian movies from the 1950s," he says, explaining how "everyone is drinking whiskey" in them and how the characters all look like they're trying hard to mimic Western ways. He describes the progression for me. His parents' generation is more religious than their grandparents', and today's generation is more religious than its forerunner. But still it's not enough. "There are a lot of Muslims," Ezzat says, "but there is no Islam."

RAMI WAS BORN in 1987 to Palestinian parents in Amman, Jordan. His mother was a biology teacher and his father an accountant. Around the time he was born, his father had been traveling back and forth to the United States, and when Rami was just eighteen months old, Abu Rami (literally "father of Rami" in Arabic) decided to move the entire family permanently to Bensonhurst, Brooklyn, where Rami grew up and his three sisters were born. Abu Rami was working in other people's groceries, mostly around the tough areas of Flatbush, to support his family, all the while saving his money with the dream of buying his own store. During this period, when Rami was a child, he and his father were virtually inseparable. After school the boy would skip over to the store where his father worked and spend the rest of the day with the men there, listening to their stories and eating candy. Other times his father would take him along for long drives to pick up supplies for the store. Conversations might touch upon school and family and miscellaneous things, but it was usually about wrestling. Rami's father and grandfather used to watch the WWF back in Jordan, and Rami took to the show, with all of its cartoon histrionics and carnival frenzy. Both father and son admired Hulk Hogan and cheered for the Ultimate Warrior, but their absolute favorite was the Canadian wrestler Bret Hart. They ordered pay-per-view matches whenever they could, and if the WWF came to Madison Square Garden or to the Nassau Coliseum, Rami's father would rearrange his schedule to take his son there. At the matches Rami always begged his father for the souvenirs and was rewarded with cheap plastic belts, wrestler T-shirts, or one of those big foam fingers.

From a young age, it was clear that Rami was both a gifted athlete and a very bright kid. By junior high school, he was playing a lot of sports, football and basketball especially, and getting excellent grades, so his parents pushed him to take the Specialized High School Admissions Test, hoping to enroll him in one of New York's exceptional academies. He scored well, and eventually he was a proud freshman in one of the city's top public schools. As soon as he got there, he tried out for the basketball team.

But Rami has a basketball handicap—he's short. With the hoop out of his reach, he turned his sights back to football. Rami moves quickly and intuitively, and the coach spotted his talents immediately. He made it onto the team as a cornerback and then a receiver, and he loved it. But as anyone who has played high-school sports will tell you, varsity athletics are consuming. Your team becomes your surrogate family. You train for three hours every day and are required to give the sport your total concentration. You are always learning how to prepare for victory and to profit from your defeats. Most important, you have to discipline yourself away from all your bad habits. Later Rami will tell me that football is like Islam, a total way of life.

But not yet. At this point Rami was a typical and not very religious teen. His family was nominally Muslim but not especially pious. They owned some random Islamic literature, bilingual Qur'ans, and a selection of prayer rugs, but the items spent most of the time stored in a closet. His mother began covering her hair after she married, but that was more out of custom than divine decree. His father didn't pray regularly, nor did he teach his son how to pray. That duty fell to Rami's maternal uncle. One summer, back when Rami was in the sixth grade, his uncle was visiting from Saudi Arabia. Having discovered that his nephew didn't know the correct prostrations or the fundamentals of the Qur'an needed for Muslim worship, he took it upon himself to instruct the boy. Rami, who spoke some Arabic, easily picked it up. But in junior high school, it was really football that was his *deen*, his religion.

Abu Rami finally saved enough money to open his own store along the sun-drenched avenues of Sheepshead Bay. He worked long hours on his feet, eking out their living from the store. But one night there was an electrical fire in the office building above, and the grocery burned down. Abu Rami was two months behind in insurance payments. In the ashes, the family searched for their lost livelihood.

Rami's father took the rest of his savings and tried a series of businesses. With a partner he opened another grocery, but foot traffic was slow and it had to close. Then he dropped his dollars on a gift shop on Fourth Avenue in Bay Ridge. He rented space in the back of a video store, where he sold baseball caps, T-shirts, purses, and costume jewelry that sat in a rotating case on the counter. Only the telephone calling cards moved, and that wasn't enough. Sales were limp, and it, too, folded. Next came an Arabic restaurant with a Yemeni partner, but the patrons only trickled in. It closed down. Money was tight.

Around the time Rami entered high school, his father began working with a group of men, Jordanian brothers he had known from the grocery business, who supplied cigarettes to other groceries around New York. They had a venture going in which they would bring the tobacco directly from Virginia to New York, scratching the Virginia state stamp off the packages. This way they would evade paying the New York taxes on the product. It is a common practice, and it is illegal. Rami's father became a distributor for them.

After terrorists attacked the World Trade Center and the Pentagon on

September 11, law enforcement blanketed the Arab and Muslim communities, especially the working-class communities of Brooklyn, Queens, and parts of New Jersey. The authorities narrowed their sights on Arab-owned convenience stores, convinced that small-scale scams involving Arab businesses must be funding international terrorism. By mid-2002 the authorities had placed an Arab informant, another Jordanian man, in their midst. He routinely bought cigarettes from the men and then started working with the brothers to pass bad checks. Next he started offering to get the brothers—but not Rami's father—weapons. After about eight months, rumors began circulating in the neighborhood that there was something suspicious about this man, and the brothers promptly cut their ties with him. The police moved in immediately to arrest all the men.

But instead of arresting Abu Rami, the police followed Rami's mother one winter morning as she made her way to Manhattan with three of her friends. Emerging from the subway, the women were swarmed by an army of officers and agents. Rami's mother, frightened nearly to death, was transported to a holding cell in downtown Manhattan. Essentially kidnapping her, the authorities then instructed Rami's mother to call her husband and advise him to turn himself in. Abu Rami quickly phoned an attorney and went downtown with his lawyer to surrender his body for that of his wife.

It happened on a Friday. Rami remembers getting a call from a Palestinian neighbor, his mother's friend, on his way home from school. (Rami's father had called her to ask for her help before heading downtown.) "Amino," she said, using a familiar name for Rami, "come to my house. There's a problem. Something's happened."

Rami called his father right away. "What's going on?" he asked.

"I'm with my lawyer right now," his father told him. "We're going to get your mother out." Rami did as he was told and went to his neighbor's house, where he found his sisters. Everyone was confused and worried. The neighbor tried to get them to go to sleep.

The next morning Rami's mother was back home. Released from custody, she returned to the house around 3:00 A.M. and never went to sleep. When Rami and his sisters walked in the front door, they saw how she was

trembling. Still visibly upset by what had happened to her, she sat her children down and explained the situation. Then she called her brothers, who
lived in California, and Rami got on the phone with one of his uncles.
"Don't worry," the man reassured his nephew, "we're going to take care of
this." Rami put the phone down, trying to understand what was happening. He was fifteen years old, and confused.

WITH HIS FATHER SWIFTLY GONE, Rami's home life was suddenly
in disarray. Even school, as easy as walking, became difficult for him now,
since it was hard to concentrate on anything. At home he would observe
his mother and see a shadow of sadness constantly drape over her face. But
he also witnessed how she took charge of her new situation. She was very
strong through it all, he thought, keeping everyone alive. And she was always on the move, running to lawyers, running to hearings, running to
visit her husband, running to pick up Rami's sisters from school. It was inspiring to him, but it was also clear that her sorrow was deep and her nerves
were raw, caused more by her own trauma at being nabbed by the police
than even by the arrest of her husband. She used to talk for hours on the
phone to her friends, and that, too, had stopped. She had become less social and more taciturn.

Money also became an issue. Lawyers demanded money, Rami's sisters
needed things, and bills began piling up. The family lived on credit for a
while, and Rami's mother watched their spending closely. When her brothers in California took turns to come and help with the family, the burden
was eased but never erased.

It was hard for Rami, too. He needed solace, direction, an anchor,
something that would satisfy his spirit and offer him purpose. One night he
decided to look to the Qur'an.

His mother had old tapes around the house of a famous Qur'anic re-
citer, Abdul Rahman al-Sudais, one of the imams at the Grand Mosque in
Mecca. Rami remembered seeing them about, but instead of searching for
them directly, he looked up Sudais on the Internet. It was night, after ev-

eryone had gone to bed, and he landed on Islamway.com. There it was—a Web site with the whole Qur'an read by Sudais. It was free, digital, and accessible. He grabbed an English translation of the Qur'an, sat with it on his lap, and in the quiet of his house listened to Sudais recite the Holy Book. Following along in the English text, he found that he understood much of what the imam, whose diction was as clear as still water, was reciting. More important, he found that something was happening to him. When it involved the Qur'an, his concentration came easily. The words flowed over him, enveloping and calming him. The feeling was ineffable.

Rami stayed up late with Sudais that night, and the next night as well. These nocturnal sessions became something to look forward to, away from the racket and screams and pressures of the day, and he found that he was slowly working his way through the entire text. He would usually begin around 11:00 P.M., listening and reading the translation, sitting comfortably in the cradle of God's words. If he had to wake up early for school the next day, he would choose a shorter sura, a shorter chapter. By early summer, with classes over but football practice still on, he was staying up until two or three o'clock, listening and reading the Holy Book's longer suras.

He liked it. He liked the idea of believing, and he began trying to keep a Muslim's required prayer schedule of five daily prostrations. But it was difficult while attending school and going to football practice. At first he would save up his missed prayers for the day and then make them up at night before sitting on the computer with Sudais. Slowly, especially in the summer with its less rigorous schedule, he got better at keeping his prayers. After about three months, he was praying regularly and had read the entire Qur'an. His nights glowed with spiritual illumination.

The solitary sessions gave him all the things he needed, what he now calls his first foundation in the religious life. For one thing he found that his Arabic improved dramatically. After a while he rarely consulted the English translation, and he could listen closely to the words and more or less follow along. Through it all he learned what was in the Qur'an (and what wasn't). He heard its poetry and read its stories and experienced an awakening. To this day he describes the feeling the Qur'an gave him as one in which his heart filled with the Holy Book's grace. Something spiritual was happening to him, and in the stillness of those nights, while the rest of the house slept, he could sense the faith rise in him as sure as the mercury climbs in a thermometer on a summer day.

IN SEPTEMBER 2003, Rami's father was released on immigration probation after spending about five months in jail. He had served his time, paid a fine, and the federal charges were dismissed. But the government was now intent on deporting him. As a condition of his release, he was barred from leaving the state and was required to sign in with an immigration officer in downtown Brooklyn every month.

With Abu Rami back home, family life returned more or less to normal. Rami's own faith leveled off at this time. He was engrossed in football practice and saw more of his teammates than he did of his family. His father was usually out when Rami was home or home when Rami was out, and he had become occupied with the thought of moving back to Amman. Only on weekends, when they would eat at local buffet restaurants, did the family spend much time together.

Football was Rami's life now anyway. When one of the seniors wasn't performing well, the coach put Rami in as a receiver for a couple of plays, and he caught his passes. The coach was impressed. "You're going to start next week's game," he told Rami, who tried not to show that he was bubbling with excitement and anticipation. Meanwhile, his mother came to every game, and she would stand up and scream for her son at every opportunity. All she knew about the rules of the game was that people hit each other, but it didn't matter. She loved seeing her son on the field. "Don't come home with a broken arm or a broken leg," she would warn beforehand, and then she would roar her approval for him—louder than any of the other parents—whenever he caught the ball.

This was life for a while. And then one day, about a year and a half after his release, Abu Rami went to sign in for his regular immigration parole and never returned. He had been arrested on the spot. This time the charges related to a check-cashing scheme that the government said originated with a man whose name was similar to his. They alleged that it was an alias. He denied the charge and called it ludicrous. He pleaded not guilty and retained another lawyer, but it didn't matter. He was back inside the labyrinth.

"IS THERE SUCH A THING as repressed memory?" Rami said when I asked about his feelings the second time his father was arrested. "I think that's what happened, because there are just blank spots during this time." He doesn't remember where he was when he learned about his father's second arrest. He doesn't recall his emotions at the time. But what he does remember is how the narrative of his faith picked up again. He started hanging out more with the other Muslim kids at school.

One Friday night at the end of his senior year of high school, he was out with a group of Arab Muslim friends from the neighborhood when on their way somewhere they decided to stop first at Beit el-Maqdis, a local mosque, for their Friday-night *halaqa,* or discussion circle. All the young men entered, removed their shoes, and sat down. The imam, Sheikh Adil, then led them in a discussion in English about the fundamentals of Islam. Rami was impressed, and he discovered that this meeting was held every week. He began attending regularly, most of the time without his friends. The material was mostly elementary—covering the proper ways to pray, basic Muslim ethics, or stories from Islam's founding era—but he took it all in.

He would arrive early at the mosque, just so he could sit alone, shoeless and cross-legged, on the carpet and absorb the building's holy calm. The rest of the kids would trail in slowly, and the sheikh would arrive and begin the lesson. Rami would listen to the stories about the Prophet—narratives highlighting his moral rectitude or the obstacles he faced in Mecca when delivering God's message—and he would surprise himself by finding his eyes regularly well up with tears. The stories taught him perseverance.

He would leave the mosque with his *iman,* his faith, soaring. And he found that it would tide him over for the weekend. But by Monday his *iman* had crested and dipped, and he would begin to forget. What would fade was his consciousness of God, his awareness that the Creator is behind all things. By midweek his *iman* was freefalling, and the world was again too much with him, until those Friday nights back at Maqdis. The *halaqa*, he said, "was like a battery that recharged me every week."

What he was picking up from the sheikh were the fundamentals of Islamic history and the essentials of moral conduct. He was learning the importance of humility, the obligation to respect your elders, and the duty to avoid talking about others behind their backs. He was discovering what it meant to require all that is good from yourself and banish all that is evil, and he was adopting the essential frame of mind that asks that you remember God, the Creator, at all times. Slowly, as he assimilated his lessons, he found he was having less in common with his non-Muslim friends and teammates. He didn't argue with them, and his differences never split them. It was just that the things he was now holding dear didn't always mesh with what they believed. When he would hang out at their houses or play pickup basketball, everything was fine. But when some of them would run off to local bars, Rami would stay behind. When others would hang out with girls, Rami wouldn't go. When they would gossip about their classmates, he would grow uncomfortable with all the ugly, ungenerous talk. He found that his priorities were slowly changing.

Rami also began visiting his father regularly in prison. He borrowed his mother's car after high school and drove for an hour to the jail in New Jersey. For the evening visits, Passaic County Jail would often allow visitors to stay for a while longer, and they would sit together, separated by Plexiglas and speaking into a phone, and talk for two hours about everything. During this time father and son became very close. They talked about Rami's school, about his father's case, about what Rami should say to his mother and what his future plans should be. They talked about his father's health—he was having heart trouble since entering prison—and also about the

people incarcerated with him. Abu Rami told Rami stories about other immigration detainees and how their detentions were tearing their families
apart. And they discoursed about Islam. Since his incarceration Rami's father also found his own faith growing. The Muslim inmates in Passaic were
a large group who were very organized and devout. They leaned on one
another, and Rami's father began praying regularly with them. Father and
son both became more religious around the same time, even if they followed two different paths. They compared notes on Islam.

Rami's mother began working outside the home to earn money for her
family. With their finances still squeezed, Rami had to consider plans for
his future based on this reality. He took the SATs—which he easily should
have aced, setting him up for an Ivy League education—but he scored
lower than expected. The reason wasn't hard to fathom: All the tumult
with his father had taken its toll on his concentration. Yet still he scored
high enough to win a partial scholarship to a local private university. The
college was expensive, but Rami convinced his mother and uncles that he
should grab it. With a major in premed, he could fulfill his childhood
dream of becoming a doctor. No one wanted to deny him his aspirations,
so his uncles agreed that they would continue to help out Rami's family
while his father's case worked its way through the maze of state and immigration courts. Everyone knew the caveats. If his father was released, Rami
could carry on with his studies and eventually apply to medical school, but
if he was deported, contingencies would have to be made, other paths
blazed. These included moving Rami to California to join his uncles in
their car business or, if the financial burden became too heavy before then,
even leaving school early.

Rami's mother was now busy constantly, so by the time he got to college, Rami had to adjust his schedule for visiting his father. His mother
needed the car, so he started taking the train from campus after classes to
New Jersey. The trip took forever, but it gave him time with his father. That
arrangement lasted through his first semester of college, but then the authorities closed the Passaic County Jail. The family hoped this would mean
that his father would again be released on immigration parole. Instead Abu

Rami was moved to a jail in Bergen County, where visiting was limited to half an hour. Now the whole family piled into the car on Sundays. They would drive an hour each way for a half-hour visit and take turns talking through the telephone to the man stuck behind the plastic partition. There was no longer any time for those long, warm, continuous conversations Rami and his father had had before. Sometimes he would visit by himself on Mondays, but with the new shorter stays, they still had to talk sparingly and in quick, comforting phrases. "How's everything?" Rami would ask. "How's the situation here?" His father would answer him simply and briefly. When Abu Rami told his son that the Muslim community in Bergen was much smaller than the one in Passaic, Rami felt that his father's *deen* was dropping. "Be more of a *masjid*-goer," Rami advised his father, using the Arabic word for mosque. "And you should have better friends." His father nodded.

"Are you praying?" he asked his father.

His father said he was, but Rami suspected otherwise.

RAMI DECIDED THAT he had to fast-track his college experience as much as possible. He would take around twenty credits a semester and summer courses if he could in order to hasten his graduation. He wanted to finish early and assume his responsibilities over his family. College life was busy but not exceptionally difficult, and Rami spent much of the rest of his time volunteering at a local Muslim youth center. At college he made friends with the other Muslim students, but also with other Arab Christians or non-Arab Muslims. They made up a large, friendly, and elastic social circle. He joined the Muslim Students Association (MSA) on campus and attended all their events.

In his MSA, Rami found scores of young Muslim men and women who were pious in outlook and settled and content in their Islamic identity. Here he met Ezzat, who was to become a big influence on the neophyte. A political-science major, Ezzat knew the political history of the Middle East backward and forward and was widely read in matters of the faith. He was also a natural debater and enjoyed pushing people's buttons to see how far they would go to defend their positions. Rami found this out one evening during his sophomore year.

It was a Thursday night in February 2006. Rami, Ezzat, and Haseeb, another friend, were sprawled out on the couches in the student lounge on campus. As was their routine, they were waiting for their friend Ahmed (not Omar's friend) to get out of his night class, and they had a few hours to kill. Since they all drove home together, they usually stayed late for one another, passing the time in conversations that often revolved around Islam. That night marriage came up as a topic, and Rami said he had no problems marrying a non-Muslim woman (something that is generally accepted by mainstream Sunni practice). Suddenly Ezzat objected. "No, you're crazy," he said. "How could you think that?" He was shaking his head in disbelief. "You're a pretty good Muslim. Your *deen* is good, and you pray," he offered almost paternally. "Why are you thinking like that?"

Rami blinked at Ezzat's vehemence. It wasn't a big a deal, he said, but Ezzat wasn't buying. Children were Ezzat's issue. What religion would they follow? he asked, then flatly stated that mixed-faith marriages are never easy. Rami was bouncing back some vague defense when Ezzat blurted out a simple question that stopped him cold.

"Why are you a Muslim?" he asked.

"What do you mean, why am I a Muslim?"

"Why are you a Muslim?" he repeated. "Why do you even care?"

Of course, by now Rami lacked nothing in religious conviction. Islam, he felt, gave him strength and discipline and nourished his spirit. It had brought him peace in times of great stress. He knew that if he was worried about anything, he could pray and find a way of getting over his problems. He had no doubt, in other words, that he was a Muslim and a proud one at that. But Ezzat was pointing to something else. No one had ever forced Rami to defend his beliefs before. It wasn't that he was offended by the question. What surprised him was that he didn't have an answer.

"Your father's a Muslim, so that's why you're a Muslim?" Ezzat was egging him on. "Did you choose to be one?"

Rami still didn't know what to say, and Ezzat didn't stop.

"The Christian is going to follow his father, right? But what if the father's wrong? Same with the Buddhist. A Buddhist is not going to say his father's wrong either! So how do you know?"

Soon Haseeb joined in, and the two of them were throwing questions at Rami, like, "How do you know God exists?" and "How do you know Islam is right?" Rami's head started spinning with the effort of fending off their interrogation. He tried explaining his views by citing verses from the Qur'an, and Ezzat scoffed. "Who wrote the Qur'an?" he asked.

"Allah!" Rami stated definitively.

You could see Ezzat's response coming all the way down the New Jersey Turnpike.

"How do you know Allah wrote the Qur'an?"

And Rami had nothing to say.

A lot of kids go through similar improvised theological discussions at some point in their college lives, but few find themselves as transformed as Rami did that night. He would emerge a changed person. "It was at that point I realized: Man! There's a lot of stuff I'm missing, even though I'm pretty religious," he later told me. "I mean, I'm praying and stuff like that. But for the first time I felt that I didn't know how to convey what my beliefs were."

Whenever Rami tried to offer a defense of his position, Ezzat or Haseeb smashed it to pieces, leaving Rami breathless and bereft. Finally he said, "Okay, let's reverse roles." They'd had their fun, asking him to defend the existence of God and challenging him on other philosophical matters for almost an hour. Now it was his turn. Rami would play devil's advocate.

Ezzat was erudite, methodical, and utterly convincing to Rami. Systematically, he charted his beliefs, which were drawn from an Islamic cosmological argument focused on first causes. He began by explaining how everything in the universe has been created and how all created things are dependent on a creator. He showed Rami how the universe itself must have started from nothing, meaning that it, too, was created, and that the beginning of the universe itself proves the independent nature of a single creator.

"If this Creator is eternal and unlimited," Ezzat asked, "how can there be two?"

Rami tried to answer, but he couldn't. Ezzat and Haseeb both smiled gently.

"And how does this Creator avail himself to us?" Ezzat inquired. Rami said nothing. "He sends people who can perform miracles," Ezzat responded.

Ezzat asked Rami if he'd ever seen a miracle or one of God's messengers, and Rami shook his head. "Prove to me that Moses or Jesus existed," he said, challenging Rami, who said he couldn't. "But can you prove that Mohammad existed?" Ezzat asked rhetorically. "You can!" he said immediately, answering his own question. "Because of the Qur'an. The Qur'an exists. It's a book that is unmatched in its poetry *and* hasn't changed in fourteen hundred years. The Qur'an is the proof and the miracle."

For another hour, the conversation continued until all the pieces had fit into place for Rami. "*Subhanallah!*" he finally said. Glory be to God! "It makes perfect sense!"

Ezzat and Haseeb looked pleased.

Rami took a breath and whistled. "Man, that's some great stuff!" He thought about how he'd been going to the *masjid* for a year and a half and nobody had ever sat him down and asked him why he was a Muslim. On the drive home, Rami suddenly felt free to question Ezzat on every issue he could imagine. "What do you think about 9/11? About terrorism?" he asked. Rami had been wondering for a long time how to confront that question if he were ever asked it, and now he wanted to hear from Ezzat how a knowledgeable Muslim would answer.

"That concept isn't part of Islam," Ezzat declared. "Killing an innocent person? Absolutely no way can you find it in Islam." And jihad? "Only an Islamic state can declare a jihad, and there is no authentic Islamic state on earth today," he explained. "Bin Laden," he joked, "is not a state." And suicide bombing? A fundamental violation of Islamic law, he said. "Killing yourself is very dangerous to one's status in the afterlife, and you are advised not to do it." He told Rami that some scholars narrate a story about an early Muslim who ran to certain death, headlong into an opposing army for reasons of military necessity. But, he stated, that scenario doesn't justify suicide bombing.

By the time Rami arrived home, everything was fitting into place. It was just one night, begun with a small comment about marriage, but it made a world of difference to him. Now the religion made more sense. Up to this point, it had given him spiritual comfort and community. From this point on it appealed to his rationalist side, and he began seeing it through the lens of knowledge acquisition. The evening made him feel that he still had so much more to learn, but he understood that he was now a changed person. Before, Rami explained, he'd had his "foot in the water and was feeling around before jumping into the pool of *deen*." But now, he said, he was gaining the confidence in himself "to take a dive headfirst and jump right in."

A FEW WEEKS LATER, Rami joined Ezzat and a group of others who were studying *aqeedah*, the creed of Islam, in their spare time. They would gather in a room in Queens and talk through various Islamic concepts, focusing on the time of the Prophet, his companions, and the following two generations for lessons. (The Prophet is reported to have said, "The best people are those living in my generation, then those coming after them, and then those coming after [the second generation].") These three generations are referred to as as-Salif as-Salih, the righteous predecessors, and they were role models for Rami and his friends. The group saw the righteous predecessors as the Muslims who built Islam from nothing, who perfected the religion, and who superintended its spread across much of the world. As they understood it, the decline of the Muslims began after these predecessors, when various corruptions and innovations from outside proper Islam began seeping into society. And according to their study, the duty of contemporary Muslims is thus to revive the religion as it once had been.

Discussions in these improvised classes and among themselves often centered on specific narratives in Islamic history. They would read in Arabic the writings of various classical Muslim scholars, people like Imam Shafi'i,

Ibn Hanbal, Ibn Taymiyya, and Ibn Qayyim. When the conversations came around to the divisions and contemporary strife in the Muslim world, they would discuss how rule by monarchs or dictators could never be considered Islamic and how they longed for a time when the worldwide Muslim community, the *umma,* would reunite and bring dignity and faith back to the people. After all, they understood Islam as the system of the Creator for His creation, the perfect way of life.

How does one revive the true Islam? The answer was self-evident, and it didn't involve Western-style democracy or political parties. It didn't blame outsiders like the United States or Europe or anyone else for the problems of the Muslim world, nor did it subscribe to the violence of radicals. Rather, the solution they sought lay in teaching Muslims the true Islam, in bringing back the true Islamic morality to the *umma.* Their evidence was the Qur'an itself, which states that "God does not change the condition of a people until they change what's in themselves."

RAMI BEGAN FOCUSING more of his efforts on *da'wa,* on propagating the faith to Muslims and non-Muslims alike. Now, besides trying to live his own proper Muslim life, he felt charged to convey the message of Islam to non-Muslims and to spread his knowledge of Islam to other Muslims so that they could carry it out. He was already going to various mosques, attending Muslim Students Association meetings at school, and helping out at his local Muslim youth center. His *da'wa* efforts, in other words, were already well under way, even while he was carrying his own full course load in college. But he now pushed himself even more, taking on a prominent role in the MSA on campus.

The MSA was its own scene, and the students organized regular social functions and public lectures. Rami helped as much as he could and found strength in their solidarity. The students were also well aware of how simplistically they were viewed by American popular culture, and they often mocked the stereotypes. It was a way of defining themselves in a society that seemed determined to define them. One night, for example, they brought the Muslim comedian Azhar Usman to campus. "I am a Muslim, but I am an American Muslim," Usman says in his routine. "And in fact I consider myself a very patriotic American Muslim, which means I would die for this country by blowing myself up," and all the brothers and sisters exploded. In laughter.

"It took me a long way to come up the hill," Rami says, referring to the distance between his old life and the new one. In fact, he would now begin to view his old life critically. It was, he says, too attached to what Muslims call matters of the *dunya*, to worldly success. Now he was learning to be satisfied with anything, whether it was a lot or a little. He was teaching himself not to be envious or jealous of others. And he was learning that he should lower his gaze in front of women and not sit beside them in class. Instead he would now choose a seat by other men or, if necessary, by himself.

He became aware of the changes he underwent as well. One day he described them to me. "I'm completely different from what I used to be," he told me. "Sometimes you just get caught up with school or with 'I gotta be this' and 'I gotta do that.' But then you're very tied down, tied down to matters of the *dunya*," he explained. "Like, I want to get a big car or how am I going to buy a big house? Stuff like that. Now it's completely different." He offered me an example. "I went from wanting to marry a non-Muslim in a huge wedding hall with dancing; from going to Las Vegas and gambling and going to Hawaii and sitting on the beach, with my wife wearing a bikini—those kinds of things. Wanting to try alcohol when I'm older. To now, where I don't think about those things," he told me. "I was born," he said, "but not aware."

It's a conservative version of Islam and not subscribed to by all Muslims of his generation. But it is the one he, his friends, and many others believe is both pure and correct.

AT THE END of the semester in his sophomore year of college and through the generosity of his uncles in California, Rami flew to Jordan for a monthlong trip to visit his extended family. It was amazing. He hadn't been back to Amman since he was an infant, so this was his first real opportunity to see Jordan and to visit with both sides of his family.

They received him with a hero's welcome, the long-lost son who had finally come home. He felt their warmth immediately, and it was entirely comfortable. And he was surprised by the mannerisms of his relatives—the way they thought or the melodies of their voices or the movements of their gestures—because he could see and hear echoes of his own parents in them. His maternal aunts and uncles told him not to get married until he finished his degree, just as his mother had advised. He was halfway around the world, and yet he felt closer to his parents. He believed he understood them and their world better now.

But perhaps his greatest surprise was that most of the cousins around his age were not nearly as religious as he. Likewise, his family was struck with his level of *deen*. "You're an American, and you don't listen to music?" they asked him incredulously. He shrugged his shoulders. It was almost as if his generation in Jordan knew more about American pop culture than he and his friends in Brooklyn, who knew more about Islam.

His cousin Jaafar was the exception. Deeply devout, Jaafar took Rami around the *masajid* of Amman, and Rami walked the city with wide-open eyes, absorbing everything around him. He wanted to go to Mecca for 'Omra (when a Muslim performs the pilgrimage but not at the appointed time of year), and Jaafar accompanied him. They boarded a bus in Jordan and rode across the desert, staying for several days in the shade of the Holy Places. He floated on his own spiritual high for weeks.

Back in Amman, Jaafar took Rami to one of the city's large *masajid*, where they attended regular Friday-night discussions. Each time they arrived around *'asr*, the time for the afternoon prayer, and stayed until after *maghreb*, the evening prayer, when the lectures began. Hundreds of people would be in the *masjid* by then, but Rami and Jaafar had been there long enough to secure a place in the front row. Rami loved it. It felt intellectual and communal, serious and spiritual. *Man, this is it,* he thought, *the full-blown Islam!* Once after the lectures, Jaafar introduced his American cousin to the scholars, and Rami shuffled in embarrassment. He was wearing his

baggy jeans and a faded T-shirt and felt he looked out of place in such honored company. Later he felt worse when he found out that the scholars
were major figures in Amman's Islamic scene, former students of Sheikh
Muhammad Naasiruddeen al-Albaani, an influential Muslim scholar who
died in Jordan in 1999.

As soon as he touched down in New York, he started thinking about the
day he could return to Amman.

WEEKS AFTER THE JORDAN TRIP, Rami and I made plans to meet
up again one evening. It was the same summer night when he introduced
me to Ezzat at Dunkin' Donuts. Later that evening three more friends, two
Lebanese Americans from Tripoli and a Coptic Egyptian American, joined
us. Politics was hanging heavy in the air that night. Israel had been raining
down bombs on Lebanon, and as soon as the rest arrived, everyone started
asking Ahmed, one of the Lebanese guys, questions. His mother and siblings were fleeing Lebanon, having just gone for a summer visit that had in
a matter of hours quickly turned horrific. Ahmed told us he had just spoken to his mother. They were scheduled to arrive back in the United States
in two days, he said, explaining their peregrinations to us: They had grabbed
a taxi over the border to Syria, but the flights from Damascus were fully
booked. The same was true from Jordan. Then they called a travel agent in
New York who was finally able to book them on a flight from Cairo. Now,
he said, they were taking a bus to Jordan in the morning and then a flight
to Cairo before boarding their plane home. Rami, Ezzat, and everyone else
shook their heads and laughed loudly at the absurdity of the trip, but I
thought Ahmed looked relieved.

"I heard taxis are charging two thousand dollars now to go to Syria,"
he said.

We all talked about the war for a while, and Ezzat offered his analysis,
arguing that Hezbollah would continue to perform well because of its organization, dedication, and discipline. The mood among the guys was less
one of outrage than of resignation. War was expected from Israel, the

United States was expected to support Israel, and the Arab leaders were expected to follow the United States at the expense of their own people.

Some of the guys wanted to smoke, so we were standing around the doughnut shop's parking lot when a black SUV roared up, a lecture in Arabic blaring from its speakers. Another Lebanese friend climbed out of the car and cut the engine, stopping the lecture, which he told us was a tape by Hezbollah leader Hassan Nasrallah. He had bought it on his last trip home. "I tell you," he said, laughing, "if they searched my car right now, I'd be learning the names of all kinds of new islands: Guantánamo, wantanamo!"

"Orange isn't my color," someone else joked.

By 1:00 A.M. everyone was hungry for some real food, and so we climbed into two cars and drove to Karam, a narrow Lebanese sandwich joint just a few blocks away. The place was almost empty, but the mood inside was somber. The workers stared silently at a TV hanging high in the corner as we walked in. Tuned to Future TV, a Lebanese channel received by satellite, the television blared Lebanese music interspersed with regular news updates. We ordered a variety of food—kebab sandwiches, rolled grape leaves, shawarmas (loquacious Ezzat chose a tongue sandwich)—and stared at the television while we ate. An old Majida al-Roumi song, "I Dream of You, O Lebanon," began playing after the news, prompting one of the guys to comment in Arabic, "When they start hauling out the patriotic songs, that's when you know you've lost your country." Everyone laughed.

RAMI AND I MET UP several weeks later to attend *juma'a,* the Friday prayer, and then hang out for the afternoon. His friend Mohammad was giving the *khutba,* or sermon, that day. Mohammad is a twenty-year-old college student and a rising star of the tristate Muslim scene. He is also a very impressive young man. Fully bilingual in Arabic and English, he can quote large parts of the Qur'an from memory and recall scholarly religious arguments with enviable ease. (He was also my student and is completing an undergraduate degree in English literature, where he enjoys the textual study of literature but is put off by all the vulgarity. His elective affinities lie with the nature poetry of the English Romantics.) In high demand, Mohammad is on the road a lot, giving the *khutba* at various *masajid* most Fridays and lecturing and teaching about Islam in his spare time. Through it all he has the patience and humility of the pious. On this day Mohammad was leading the prayer in lower Manhattan, in a *masjid* that is steps away from City Hall.

I took the subway there and waited for Rami. The prayer hall was very simple, with piles of shoes stacked by its doors and a cross section of humanity—from all classes, professions, and countries—sitting quietly on the carpeted floor. Rami and Mohammad arrived late, and the prayer began immediately. Mohammad climbed the minbar and lectured on the lost glory of the Islamic age, particularly from al-Andalus, Islamic Spain. After the prayer, middle-aged men crowded around him as if he were a rock star, handing out their business cards and asking him to lecture at their *masajid* in the future. Rami stood beside him, and I approached, tapping him on his shoulder. We hugged a hello. Rami had grown a woolly beard.

"I'll go get the car," Rami told Mohammad, and he disappeared while Mohammad used me as an excuse to get away from his admirers. We exited the building a few minutes later, and Rami picked us up on the busy Manhattan street. We climbed into the car, and I commented on Rami's facial hair. Mohammad smiled. "His family calls him an extremist," he said, laughing from the backseat. I looked to Rami inquiringly. "Nah, it's not really like that," he said.

Later he explained what Mohammad was referring to. Rami had recently returned from a Muslim youth conference in California, where he'd stayed with his uncle and was busy from early in the morning until late at night with conference activities. The event was incredible and inspiring to Rami. He saw Muslims his age from all over the country. They compared their activities, especially their *da'wa* efforts, in each of their cities, and the conversations would often turn into friendly competitions. The whole gathering was very social and loads of fun, and Rami felt linked to a movement and to a national community of Muslims. His uncles didn't see him much at home, however, and one night, in the garage of his house, one of his uncles asked him what he was in California for.

"A meeting," Rami said.

"What kind of meeting?" his uncle asked.

"A MAS conference," he said, referring to the Muslim American Society. His uncle then asked him what he was up to in New York, and Rami explained that he was active with his studies, his leadership work with Muslim youth, and his *da'wa* efforts. His uncle paused and looked at him. "Are you sure you know what you're doing?"

"Yeah," Rami responded. "I'm not doing anything. Just hanging out with kids."

"Well," his uncle said, "just make sure you know what you're doing. Watch who you're hanging out with. Watch what you're saying."

Rami looked at him. "Is it because I have a beard now?" he joked.

His uncle explained that he didn't want Rami to fall into any trap with the government the way his father had. That was the source of his concern. In narrating the story, Rami then told me that his father had expressed a similar caution to him on a recent prison visit. "It's like they did with us," Abu Rami told his son. "They bring in undercover guys, and they're always pushing you, pushing you," his father warned. "And then you slip. And once you slip, that's it. It's downhill for you."

BOTH RAMI AND MOHAMMAD dress the part of the practicing Muslim. Both have religiously sanctioned beards, following the example of the Prophet, and Mohammad is always in a flowing *jalabiyya* and kufi, with tennis shoes on his feet. Mohammad can needle Rami about his appearance because he gets it himself. He is Egyptian American, but he hasn't visited Egypt since he was an infant, and he deeply desires to go there. He wants to see firsthand how the Egyptian Muslims live and maybe even meet Abu Ishaq Al Heweny, an Islamic scholar he greatly respects. His mother, however, has laid down a rule: He can go to Egypt only if he shaves his beard.

"It's because she's worried about you," I told him one day as he drove me to the subway after prayers.

He sighed. "I know."

But both Rami and Mohammad gain strength from the outward manifestations of their faith. Mohammad told me that "people think hiding their Islam will protect them. It's exactly the other way around." He says that his traditional appearance regularly prompts people to ask him about Islam, and so he sees it as part of his *da'wa*. For Rami and Mohammad, publicly expressing their faith is a major difference between their generation and the previous one.

"Thirty years ago," Rami explained to me one day, "the Muslims were more cultural." They confined their faith to the *masjid,* he said, and didn't talk openly about their *deen*. "They were new to the country, and it was their way of fitting in." But today, he said, "their kids have grown up here, their English is good, and they interact with people as Muslims."

I was reminded of an article I had recently read about piety among French Muslim women today. Jeanette Jouli, the author, explains that many pious French Muslim women attempt to render themselves visible to the world at large by donning the *hijab* or praying out in the open while at work or at school. They do so in an attempt to mark and claim a presence in the public sphere. "This hints at a typical feature of the struggle for recognition by minority and stigmatized groups," Jouli writes. "Visibility is considered a source of power whereas its opposite, invisibility, becomes a sign of oppression."

Da'wa, she explains, thus takes on a newly invigorated urgency, the struggle to represent Islam positively to non-Muslims, to counter its negative image. Since *da'wa,* according to Jouli, is "now perceived to be the precondition for the (social, political, and spiritual) well-being of the Muslim umma [community] in the West, it has thereby been elevated to the status of religious obligation."

RAMI AND MOHAMMAD took me along for some of their *da'wa* work, and I learned more about it driving with them on the highway to Staten Island after the Friday prayer one day. We were going to what they call simply "the office," two small rooms in Staten Island from which they host a Web site called FreeQuran.org. As the name promises they send Qur'ans to whoever wants one, Muslim or non-Muslim. It's a shoe-box organization, supported by private donations, most of which Mohammad raises by asking his Friday prayer attendees to contribute. I asked him how many Qur'ans they send a month, and I whistled when he told me the number is about three thousand. "It's the *kuffar*"—the nonbelievers—"who are doing our work for us!" Mohammad said happily as we turned off the highway. He explained that hits to the site crest every time some public figure speaks ill of Muslims, the last being after the pope's controversial comments on Islam. One woman, he said, even embraced Islam after watching Showtime's *Sleeper Cell* on television.

We arrived at the office, which is attached to a residence in a sleepy Staten Island neighborhood that looks like a sterile Canadian suburb, all closely shaved lawns and big-box stores. The office itself appeared as a mix between a nonprofit organization and a 99 Cents Only Store. Shelves were stacked full of Qur'ans in various languages—English, Spanish, French, Turkish, Russian, Bosnian, and more. One wall was taken up with CDs of various lectures, another with literature and pamphlets about such things as how to perform your prayers correctly and why Islam condemns terrorism. By the window were perched an old computer and printer. Mohammad sat down at the computer, and Rami started sticking labels onto envelopes and stuffing Qur'ans into them while I inquired more about their work.

New Muslims who visit the site are asked to fill out a brief questionnaire before receiving a free package of literature on Islam. Mohammad showed me the questions, which are straightforward, asking things like "How long have you been a Muslim" and "What was it that made you make this decision?" Then he pulled up some answers he had received to the latter question, which fell broadly into three categories: for a future husband or wife (usually a husband), because the respondent found Islam more "logical" than Christianity (primarily because of the concept of the Trinity), or because of the past glories of Islamic history.

Mohammad then shared some of the personal e-mails that had landed in the organization's in-box, including the one from the woman who'd converted because of the TV show. To the question asking her why she embraced Islam, she wrote, "Sounds crazy, but the Showtime show Sleeper Cell opened my eyes to the preachings of the Quran. Not the extremist views, but the ones of the main character."

Next he drew my attention to another e-mail, from a woman in Mississippi who wrote that she had been a Muslim now for five months. "Being a Muslim in Mississippi is not easy, that's for sure," she stated. "Most people do not know that I am a Muslim. I live in the Bible Belt, for goodness sakes." The daughter of a Christian evangelist, this woman had her first introduction to Islam through a friend who she later found out was Muslim. "If I had known that she was Muslim up front, I truly believe I would not have befriended her. I was sincere in my thinking that she was going to hell. I didn't hesitate to tell her so, either. OHHHH. How many times did I say, 'Sweety, you are gonna go to hell, if you don't accept Christ as your savior. I am sorry to tell you that.' Gosh, I was so condescending, I don't know why she stayed my friend." Her own family took her conversion hard, she explained, and they "seemed to fall apart during that time." She described how "they talked among themselves," expressing sentiments like, "She's gone mad," "What is she thinking?" and "WE MUST SAVE HER." They even held "prayer circles" for her, which she characterized as being "almost like a funeral."

As I was reading, Rami was stuffing more Qur'ans into envelopes. I asked Mohammad if he got any hate mail as well. He pulled up an e-mail that I begin reading on the screen.

"Why are you assholes still stuck in the seventh century?" it begins, and gets worse from there. "Validate Darwin, and the Serbs (whose only sin was to be right too soon about the ethnic cleansing issue) and die, before someone else has the bright idea of nuking the K'aaba [sic] down through the earth's mantle." (It continues and gets worse, but I won't bother to quote it in full.) The writer ends his missive with the statement that "killing muslims [sic] has to be the ultimate victimless crime." After I finished reading it, I looked at Mohammad, who just shrugged it off. The work was clearly too important for him to allow himself to get sidetracked by a few ignorant people.

Rami's routine is to spend Friday mornings at the office, printing labels, packing envelopes, and shipping Qur'ans with Mohammad. I accompanied them for several weeks and noticed the obvious, that a lot of the inquiries for free Qur'ans come from various prisons and other institutions from around the country. On just one day that I was there, for example, they received requests from Lackland Air Force Base, Lycoming County Prison in Pennsylvania, the State of New Jersey Department of Corrections, the Goodhue County sheriff in Minnesota, the Piedmont Correctional Institute in North Carolina, the Lake County sheriff's office in Florida, the Jefferson County sheriff's office in Colorado, and the Cincinnati Children's Hospital. A large number of the letters from prison authorities ask for Qur'ans in Spanish. I remarked to the guys how many of the letters come from correctional facilities and they nodded.

Ten minutes later Rami said, "I should send Qur'ans to my dad's prison," He said it more to himself than anyone else. "Why didn't I think about it before? I'll ask him on Sunday," he said, filing away the idea.

His father has been moved again, to another facility deeper in New Jersey. It's farther away, but at least now the visitations occur in a large common room. They sit as a family and interact like regular human beings. It's a much better arrangement, Rami told me. And there are also a good number of Muslims with his father, which Rami believes buoys his faith. Moreover, his father's health is getting stronger. But since the family visits all at once, Rami and his father don't spend intimate time together as they once did in Passaic. Still, it's a clear improvement over the Bergen County Jail.

We stuffed six enormous bags full of Qur'ans and other literature and dropped them off at the bulk-mailing center of the post office before driving quickly to a *masjid* in Queens. All the Muslims there were waiting patiently for Mohammad to climb the minbar and begin his lecture. The topic of the day was the gift of the Qur'an.

———

I SPENT A BUNCH OF FRIDAYS with Rami and Mohammad. Usually this meant getting up early in the morning for some breakfast with them after the dawn prayer. Then we would tumble back into Mohammad's car and stay in the office for a few hours before leaving again for a *masjid* somewhere in the five boroughs. Mohammad would then lead the Friday prayer, and we would usually have to wait for him to finish talking to the congregants before climbing back into his car. ("He's both sheikh and chauffeur," I said to Rami one day as we stood around waiting for Mohammad at a *masjid* in Queens. "But that's good!" Rami responded.) After the prayer Rami will usually go see the kids waiting for him at the youth center or prepare for a *halaqa* that night at another *masjid*.

As we drove between boroughs, our discussions often revolved around the finer points of Islamic thought. Mohammad would narrate the dispute in the fourteenth century between the conservative scholar Ibn Taymiyya and the Sufi philosopher Ibn Arabi (taking Ibn Taymiyya's side) or tell us why he doesn't respect the popular Egyptian televangelist Amr Khaled (not scholarly) or why the commentary on the Qur'an by the Islamist intellectual Sayyid Qutb is totally wrong in its approach. (It ought to be considered only as one man's reflection on the Holy Book, he explained, not admired as a piece of scholarship.) Far more often, however, the conversations were about various success stories of bringing new people to Islam. The guys would compare notes, suggest strategies, and narrate conversion stories to one another with joy.

One morning we picked up another Mohammad, a young Egyptian immigrant from Bedford-Stuyvesant, before going for a fava-bean breakfast at a Yemeni diner on Atlantic Avenue. (It was delicious!) As we drove, the conversation turned to family, and I asked the first Mohammad how big his was. He responded by saying that he has three sisters and two brothers.

"I have more brothers than you," Mohammad II said from the backseat.

"No you don't," Mohammad I said flatly.

"I do! I have eight."

"No you don't."

"Yes, I have eight brothers and four sisters," he said, his voice rising in confusion.

"And I have 1.5 billion brothers and sisters." Mohammad said, grinning while the rest of us groaned our approval.

On another day we drove back to the office after the Friday prayer, and Mohammad slipped in a cassette of Qur'anic recitation. Rami asked Mohammad if he had any cassettes by Sudais, and Mohammad thumbed through his cassettes while driving as he told us how he also likes the recitation styles of Saud Ash-Shuraim and Mishary Rashid. Rami commented on how he finds Sudais much more understandable than Rashid, and I asked where these reciters are from. Rashid is Kuwaiti, and Shuraim is one of the imams at the Great Mosque in Mecca, they told me, which got Rami thinking and he fell quiet. Suddenly he spoke up from the backseat. "Imagine giving a *khutba* [sermon] in Medina?" he said to Mohammad. "Man!" Rami sighed in reverie.

Mohammad smiled as he drove. "Were it not for the obligations of *juma'a*," Mohammad declared, referring to Friday prayer, "no one should climb that minbar!"

The conversation jammed as we passed a car on Ocean Parkway that had been stopped by plainclothes police officers. The trunk was wide open, and the cops were searching the men in full view of everyone. We all looked out the windows. "They opened the trunk," Rami said. "Can they do that? They can't, right, unless they have probable cause?"

"We're in martial law, brother," Mohammed deadpanned. "No more probable cause."

ON ANOTHER FRIDAY we met up early in the morning and headed out to Staten Island, where we packed up Qur'ans in the morning and then picked up another of their friends, Jihad, a half-Palestinian half-Jamaican brother who speaks in full hip-hop cadences. Jihad had cut up some mango for us as we drove to Bed-Stuy. We had a full schedule that day. Mohammad was leading the prayer at Masjid at-Taqwa, a prominent Brooklyn *masjid,* and was then scheduled to speak to the Muslim Students Association at FDR High School in Bensonhurst, Mohammad's alma mater. Time was tight, he told us, and he asked us all to hurry outside to the car after the prayer.

We did, but we arrived late to the high school anyway. We surrendered our IDs to enter, and the security guard recognized Mohammad and smiled broadly at him, telling him he looked exactly as he did in high school but for his beard. They traded news politely while the rest of us were signed in. Eventually we proceeded into the high-school fortress, and we walked the hospital-like hallways to the classroom. On the way, we passed a large banner advertising all the clubs in the school. "Yo, look at that," Jihad observed. "The 'Muslims Students' is written in bigger letters than 'The Christian Club.' *Subhanallah!*" I looked at the sign and saw that he was right.

The classroom looked just like the typical English class that I remember from high school. I could make out their curriculum from the wall art. Hand-drawn posters illustrated scenes from *Fahrenheit 451* and *A Midsummer Night's Dream,* and a large scroll across one wall threatened that BIG BROTHER IS WATCHING YOU. About fifty students were sitting patiently for us, while three teachers stood in the back of the room. There were about equal numbers of boys and girls present, with the boys sitting on one side of the room and girls on the other. About two-thirds of the girls covered their hair, and most of both sexes were dressed in jeans and sweatshirts. Rami looked almost exactly like them, with a Guess Jeans sweatshirt, baggy pants, and white Nikes, but he was also wearing a white kufi, and his beard showed his difference in age. The kids began buzzing as soon as we walked in. Rami salaamed a bunch of them, telling me later that he knew them from the youth center. I saw admiration shine in their faces as they looked at him.

Mohammad quieted everyone down and began with a brief Qur'anic recitation before starting his lecture. "Just to let you know that I'm not from another planet," he said, "I also went to FDR. Graduated four years ago. I can't tell you if I liked it, because I see there are teachers here."

The kids ate this up.

"Islam began as something strange, and it's going to return as something strange, the way it began," he said, launching into the lecture proper. "Because if there was no test, no pressure, then what are we being given Jenna"—heaven—"for?" he asked. For the next forty-five minutes, he carefully explained the virtues of nonconformity in the name of Islamic principles. "Be strange," he advised them. "Practice your *deen*. Dress like this." He motioned to himself. "Ask the school for places to pray. Do all of that and you will be strange. But this doesn't come anywhere close to the strangeness of the first Muslims."

He had the complete attention of everyone, including the teachers. He was very good.

"People will look at you funny? Big deal! They say it's oppression. Allah says it's an honor for me."

He told a story about how he was "strange" in high school. When he played on the basketball team, the cheerleaders had a routine where they always kissed the players on the cheek before a game, but Mohammad refused to be kissed. When he stopped a cheerleader from her peck one day, she looked at him in shock and confusion.

"I'm not gay or anything," he told her.

This comment drew the loudest laughter of the day from the high-school students.

"I just don't have the right to touch you," he continued.

He told the students how he in fact gained her respect by his comment and how such actions built his strength, his remembrance of Allah, and his faith, which constantly has to be fed. "Your faith is like water to a fish," he said. "Without water, the fish dries up and eventually dies."

Then he advised the students to build community with other Muslims. "You're as strong as the people you're around," he intoned. "Find the best companions. Stick together. Don't isolate yourselves. Interact, but help one another."

The students listened carefully, and he soon concluded, asking if anyone had any questions. "But don't ask me about Osama bin Laden," he joked. "I've never met the man."

Questions were few, and we departed as quickly as we arrived. Mohammad had another *da'wa* conference on Long Island to attend that evening, and Rami was leading the *halaqa* that night at his *masjid*.

The week before, Rami had spoken to the younger kids there, asking them, "Who are our role models today?"

The kids shouted back "Kobe Bryant!" and "Jay-Z!"

"And who should our role model be?" he asked.

"The Prophet!" everyone yelled.

We climbed back into the car and then scattered to our various obligations. In the subway on my way home, a young man in a stiff white shirt and ink-black pants handed me a pamphlet that I began reading. "Are you going to heaven or to hell?" it asked. "Jesus Christ awaits your choice."

OVER THE COURSE of several weeks, I met Rami at the Muslim youth center near his house. The center is a converted old Italian banquet hall sandwiched between a concrete playground and a police station. Across the street is an Irish bar. A bulletin board just inside the center's main door has postings from people looking for apartments and job opportunities. "Looking for a halal job. Abdullah," says one, with a cell-phone number attached. A vending machine full of candy has a sign stuck to it. BEEF GELATIN ONLY, it reassures prospective buyers. Rami and I climbed the winding, rococo staircase to the prayer hall. With its faded carpet, low-slung chandelier, and mirrored walls, the center betrays a riotous past of Italian parties and loud Catholic weddings. On the occasions of our meetings, only Rami and I were there, and we sat together on the carpet in the quiet room.

I had been struck by how whenever he talked about his recent past, the most religious time he has lived, I always saw joy and purpose illuminate Rami's face. I asked him if this had been the best year of his life. "Yeah," he said immediately. "By far. A lot," he added. Why? Because, he said, he has finally found himself. "At one point everybody finds themselves," he explained. "Finally you know what the next twenty or thirty years will be for you." An Islamic way of life is what he's chosen. "That's the path that opened up, and that's the path that I'm trying," he said.

I asked him if this is the happiest he has ever been. He paused.

"I think that after I get married, I'll be a little happier," he said.

But other plans for the future had changed. Medical school was now off the table, because his family can't afford for him to be in school that long. He has been looking into becoming a high-school biology teacher or a lab assistant. A job like one of these would provide him with an income and, God willing, the opportunity to study for a master's degree at the same time, he said. He expected his father to be out of prison by the fall, but the deportation order would likely still be enforced. If it was, that, too, would be some kind of mercy. At least his father's fate would finally be decided, and they could plan around that fact. His mother and sisters might move to California, he said, but he would likely stay in New York. Nothing was certain.

Maybe he would go to Saudi Arabia, he said, to study the language and religion for a few years. He would like to. He also wants to get married, find a good job, and save his money. His wife could work too, he said, so they could save their money together. That way he could afford to take a cut in pay to devote his life to Islam through working with an American Muslim organization. *Da'wa*, he told me, is more important to him than traditional American definitions of success.

For the moment, however, his efforts were aimed at something smaller, being at home more. His mother has begun complaining that he's always out. Usually he was at the *masjid* or the youth center. He volunteered there for two years before they put him on staff. It was satisfying to get paid for doing something you love, he explained, and Rami really enjoys working with the youth there. "They're good kids," he said. "They look up to you and pay attention to every word you say." He explained that he has to act accordingly around them. "You don't want them to curse, so you don't curse. You don't want them to lie, so you don't lie." The kids call him often on his cell phone, asking him about soccer practice—he's their coach—or the date for their next event or what they should bring for the white-water-rafting trip they take during the summer. "It's good," Rami said. "It shows you where you are and how thankful you should be for where you are." I asked him if his time with these young people had anything to do with the absence of his own father. "Right," he said, taking off on my question before I even finished. "So I relate to the kids like that," meaning like a father. I nodded. "Yeah," he continued. "I kind of feel that way."

A COUPLE FRIDAYS LATER, I was at a cramped *masjid* on Church Avenue. This is a bleak, working-class neighborhood full of abandoned lots and auto-body shops, their garage doors always open wide to the streets. Half-built cars and litter are everywhere. A Western Union sits on the corner, and the restaurants nearby are quick-fix Mexican taquerías and a halal pizzeria run by Bangladeshis. The *masjid*, beside a Central American travel agency, is in a simple two-story brick building on another corner. The call to prayer echoes regularly from tinny speakers bolted to the roof.

Rami was inside, dressed in a powder blue *jalabiyya* and a white kufi. It was afternoon, time for the *juma'a* prayer. But on this day we were not meeting Mohammad. Today was different, another signpost in the path Rami is on. On this day Rami was leading the prayer. Rami was the *khateeb*.

I arrived just as the main room filled up to capacity with its mostly Pakistani and Bangladeshi congregation, so I had to stay downstairs, where classes are held during other hours but where the overflow worshippers from the Friday prayers go. From here I will have to watch Rami on two small TVs that broadcast what happens on the floor above. In front of me was a whiteboard with a message on it. "Please do not talk during the khutba," it pleaded. "And do not fall asleep." After a few minutes, I saw Rami climb the minbar on the TV, and he began his lecture on a topic familiar to religious people everywhere: readying yourself for the end of your days. He spoke into a microphone that, typical of *masjid* aesthetics, echoed with reverb, making him sound as if he were in a cavernous thousand-person hall. "We will all drink from the cup of death," Rami warned the assembled Muslims. "Are you prepared?"

He continued. "If your mother or father had heart disease, you would spend all the money in the world on the best doctors," he lectured. "But the diseases of the heart that can destroy this life *and* the next, diseases like arrogance and jealousy, don't cost a thing to cure." He spoke about what he called the persistence of minor sins and their destructive power. "If you have a boulder and you splash a bucket of water on the boulder, the boulder will withstand the water," he said by way of analogy, "but small drops of water on one point can create a hole in that boulder over time. It's the same with the persistence of minor sins. They will create a hole in the heart of the believer." Then he explained how "you die on that which you love. If you're in love with drinking, you will die with a beer in your hand. But if you're in love with reading the Qur'an, you will die with the Qur'an in your heart. Your end will come with whatever you love doing the most."

He was not yet polished in his delivery, and he stumbled occasionally, but his sincerity was entirely evident. After about fifteen minutes, in the second part of his sermon, he moved toward a conclusion. "Brothers and sisters," he said, "look at the conditions of the Muslims today. Look at Palestine, Iraq, Afghanistan, Darfur, Pakistan. What are we waiting for? Are we waiting for someone else to help the conditions of the Muslims? What are we doing today to rebuild Islam so that the children don't die and the people don't starve?" And then he offered the Muslims his advice about how to change the state of the world today. His prescription was simple. "Purify your hearts," he said, and the sermon, rather abruptly, ended.

Afterward, we ate lunch at a lonely Pakistani restaurant nearby and talked about his lecture. In the middle of our conversation, Rami suddenly stopped. "Oh, man," he said. "I forgot a good ending!" He pursed his lips. "Sometimes you just forget," he explained.

"How did you want it to end?" I asked.

He paused to get the expression just right. "You come into the world crying while everyone around you is laughing," he said. "But when you leave this world for the next life, and everyone else is crying, you should be laughing." He summed up what he meant. "You've done good. Now all you have is bliss," he explained with wide eyes. "That's what I should have said."

The young imam was kicking himself and smiling.

AFTERWORD

What does it mean to be young and Arab in America today? The popular image we hold of American youth in general is one of carefree innocence, living out a time of breezy self-indulgences and creative self-inventions. This is a stage of life to be treasured, we are told, because it lies far away from the pressures of adult responsibilities and the burdens of politics. But the stories here suggest that being young and Arab in America can never be so simple, as the "war on terror" encroaches on young Arab and Muslim Americans and complicates their lives in ways that are often invisible to the general public. Far away from the headlines of the moment, young Arab and Muslim Americans face a volatile mixture of fear, suspicion, curiosity, and misunderstanding, all the while seeking to discover who they are. In this environment they have to deal with a slew of new realities uncomfortably born out of the age. National security can mean fundamental disruptions of their family life, where they may have to take care of their parents instead of the other way around. Jobs and careers become more worrisome, as they must now be concerned that the ring of their names or the misbegotten assumptions people carry about them will shove them down opportunity's ladder. In the hostilities they encounter is the lingering possibility of outright violence. The upheavals in the Middle East can dictate the direction of their lives, as can the pendulum swings of federal law enforcement, now completely overhauled to terrorism prevention. Even high school, with all its highs and lows, becomes not merely a popularity contest but a political trial of tolerance and respect.

In this rocky terrain, young Arab and Muslim Americans are forging their lives as the newest minorities in the American imagination. In their circumstances and out of their actions, they are also shaping the contours of a future American society. And though they don't always succeed in their efforts, the human drama of their predicament has now become a part of what it means to be an American.

The burning question really is whether American society will treat them as equals. The answer is not entirely clear. Simply put, the general public seems divided about the Arabs and Muslims in our midst. On the one hand, the last few years have seen a spirit of inclusion and desire for mutual cooperation spread across the country. Arab and Muslim organizations have matured in this environment, as they engage the general public more openly and fully than before, and the results are evident. Islam is increasingly understood as an American religion—in 2006 the first American Muslim, Keith Ellison, was elected to Congress—and Arab Americans are now frequently acknowledged to be an integral part of the United States. Despite an unwarranted controversy, the first dual-language Arabic-English New York City public high school opened its doors in Brooklyn in 2007. Arabs and Muslims are successfully integrating themselves into the institutional framework of American society.

Yet too many people continue to see Arabs and Muslims in America—particularly the young generation—through narrowed eyes, as enemies living among us. Key members of the political class, an often shrill news media, and a law-enforcement establishment that succumbs to ethnic and religious profiling lead the charge, and Muslims and Arabs are scrutinized for sedition at every turn. Even the most mundane facts of their lives, such as visiting mosques and *shisha* cafés, are now interpreted as something sinister and malevolent. On any given day, popular feelings seem to swing wildly between these poles of fear and acceptance, illustrating what the sociologist Louise Cainkar has called "the apparent paradox of this historical moment: [where] repression and inclusion may be happening at the same time."

It's a strange place to inhabit, and it reveals not only the bifurcated nature of contemporary American society but also the somewhat precarious condition of Arab and Muslim Americans. Because their situation here is ultimately dependent less on what happens on the home front and more on what happens in the Middle East, Muslim and Arab Americans know that their own domestic security and their ability to live full American lives turn on the winds of global conflicts and on America's posture in the world and its policies abroad.

In *The Souls of Black Folk*, W.E.B. Du Bois observed that the treatment of African Americans stands as "a concrete test of the underlying principles of the great republic." In fact, the same can be said about Arabs and Muslims today. However, the principles currently at stake revolve not only around issues of full equality and inclusion, but fundamentally around the consequences that American foreign policy has on domestic civil rights. This condition is not new, and the history is important to remember.

ISLAM WAS PRACTICED in this land centuries ago. As far back as the colonial era, many West African Muslims were sold into slavery, making Muslim-American history older than the republic itself. Mustapha, historians tell us, was actually a fairly common name among slaves in colonial South Carolina. For their part, Arabs have been arriving on these shores since the latter part of the nineteenth century, when mostly Christian Arabs from Mount Lebanon packed up their belongings and landed on Ellis Island with an average of $31.85 in their pockets, more than the $12.26 that Polish immigrants carried or the $21.32 of the Greeks. The migrations of both Arabs and Muslims have ebbed and flowed over the years for many reasons, primarily because of the vicissitudes of American immigration law.

In the late nineteenth century, a few years after they began arriving in the United States, Arab Americans established themselves on Washington

Street in Lower Manhattan (dubbed "Little Syria"), where they opened stores, published lots of newspapers, lived closely, fought among themselves, and worried about being too different from other Americans or about becoming too American. (The move to Brooklyn happened mostly in the 1940s, with the construction of the Brooklyn Battery Tunnel, which razed much of Little Syria.) The early community thrived mostly as pack peddlers who, after stocking up on jewelry and notions from the stores on Washington Street, would then set off to sell their Holy Land wares, crisscrossing the country, often on foot.

The Washington Street shops spawned a certain amount of nineteenth-century exotic curiosity. An 1892 *New York Tribune* article noted that in them were boxes piled high with gossamer silks, olivewood trinkets, and luxurious satins. "In the midst of all this riot of the beautiful and odd," the article says, "stands the dealer, the natural gravity of his features relaxed into a smile of satisfaction at the wonder and delight expressed by his American visitor. But the vision ends, and with many parting 'salaams' one goes back to the dust and dirt, the noise and bustle" of Washington Street.

The early Arab-American community also encountered ethnic bigotry typical of the period. An 1890 *New York Times* article, for example, manages to illustrate this in a few words, while insulting a few others along the way. "The foreign population in the lower part of this city has of late years been increased by the Arabic-speaking element from the Lebanon, in Syria," it begins. "In clannishness and outlandish manners these people resemble the Chinese and what are called the Diego Italians. Nearly all of them are Maronite [Christians], and in many respects they are inferior to the Chinese and Italians, who do possess a certain amount of self-respect and are willing to work honestly and work hard for a living." The comments seem antiquarian today ("Diego Italians"?), but what we find here, between exoticism and chauvinism, is precisely the nation's early-twentieth-century spirit, which welcomed and reviled foreigners simultaneously. (Like any ethnic story, really, Arab-American history reveals as much or more about *American* culture as it does about immigrant ethnic mores.)

The second phase of Arab-American history dates from around 1909 until 1944. During this period the main issue plaguing the Arab-American community, beside the growing unrest in Palestine, was whether Arabs could naturalize as American citizens. According to the citizenship laws of the period (and until 1952), only "free white persons" could qualify for naturalization, and laws were passed explicitly to bar "Asiatics" from American citizenship. Confronted with this reality, the Arab-American community from across the nation mobilized to prove that they were indeed "free white people," and a series of court rulings eventually affirmed that position. A close examination of these years similarly reveals much less about the genetic makeup of Arabs and much more about America's domestic racial politics between the wars.

When an immigration judge ruled in 1942 that the Yemeni Ahmed Hassan—perhaps the first Arab Muslim to face the court (the others had been Arab Christians)—could not petition for citizenship, the community faced a setback. "Arabs are not white persons within the meaning of the [Immigration] Act," wrote Judge Arthur Tuttle, who heard Hassan's petition, citing Hassan's Muslim background as proof of his racial difference. "Apart from the dark skin of the Arabs," he explained, "it is well known that they are a part of the Mohammedan world and that a wide gulf separates their culture from that of the predominately [sic] Christian peoples of Europe."

Yet less than a year and a half later, the court changed its mind. In 1944, Mohamed Mohriez, "an Arab born in Sanhy, Badan, Arabia," who had been in the United States since 1921, succeeded in his case. Why the change? District Judge Charles E. Wyzanski explained. The "vital interest [of the United States] as a world power" required granting Mohriez's petition, wrote the judge, because it was now necessary "to promote friendlier relations between the United States and other nations and so as to fulfill the promise that we shall treat all men as created equal." Part of these warmer ties included a controversial aid package made in February 1943 under the Lend-Lease Act to Saudi Arabia, as the United States was now eager to secure access to kingdom's massive oil reserves. In other words, as the United States assumed its leadership role on the world stage, the domestic understandings of America's racial-classification system and where Arabs fit within it altered alongside. The exigencies of international politics changed the supposedly immutable facts of the Arab "race," all within the span of seventeen months.

The decision was significant, but it had little effect on the Arab-American community, since immigration was still mostly a closed door until 1965. But when the immigration laws changed again in that year, abandoning the quota system that had favored European immigrants, the community grew substantially with new arrivals. (The parents of all the characters in this book, except for Sami's father, entered the United States after 1965.) This is also a period when two other important things were happening in the United States: the civil-rights movement and, after 1967, the deepening role of the United States in the Middle East in the wake of the 1967 Arab-Israeli War. Now, unlike in the earlier periods of Arab-American history, it will be American foreign policy and its designs on the Middle East—and not America's domestic ethnic or racial hierarchies—that define the parameters of Arab American life.

And what are those parameters? They include substantial government surveillance and repression, a history that is generally little known outside the Arab-American community. In October 1972, Abdeen Jabara—a Michigan civil-rights attorney and one of the founders of the Association of Arab American University Graduates, the first politically active Arab-American organization created after the 1967 war—suspected that his phone was being tapped. He filed a lawsuit against the FBI, only to discover that his communications had been monitored since 1967. Jabara's suit also led to the disclosure of a secret Nixon plan dubbed "Operation Boulder," a series of presidential directives demanding that every person with an Arabic surname undergo a security check before receiving a visa to the United States. Operation Boulder further authorized the FBI to spy on the Arab-American community through compiling dossiers on people's lawful political activities and even monitoring the magazines they read, resulting in the general harassment of the community. The FBI's Mark Felt, later revealed to have been Woodward and Bernstein's Deep Throat, also approved an illegal burglary at the Bureau of the Arab Information Center in the fall of 1972, in the middle of the Watergate scandal. And government intimidation and repression continued throughout the 1970s and 1980s. By 1986, the same year President Reagan claimed that Libyan "hit squads" had entered the country to assassinate him (a charge later revealed as a "complete fabrication" by FBI assistant director Oliver Revell), the Immigration and Naturalization Service (INS) circulated an internal document titled "Alien Terrorists and Undesirables: A Contingency Plan." The program called for the wide-scale registration and detention of nationals from Iran and seven Arab nations in an Oakdale, Louisiana, camp that had already been prepared with fencing and sanitation facilities in the event of a major conflict in the Middle East. With shades of Japanese internment (and a precursor to post–September 11 policies), the INS contemplated housing large numbers of people on the camp's thousand acres, conceding in the memo that the plan "indiscriminately lumps together individuals of widely differing political opinions solely on the basis of nationality."

The disclosure of the Contingency Plan came in the wake of the arrests of eight student activists, seven Palestinians and one Kenyan woman, in Los Angeles in 1987. The L.A. 8, as they came to be known, were arrested not for criminal or terrorist activity but explicitly for their political opinions. The FBI had been monitoring the group for years, even renting an apartment adjacent to one couple and drilling a hole in their bedroom wall to spy on them, but by the government's own admission it never discovered any criminal activity. Still, the government ordered their arrest and then sought their deportation, manipulating McCarthy-era laws to show that the L.A. 8 promoted "the doctrines of World communism." The group was distributing literature of the Popular Front for the Liberation of Palestine, but the same pamphlets and newspapers were commonly found in public libraries around the country. Such activities would normally be constitutionally protected by the First Amendment, but the eight were not U.S. nationals, and FBI director William Webster himself later admitted that "if these individuals had been United States citizens, there would not have been a basis for their arrest."

Then, in the 1990s, immigration courts expanded their use of "secret evidence" in key deportation cases. Since the Constitution guarantees people the right to confront the evidence against them, including the right to examine exculpatory information, evidence cannot be kept secret from defendants (except perhaps in extraordinary circumstances). But immigration courts are not held to the same standard, and the INS pursued at least two dozen deportation cases based on "secret evidence" in this period. Although it claimed it was not engaged in selectively prosecuting Arab or Muslim immigrants, the agency was unable to name a single "secret evidence" case that didn't involve an Arab or a Muslim.

All these actions stemmed neither from domestic race relations nor from how Arab Americans fit into America's enduring ethnic hierarchies. Rather, they originated from U.S. foreign-policy interests in the Middle East. At times such policies and programs were reactions to nationalist terrorism (before "Islamic" terrorism was the foe), but—as with the L.A. 8— they were more often used to limit the speech of Arab Americans in order to cement U.S. policy on the Israeli-Palestinian conflict.

With the terrorist attacks of 2001, a new era began and the "war on terror" was launched. There is a crucial difference between this earlier period and today. Before 2001 the government focused its efforts almost exclusively on a handful of immigrants and activists and especially on immigrant activists. Today everyone—immigrant and citizen, activist and spectator— has become vulnerable. Group membership alone, through national origin, religion, or ethnicity, suffices as grounds for broad legal and cultural suspicion as a new category of "the Muslim," resembling with more than a few brushstrokes the image of "the Jew" in classical anti-Semitism, has been painted into existence in the wake of our policies and fears.

Osama bin Laden and al-Qaeda are to blame for the terrorist attacks, but we are responsible for the kind of society we live in, and since September 11, 2001, Arab- and Muslim-American civil rights have been even further eroded. First there was the preventive detention of at least 5,000 men and a few women and entire families, as Rasha's story shows, grabbed almost exclusively because of birthplace. The government then sought 19,000 "voluntary" interviews between the wars in Afghanistan and Iraq. They instituted the program of "Special Registration," begun a year after 9/11, which required the interviewing, fingerprinting, and photographing of more than 170,000 men from twenty-four Muslim-majority countries (and North Korea). Special Registration initiated deportation proceedings for almost 14,000 people, many times more than the 556 foreign nationals deported between 1918 and 1921, during the infamous Palmer Raids that followed several bombings in the country, including one on the house of Attorney General A. Mitchell Palmer. None of these policies produced a single terrorism conviction.

At least five major Muslim charities in the United States have been shut down by the government, even though the authorities have never shown any significant evidence of terror financing by any United States–based charity, according to the nonpartisan OMB Watch. Spies and government informants have penetrated Muslim-American communities, "material witness" warrants have led to the prolonged and indefinite incarceration of individuals without charge, immigration hearings were routinely held behind closed doors, and there has been the dangerous expansion of the use of "secret evidence" in our courts. There was also the ruling by Brooklyn District Court judge John Gleeson in 2006 stating that the U.S. government has the right to detain immigrants on the basis of their race, religion, or national origin and that it can legally imprison immigrants indefinitely as long as their eventual removal from the country is "reasonably foreseeable." This is a district court's decision, and it is currently on appeal, but if the judgment is allowed to stand as good law, the implications are profound and chilling, paving the way for future selective prosecutions and incarcerations of any immigrant community based solely on its collective attributes.

AT LEAST since the Second World War and especially since 1967, the United States has become progressively intertwined in the affairs of the Middle East. ("Whoever controls the Middle East controls access to three continents," counseled British ambassador Sir Oliver Franks to American officials in 1950.) But that involvement has been far from benign. For several long decades and through a series of security pacts, arms sales, military engagements, covert actions, and overt wars, the United States has followed a course that supported one dictatorial regime after another, sought control of the natural resources of the region, attempted to forge client states amenable to U.S. interests, and, with the cooperation of native elites, engaged in a policy of neorealist stability at the expense of the aspirations of the vast majority of people who live in the region. The core issue remains the rights of the Palestinian people to self-determination.

One can debate whether this history since 1967 constitutes an "imperial" or "hegemonic" posture of the United States concerning the Middle East. (I believe it to be imperialism, American style.) But since the terrorist attacks of 2001, things have taken a decidedly imperial turn, culminating now in the direct military occupation of a major Arab country, an adventure labeled a "colonial war in the postcolonial age," by former national security adviser Zbigniew Brzezinski. And the political theorists of empire have repeatedly cautioned that the consequences of imperialism can reach far beyond the colony.

In the middle book of *The Origins of Totalitarianism,* titled *Imperialism,* Hannah Arendt explores the political history and implications of imperial rule, noting its bases of authority and actions in the world. She draws attention precisely to many of those pursuits and tactics of imperialism that confront us today: the establishment of penal colonies, the horrors of conquest, wild profiteering, colonial lawlessness, arbitrary and exceptional exercises of power, and the growth of racism along with its political exploitation. Arendt and others also have warned that in the long run imperialism tends not to be exercised solely in some blank, foreign space "out there" but has the dangerous capacity to return home and undermine the nation. She borrows this observation in part from the historian of the British Empire J. A. Hobson, who observed long ago that imperialism corrodes a nation's psyche and endangers its republican institutions. Arendt labels her caution the "boomerang effects" of imperialism.

The current erosion of domestic civil rights in the age of terror ought to be viewed through this lens. This is not only about the ways that torture has been normalized into American culture or how the moral questions raised by maintaining the penal colony at Guantánamo Bay cost the Republic's soul dearly. It is also about the specific ways that imperialism is boomeranging back directly to the home front. With the passage of the Military Commissions Act, for example, the concept of indefinite detentions—even of United States citizens—has now been enshrined into law. The government claims a national security exception in key legal cases and further employs the use of "secret evidence." Warrantless wiretapping is now legal and pervasive. The government's use of all these instruments of law has been detailed by others, most notably by the *Boston Globe*'s Charlie Savage in his book *Takeover: The Return of the Imperial Presidency and the Subversion of American Democracy.* But each of them has been used before the "war on terror" on certain members of the Arab-American community, as the United States sought to impose its will over the Arab region. What we are currently living through is the slow creep of imperial high-handedness into the rest of American society, performed in the name of national security and facilitated through the growth of racist policies. This fact alone menaces the foundations of American society far beyond what has happened to Arab- and Muslim-American communities. "It is indeed a nemesis of Imperialism," writes Hobson, "that the arts and crafts of tyranny, acquired and exercised in our unfree Empire, should be turned against our liberties at home."

Yet Hobson calls the crush of domestic liberty a "nemesis" of imperialism precisely because the desire to preserve a republican civil society is, in the end, a powerful one that must outweigh the imperial agenda. In fact, what many of the stories in this book illustrate is that the fight to retain standards of fairness and to mine human compassion are themselves acts of resistance, ways of opposing the imperial push in the age of terror. Hundreds of people signed a petition for the release of Rasha and her family from detention. Yasmin reached out to Advocates for Children and found a receptive ear based on principle. Akram discovered a supportive community around his store when the danger of retributive violence was high, and Rami is learning much about the possibilities of religious freedom in the United States as he engages the general public to educate them about Islam. There are countless other stories like these around the country and in fact across the world today, where people connect to each other on the basis of equality and coexistence and through the universal values of a shared humanity.

Such actions remind me of the spirit of a summer Saturday afternoon in Brooklyn, when two cars park kitty-corner across the street and halt the traffic, and suddenly there's a block party on the pavement. People begin streaming out of the town houses, stores, and restaurants. Some bring guitars with them, others carry food, and still others are holding their babies. People laugh about politics and delight in the differences in religions while others set up the stage for the band. Everybody eats one another's food. More tables have to be found, the lights blaze, and out of nowhere the street has been transformed into a celebration. Before long it has become a party of everyone for everyone and by everyone, and it lasts late into the night.

ACKNOWLEDGMENTS

A book such as this one depends entirely upon the generosity of many people. Foremost among them are the seven people whose stories I tell, and I extend my deepest gratitude to Rasha, Sami, Yasmin, Akram, Lina, Omar, and Rami. They shared their time and their lives with me, and they continue to inspire me in a multitude of ways.

Many other people offered crucial support along the way. I thank Kaled Alamarie, Kareem Abdelaziz, Jonathan Blazon, Lamis Deek, Hussam Alharash, Yasmin Hamidi, Faozia Aljibawi, Sarab Al-Jijakli, Shane Kadidal, Robert Ji-Song Ku, Cynthia Lee, Neil Levi, Sunaina Maira, Wael Mousfar, Sana' Odeh, Betsy Reed, Jennifer Ridha, Andrew Rubin, Hussein Saddique, Linda Sarsour, and Karam Tannous. I am grateful to the Professional Staff Congress of the City University of New York and Brooklyn College's Provost's Committee on Reassigned Time for their assistance. I very much appreciate invitations from colleagues who asked me to share pieces of this work at their institutions while it was coming together. Thanks to Patrick McGreevey at the American University of Beirut; Lisa Lowe at the University of California, San Diego; Ghada Osman at San Diego State University; Ezra Mirze at the University of Tampa; Iftikhar Dadi at Cornell University; Linda Herrera at the Institute of Social Studies in the Hague, Asef Bayat at the Institute for the Study of Islam in the Modern World; Jae H. Roe at Sogang University in South Korea; Emma Teng at the Massachusetts Institute of Technology; and Margaret Pappano at Queen's University in Kingston, Canada.

I am deeply indebted to Zein Rimawi, a tireless activist, community organizer, and dear friend. Ellen Tremper is a constant source of moral and intellectual support. Rob Nixon taught me what writing is all about. He has offered me so much encouragement and wisdom over the years that I will never be able to thank him enough. Thanks also to Christian Parenti, who is always there when needed and is a model of the engaged intellectual.

Katherine Fausset, my brilliant and magnificent agent, believed in this project from the beginning, and I offer her all my gratitude. Vanessa Mobley, my editor, has one of the sharpest minds in New York City, and I have benefited tremendously from her insights, her questions, her intuition, and her craft. I am honored and pleased beyond words to have worked with her.

Two people in particular have made this book possible, and they deserve special thanks. Corey Robin, from whom I never stop learning, was the first person to hear the idea that became this book. His help and support proved invaluable in all sorts of ways. Zohra Saed was instrumental at every turn, and I wish to thank her not only for her assistance but also for her creativity, humor, and friendship.

Finally, my greatest debt is to Shara Richter, whose intelligence and heart continue to enchant and exhilarate me in ways that defy gravity. She helped me find my shoulders, and so much more.

NOTES

PREFACE

2 "Being a problem is a strange experience": W.E.B. Du Bois, *The Souls of Black Folk* (Mineola, NY: Dover, 1994 [1903]), 1. By linking the African-American experience with the Arab-American present in this book, I mean to draw attention to how difference operates in American society, but this certainly does not mean that Arab-American life since September 11, 2001, is in any way equivalent to the ravages of slavery and segregation.

2 "the meaning of its religion, the passion of its human sorrow": Ibid., v.

2 Native Americans, labeled "merciless Indian savages": Richard Drinnon, *Facing West: The Metaphysics of Indian Hating and Empire Building* (Norman: University of Oklahoma Press, 1997), 90–98.

2 With the rise of Catholic immigration: Roger Daniels, *Guarding the Golden Door: American Immigration Policy and Immigrants Since 1882* (New York: Hill and Wang, 2004), 7–10.

3 German Americans were loathed and reviled: John Higham, *Strangers in the Land: Patterns in American Nativism 1860–1925* (New York: Atheneum, 1977), 208.

3 anti-Semitism drove Jewish Americans: Leonard Dinnerstein, *Anti-Semitism in America* (New York: Oxford University Press, 1994), 78–104.

3 Japanese Americans were herded like cattle: Roger Daniels, *Prisoners Without Trial: Japanese Americans in World War II* (New York: Hill and Wang, 2004).

3 Chinese Americans were commonly suspected: Iris Chang, *The Chinese in America: A Narrative History* (New York: Penguin, 2004), 236–260.

3 Hispanic Americans have long been seen as outsider threats: Juan Gonzales, *Harvest of Empire: A History of Latinos in America* (New York: Penguin, 2001).

3 Bias crimes against Arabs, Muslims, and those assumed to be: Office for Victims of Crime, Hate and Bias Crimes Report, (U.S. Department of Justice, 2003), http://www.ojp.usdoj.gov/ovc/ncvrw/2003/pg5j.html; and Human Rights Watch "We Are Not the Enemy: Hate Crimes Against Arabs, Muslims, and Those Perceived to Be Arab or Muslim After September 11," (2002), 4.

3 39 percent of Americans admit to holding prejudice against Muslims: Marilyn Elias, "USA's Muslims Under a Cloud," *USA Today*, Aug. 10, 2006.

3 Different studies: The studies are discussed in Solana Pyne, "Making Enemies: Post 9-11 Crackdowns Spurring Prejudice," *Village Voice*, July 9, 2003.

4 Mass arrests following the attacks: See Amnesty International, *Amnesty International's Concerns Regarding Post September 11 Detentions in USA*, Mar. 2002.

4 deportation proceedings against almost 14,000 people: See Moustafa Bayoumi, "Racing Religion," *New Centennial Review* 6:2 (2006): 267–293.

4 "exceptions permitting use of race and ethnicity": CBS News/Associated Press, "Bush Orders Racial Profiling Ban, Critics Worry Loopholes Will Still Allow Profiling of Some Groups," June 18, 2003. The article quotes Miriam Gohara, an attorney with the NAACP Legal Defense Fund: "It looks to me that [the policy] is more interested in carving out exceptions to racial profiling than it is in enforcing a ban," she said.

5 Prince sings an ode: The song is "Cinnamon Girl" from Prince's 2004 album *Musicology* (NPG Records). The song's video sparked controversy for its depiction of a young woman who, after enduring post–September 11 racist abuse, dreams of enacting terrorist violence herself. She decides against it by the video's end. See Associated Press, "Prince Video Courts Controversy: Depicts Teenage Girl Dreaming about Carrying Bomb into Airport," Oct. 15, 2004.

5 "Arab and Muslim Americans have been compelled": Sally Howell and Andrew Shryock, "Cracking Down on Diaspora: Arab Detroit and America's 'War on Terror.'" *Anthropological Quarterly* 76, no. 2 (2003): 443–462.

5 Japanese-American groups speaking out: Center for Constitutional Rights, "Descendents of Japanese American Internees File Amicus Brief in Support of Muslim Immigrants." April 3, 2007, http://ccrjustice.org/newsroom/press-releases/descendents-japanese-american-internees-file-amicus-brief-support-muslim-imm. Also see Nadine Naber, "So Our History Doesn't Become Your

Future: The Local and Global Politics of Coalition Building Post September 11," Journal of Asian American Studies 5 (Fall 2002): 217–242.

7   Twenty-one percent of the American public: Pew Research Center, *Muslim Americans: Middle Class and Mostly Mainstream*, May 2007, p. 16.

7   30 percent of American Muslims: Helen Samhan, "By the Numbers," *Arab American Business*, Oct. 2003, 27–35. Also see G. Patricia de la Cruz and Angela Brittingham, "We the People of Arab Ancestry in the United States," Census 2000 Special Reports, U.S. Census Bureau (March 2005), 19.

7   The median age of 30.8 is derived by factoring in Arab Americans with mixed ancestries with Arab Americans generally. Arab Americans alone, according to the 2000 Census, have a median age of 33.1.

7   the Muslim-American experience is capacious and sprawling: Studies estimate that only 25 percent of the American Muslim community is Arab. See Ishan Bagby, et al., "The Mosque in America: A National Portrait" (Washington, DC: Council on American-Islamic Relations, 2001), 3. Also see Pew Research Center, *Muslim Americans: Middle Class and Mostly Mainstream* (May 2007), 1.

7   a majority Christian population: According to the Arab American Institute, about 25 percent of Arab Americans are Muslim; see "Demographics," http://www.aaiusa.org/arab-americans/22/demographics.

8   the census underreports Arab Americans: U.S. Census Bureau, Census 2000 Summary File 3 puts Arabs in Brooklyn at 35,739 or 1.4 percent of Brooklyn's population. Dearborn's Arab population, according to "The Arab Population: Census 2000 Brief," is 29,161 or 29.85 percent of Dearborn's population. See G. Patricia de la Cruz and Angela Brittingham, "The Arab Population: Census 2000 Brief." U.S. Census Bureau (December 2003), 7. Also see the population pamphlet titled "New York" by the Arab American Institute (2003), which estimates a population of 405,000 Arab Americans in New York with 29 percent, or 117,450, living in Brooklyn.

8   Brooklyn is "chiefly no whole or recognizable animal": James Agee (with a preface by Jonathan Lethem), *Brooklyn Is: Southeast of the Island, Travel Notes* (New York: Fordham University Press, 2005), 5.

10 crisis in local charitable donations: A local private Islamic school in Sunset Park, for example, was easily collecting between $100,000 and $200,000 annually in donations prior to the terrorist attacks. After September 11, however, donations trickled to less than $30,000 in 2006. See Laila Al-Arian, "Where Two Worlds Meet: An Islamic School in Brooklyn" (Columbia University Journalism School Master's Thesis, 2006), 7. My thanks to Laila Al-Arian for sharing her thesis with me.

10   the no-fly list: Many experts now see the no-fly list as sprawling and ineffective. See Mimi Hall, "Terror Watch List Swells to More than 755,000," *USA Today*, Oct. 23, 2007.

CHAPTER ONE: RASHA

37   stopped for driving four miles over the speed limit: David Cole, *Enemy Aliens* (New York: New Press, 2003), 31.

37   without even his own clothes: Amnesty International. *Amnesty International's Concerns Regarding Post–September 11 Detentions in the USA* (Mar. 2002), 28.

38   "presumption of innocence": Ibid., 1.

38   "more objective criteria": U.S. Department of Justice Office of the Inspector General, *The September 11 Detainees: A Review of the Treatment of Aliens Held on Immigration Charges in Connection with the Investigation of the September 11 Attacks* (Apr. 2003), 187.

38   Religion and ethnicity: In a troubling development, the courts later ruled that the government has the right to detain immigrants on the basis of their race, religion, or national origin, and it can legally imprison immigrants indefinitely, as long as their eventual removal from the country is "reasonably foreseeable." See David Cole, "Manzanar Redux? In an echo of Japanese internment, a judge's ruling allows foreign nationals to be rounded up on the basis of their race or religion." *Los Angeles Times*, June 16, 2006. Also see Moustafa Bayoumi, "Court Wrongly OKs Profiling," *Pittsburgh Tribune-Review*, July 2, 2006.

38   arrests "might require some level of evidence": U.S. Department of Justice Office of the Inspector General, *The September 11 Detainees: A Review of the Treatment of Aliens Held on Immigration Charges in Connection with the Investigation of the September 11 Attacks* (April 2003), 187.

38   THESE COLORS DON'T RUN: U.S. Department of Justice Office of the Inspector General, *Supplemental Report on September 11 Detainees' Allegations of Abuse at the Metropolitan Detention Center in Brooklyn, New York* (December 2003), 47.

38   "goosenecking": Ibid., 17.

39   "you have to establish who is in charge": Jeff McDonald, "Beatings Used to Show Who Was in Charge, Witness Says; Marine's Court-martial in Iraqi's Death Goes On," *San Diego Union-Tribune*, Aug. 31, 2004.

39   the Justice Department announced 1,182 arrested: David Cole, *Enemy Aliens* (New York: New Press, 2003), 25.

39   of these 762, only 6 percent: U.S. Department of Justice Office of the Inspector General. *The September 11 Detainees, 74.*

39   an unspecified "reasonable" amount of time: Neil A. Lewis and Philip Shenon, "Senate Democrat Opposes White House's Antiterrorism Plan and Proposes Alternative," *New York Times,* Sept. 20, 2001.

39   The average length of detention: U.S. Department of Justice Office of the Inspector General, *The September 11 Detainees, 46, 52, 56.*

40   Those detainees included community leaders: Peter J. Irons, *Justice At War: The Story of the Japanese Internment Cases* (Berkeley: University of California Press, 1993), 22.

40   "the FBI was turning many aliens over": John Joel Culley, "Enemy Alien Control in the United States during World War II: A Survey," in Kay Saunders and Roger Daniels, eds., *Alien Justice: Wartime Internment in Australia and North America* (St. Lucia, Queensland: University of Queensland Press, 2003), 143.

40   Herbert Nicholson, pastor of the West Los Angeles Methodist Church, objected: Michi Weglyn, *Years of Infamy: The Untold Story of America's Concentration Camps* (Seattle: University of Washington Press, 1996), 46.

40   "we picked up too many": Ibid.

40   Historians of Japanese internment: See Greg Robinson, *By Order of the President: FDR and the Internment of Japanese Americans* (Cambridge: Harvard University Press, 2003), and Roger Daniels, *Prisoners Without Trial: Japanese Americans in World War II* (New York: Hill and Wang, 1993), Daniels (p. 3) cites the 1981 report by the Presidential Commission on the Wartime Relocation and Internment of Civilians, which read that the relocation and internment of Japanese and Japanese Americans "was not justified by military necessity, and the decisions which followed from it . . . were not driven by analysis of military conditions. The broad historical causes which shaped these decisions were race prejudice, war hysteria, and a failure of political leadership."

40   "After 9/11, headquarters encouraged more and more detentions": "Full Text of F.B.I. Agent's Letter to Director Mueller," *New York Times,* Mar. 5, 2003.

41   the 314,000 people in the United States who had "absconded": Kevin Lapp, "Pressing Public Necessity: The Unconstitutionality of the Absconder Apprehension Initiative," New York University School of Law, *Review of Law and Social Change* 29 (2005): 573.

42   people were often taken into custody regardless: Susan Sachs, "U.S. Begins Crackdown on Muslims Who Defy Orders to Leave Country," *New York Times,* Apr. 2, 2002.

42 "affords a convenient pretext": David Cole, *Enemy Aliens* (New York: New Press, 2003), 24.

42 Just because the government has "charged a foreign national as deportable": Ibid., 19.

42 as Mark Dow has shown: Mark Dow, *American Gulag: Inside U.S. Immigration Prisons* (Berkeley: University of California Press, 2005), 25.

42 In 1995 approximately 5,500 people: Bryan Lonegan, et al., "Immigration Detention and Removal: A Guide for Detainees and Their Families" (Legal Aid Society, Oct. 2004), 1.

42 By 2006, the number was over 27,000: ICE Office of Detention and Removal Fact Sheet, Nov. 15, 2006, http://www.ice.gov/pi/news/factsheets/dro110206.htm

42 contract out beds to county jails: Meredith Kolodner, "County Jails Boost Their Income," *News 21,* July 26, 2006. Brian Donohue and Tom Feeney, "Federal Detainees, County Headaches," *Newark Star-Ledger,* June 3, 2005.

CHAPTER TWO: SAMI

50 something quite rare in the United States: *Parade* magazine reported in 2005 that in the entire U.S. armed forces of 2.6 million people there are "an estimated 3,500 Arab Americans" serving, pointing out that "the Pentagon doesn't keep official figures." Lyric Wallwork Winik, "Don't Ask Me to Take Off the Uniform," *Parade,* Apr. 17, 2005.

The military advertises regularly in Arab-American community newspapers in Brooklyn, as do independent military contractors (in fact, I regularly receive mail solicitations from both). The military ads promise "quick advancement in rank" if you speak Arabic and private contractors offer "up to $160,000/year" with a small line on the bottom of the ad that reads, "All work to be performed in Iraq." The war is almost universally unpopular among the Arab-American community in Brooklyn, and there have been few takers.

CHAPTER THREE: YASMIN

97 "Those who stand for nothing": The maxim is commonly and mistakenly attributed to Alexander Hamilton. It was identified simply as "graffiti" by *Reader's Digest* in 1922. Lila Bell Acheson Wallace and De Witt Wallace, *The Reader's Digest* (Pleasantville, NY: Reader's Digest Association, 1922), 77.

CHAPTER FOUR: AKRAM

122 Arab-owned grocery stores in New York City: There is no official figure on the number of Arab-owned grocery stores in New York City. In 1995 the Arab American Institute estimated that there are over 2,000 Arab-American small store owners in the New York City area. See "Discrimination at the Arizona Iced Tea Company and the Power of Arab Americans," Sept. 18, 1995, available at http://www.aaiusa.org/washington-watch/1250/w091895. Also see Yinon Cohen and Andrea Tyree, "Palestinian and Jewish Israeli-born Immigrants in the United States," *International Migration Review* 28, no. 2 (1994): 243–255. Cohen and Tyree claim that "Palestinian Arabs tend to own small businesses more than any immigrant group in America" (p. 253). Another study of patterns of self-employment in the United States puts Palestinians (20 percent) just behind Koreans (24 percent) and Israelis (22 percent), who could also be Palestinian. See Pyong Gap Min and Mehdi Bozorgmehr, "Immigrant Entrepreneurship in the United States: Trends, Research and Theory," in *Venturing Abroad: Global Processes and National Particularities of Immigrant Entrepreneurship in Advanced Economies,* ed. Robert Kloosterman and Jan Rath (Oxford and New York: Berg and New York University Press, 2003).

122 She cites the Jews in Europe: Edna Bonacich, "A Theory of Middlemen Minorities," *American Sociological Review* 38, no. 5 (1973): 583–594. Also see Walter P. Zenner, *Minorities in the Middle: A Cross-Cultural Analysis* (Binghamton: SUNY Press, 1991).

131 "You Arabs get out": American Arab Anti-Discrimination Committee (ADC), *Report on Hate Crimes and Discrimination Against Arab Americans: The post–September 11 backlash, September 11, 2001–October 11, 2002* (2003), 66.

131 breaking his dentures: Ibid., 62.

131 convenience store owned by a Palestinian-American man in Missouri. "Violence Against Arab and Muslim Americans: Michigan to Wisconsin," Tolerance.org, a Web project of the Southern Poverty Law Center (2002), http://www.tolerance .org/news/article_hate.jsp?id=412.

131 three men attacked the Iraqi-American storeowner: Ibid., "Alabama to Massachusetts." http://www.tolerance.org/news/article_hate.jsp?id=278.

131 "get those Arabs for what they did": American Arab Anti-Discrimination Committee (ADC), *Report on Hate Crimes and Discrimination Against Arab Americans,* 51. Also see "Police Charge 3 Youths with Hate Crime in Somerset," *Providence Journal Bulletin,* Sept. 13, 2001.

131 shot four times in the back: CAIR Research Center, "American Muslims: One

Year After 9-11" (Washington, D.C.: Council on American Islamic Relations [CAIR], 2002), 30.

131   the tragedy that befell Adel Karas: Human Rights Watch, "We Are Not the Enemy: Hate Crimes Against Arabs, Muslims, and Those Perceived to Be Arab or Muslim After September 11" (2002), 18.

131   "I did it to retaliate on local Arab Americans": Ibid., 17.

131   Yemeni immigrant Abdo Ali Ahmed: Ibid., 18.

133   a Harris Poll conducted in June 2007: Compared to 65 percent of whites and 10 percent of Hispanics. See "Fighting the War on Terror: Republicans Giuliani and McCain Get Higher Ratings Than Clinton, Obama or Edwards." Harris Poll #58, June 19, 2007, http://www.harrisinteractive.com/harris_poll/index .asp?PID=773.

134   "Black New Yorkers joke among themselves": Somini Sengupta, "Sept. 11 Attack Narrows the Racial Divide," *New York Times,* Oct. 10, 2001.

134   "within two weeks after the WTC and Pentagon bombings": Ishmael Reed, "Civil Rights: Six Experts Weigh In," *Time,* Dec. 7, 2001.

134   "Is anyone with dark skin Arab-American?": Ibid.

134   cultural studies scholar Sylvia Chan: Sylvia Chan (in conversation with Jeff Chang), "Can Hollywood Get Race Right?" Alternet.org, July 19, 2005, http:// alternet.org/movies/23597/?page=3.

CHAPTER FIVE: LINA

153   After Saddam's 1990 invasion of Kuwait: Sarah Graham-Brown, *Sanctioning Saddam: The Politics of Intervention in Iraq* (London: I. B. Taurus, 1999).

153   Most families were sold monthly supplies: Rajiv Chandrasekaran, "Stockpiling Popularity with Food: Rations Quell Iraqi Discontent," *Washington Post,* Feb. 3, 2003.

153   Under sanctions, however, medicines became scarce: "UN Says Sanctions Have Killed Some 500,000 Iraqi Children," Reuters, July 21, 2000.

153   "I am resigning": Quoted in John Pilger, "Why We Ignored Iraq in the 1990s," *New Statesman,* Oct. 2, 2004.

153   To ensure compliance: Charles Levinson, "Cautiously, Iraqis Open for Business," *Christian Science Monitor,* Jan. 4, 2006.

178   "In or about December 2001": United States District Court, Southern District of New York, Indictment s1 03 Cr. 807 (MBM).

178   The fourth count of the indictment charged: Ibid.

178   the man known as "The Scorpion": Robert Gearty and Greg P. Smith, "Diplo's

Son Seeks Haven, Says He's Innocent of Spy Charges," *Daily News* (New York), Apr. 16, 2003.

178   the FBI had long pressured their father: Benjamin Weiser, "Former Iraqi Diplomat's Son Is Charged as Illegal Agent," *New York Times*, Apr. 15, 2003. Greg P. Smith, "Judge, Iraqi Diplo's Son No Threat to U.S.," *Daily News*, July 8, 2003.

179   "It is difficult for the court to believe": Greg P. Smith, "Judge, Iraqi Diplo's Son No Threat to U.S.," *Daily News*, July 8, 2003.

180   The main charge against them: Robert Gearty, "Iraqi Brothers Guilty of Lying," *Daily News* (New York), Jan. 12, 2005.

183   But exile is usually characterized as: Edward W. Said, "Reflections on Exile," in *Reflections on Exile and Other Essays* (Cambridge, MA: Harvard University Press, 2002), 173.

184   2 million other Iraqis: "Nearly 4.5 Million Displaced and Refugees in Iraq, says UNHCR," Associated Press, Oct. 23, 2007. Also see Madona Mokbel, "Refugees in Limbo: The Plight of Iraqis in Bordering States," *Middle East Report* 244 (Fall 2007): 10–17.

CHAPTER SIX: OMAR

193   In the first eight months after the attacks: "EEOC Provides Answers About Workplace Rights of Muslims, Arabs, South Asians, and Sikhs," U.S. Equal Employment Opportunity Commission press release, May 15, 2002, http://www.eeoc.gov/press/5-15-02.html.

193   the American Arab Anti-Discrimination Committee had cataloged: American Arab Anti-Discrimination Committee (ADC), *Report on Hate Crimes and Discrimination Against Arab Americans: The post-September 11 backlash, September 11, 2001–October 11, 2002* (2003), 20.

193   According to a report aired on December 15, 2006: Alix Spiegel, "Which One of Them Is Not Like the Other?" From "Shouting Across the Divide," *This American Life* no. 322, WBEZ and Public Radio International, Dec. 15, 2006.

193   "severe and pervasive harassment": "EEOC Sues Plaza Hotel and Fairmont Hotels and Resorts for Post 9/11 Backlash Discrimination," U.S. Equal Employment Opportunity Commission press release, Sept. 30, 2003, http://www.eeoc.gov/press/9-30-03b.html.

194   In 2003, the luxury hotel chain agreed: "The Plaza Hotel to Pay $525,000 for Post-9/11 Backlash Discrimination Against Employees." U.S. Equal Employment Opportunity Commission press release, June 8, 2005, http://www.eeoc.gov/press/6-8-05.html.

194   "Heidi McKenzie" garnered: "Names Make a Difference: The Screening of Resumes by Temporary Employment Agencies in California," Discrimination Resource Center. Berkeley, Cal., Oct. 2004, http://drcenter.org/studies/resume_study_04.pdf.

194   "The unanticipated events of September 11th, 2001": Alberto Davila and Marie T. Mora, "Changes in the Earnings of Arab Men in the US between 2000 and 2002," *Journal of Population Economics* 18 (2005): 587–601.

194   earnings fell 9 to 11 percent: Neeraj Kaushal, Robert Kaestner, and Cordelia Reimers, "Labor Market Effects of September 11th on Arab and Muslim Residents of the U.S.," *Journal of Human Resources* 42, no. 2 (Spring 2007): 275–308. My thanks to Professor Kaushal for sharing her article with me before its publication.

196   "vicious, inaccurate, and inexcusable": Jeremy Scahill, "The War on Al Jazeera," *Nation*, Dec. 1, 2005.

198   "Right away on the road": Beth Sanders, dir., *Fear and Favor in the Newsroom*, California Newsreel/KTEH-PBS San Jose documentary, 1996.

198   While the footage was damning: Beth Sanders and Randy Baker, "Fear and Favor in the Newsroom," in *Censored 1998: The News That Didn't Make the News*, ed. Peter Phillips (New York: Seven Stories Press, 1998), 167.

206   the United States has become a far less welcoming place: Sam Dillon, "US Slips in Attracting the World's Best Students," *New York Times*, Dec. 21, 2004.

206   This is especially true for students from the Middle East: The sharpest declines were reported in the 2003–04 academic year. There were 15 percent fewer students coming from Jordan that year and 30 percent fewer coming from the United Arab Emirates. See "International Student Enrollments Declined by 2.4% in 2003/04," Institute of International Education press release, Nov. 10, 2004, http://opendoors.iienetwork.org/?p=50137.

206   Total enrollments were down almost 20,000 students: By the 2005–06 academic year, the number of international students enrolled in U.S. higher-education institutions had declined by 21,557 students since its high in the 2002–03 academic year. See "International Student and Total U.S. Enrollment," *Open Doors 2006* table, Institute of International Education, http://opendoors.iienetwork.org/?p=89192.

211   the entire FBI staff of 12,000 agents: Dan Eggen, "FBI Agents Still Lacking Arabic Skills," *Washington Post*, Oct. 11, 2006.

211   only 54 of them could be considered fluent: Souheila Al-Jadda, "Lost in Arabic Translation," *Christian Science Monitor*, Sept. 16, 2004.

212   The Iraq Study Group pointed out: James A. Baker III and Lee Hamilton, *The*

Iraq Study Group Report: The Way Forward–A New Approach, United States Institute of Peace, 2006, 60.

212 Special Agent Bassem Youssef: John Solomon, "FBI Terror Expertise Papers to Come Out," Associated Press, Dec. 13, 2006.

212 "Has the U.S. threatened to vaporize Mecca?": Niall Stanage, "A Sure Way to Undermine Anti-Terrorism Efforts," *New York Observer,* Dec. 17, 2006.

212 "all Arabs are animals": Larry Neumeister, "Lawsuit Says NYPD Anti-Terror Cyber Unit Filled with Muslim Hate," *New York Newsday,* Dec. 5, 2006. William K. Rashbaum, "Police Antiterrorism Analyst Sues City, Citing Anti-Muslim E-mail," *New York Times,* Dec. 6, 2006.

CHAPTER SEVEN: RAMI

223 Abu Rami: It is a common practice among Arabic speakers to refer to people who are parents by their relationship to their firstborn sons. Rami's mother would thus be Umm Rami.

226 The authorities narrowed their sights: John Mintz and Douglas Farah, "Small Scams Probed for Terror Ties: Muslim, Arab Stores Monitored as Part of Post– Sept. 11 Inquiry," *Washington Post,* Apr. 12, 2002. A 2004 study performed for a Queens College master's class in Urban Research Methods examined the New York State Department of Taxation and Finance Audit's focus on Arab-American small businesses, primarily grocery stores. The study discovered that since 2001 a widespread practice on the part of the taxation department has emerged, in which the department now routinely and often punitively audits Arab-American small businesses. The author of the study told me that of the approximately one hundred stores he approached, all had been audited since September 11, 2001, and none had been audited prior to then. High fines have forced some to close their businesses. His study argues that this practice targets business owners "from the Middle East under the assumption that they are contributing financially to terrorism." See Kaled Alamarie, "New York State Department of Taxation and Finance Audit Discrimination Against Arab American Businesses," Urban Research Methods, Professor Nathalis Wamba, Queens College, City University of New York, Dec. 2, 2004, p. 7. My thanks to Kaled Alamarie for sharing his work with me.

233 pious in outlook: Many contemporary observers want to date this tendency of young Muslims toward their religion to a domestic response to the September 11 attacks, but if you have spent any time with Muslim youth prior to 2001 (as I have), you will know that this direction was evident long before. The effect of

September 11 has been not to mark a rupture between one period and the next so much as to accelerate and expand upon a previous trend. In fact, the rise of a faith-based identity may chart with the expansion of Islam in the Muslim world, but it also and perhaps more significantly correlates with the growth of religion in all aspects of American society, including in college life.

245 "Visibility is considered a source of power": Jeanette S. Jouli, "Being a Pious French Muslim Woman," International Institute for the Study of Islam in the Modern World, *ISIM Review* 19 (Spring 2007), 32–33.

245 "now perceived to be the precondition": Ibid., 32.

AFTERWORD

260 Despite an unwarranted controversy: The school is the Khalil Gibran International Academy, one of the sixty-five dual-language programs in New York City public schools. (See Julie Bosman, "French Gains Foothold on New York City's Dual-Language Map," *New York Times*, Aug. 22, 2007.) Despite what many detractors have held, the school will teach the Arabic language and Arab culture, not the religion of Islam. On the school and the controversy, see Samuel G. Freedman, "Critics Ignored Record of Muslim Principal," *New York Times*, Aug. 29, 2007. One of the most interesting and perceptive treatments of the controversy surrounding the school was from Larry Cohler-Esses, "Jewish Shootout over School: Fall of Jewish-supported Principal Exposes Bitter Fault Line on Approach to Muslims," *Jewish Week*, Aug. 17, 2007.

260 Even the most mundane facts of their lives: The New York City Police Department released a report in August 2007 which claimed that the "emerging threat" to law enforcement resides with "unremarkable" Muslim men under thirty-five who visit what the reports dubs "terrorism incubators": mosques, "cafés, cab driver hangouts, flophouses, prisons, student associations, non-governmental organizations, hookah (water pipe) bars, butcher shops and book stores," in other words, precisely the places where I have been hanging out. I can attest from my experience to the false conclusions of the report, which it seems to me seek to justify the NYPD's antiterrorism budget. But perhaps the more pertinent question about the report concerns how we have arrived at a place where the NYPD assumes that every average Muslim under thirty-five is a potential terrorist. Something has surely gone terribly wrong when law enforcement premises its work on policing the ordinary and the unremarkable. See "Radicalization in the West: The Homegrown Threat," New York City Police Department Intelligence Division, Aug. 2007, 20.

261   "the apparent paradox of this historical moment": Louise Cainkar, "No Longer Invisible: Arab and Muslim Exclusion After September 11," *Middle East Report* 224 (Fall 2002): 29.

261   "a concrete test of the underlying principles": W.E.B. DuBois, *The Souls of Black Folk* (Mineola, NY: Dover, 1994 [1903]), 7.

261   many West African Muslims were sold into slavery: Sylviane A. Diouf, *Servants of Allah: African Muslims Enslaved in the Americas* (New York: New York University Press, 1998).

261   Mustapha, historians tell us: John C. Inscoe, "Carolina Slave Names: An Index to Acculturation," *Journal of Southern History* 49, no. 4 (November 1983), 533. Michael A. Gomez, *Exchanging Our Country Marks: The Transformation of African Identities in the Colonial and Antebellum South* (Chapel Hill: University of North Carolina Press, 1998), 68. According to John Inscoe, "Quite a few slaves [brought from abroad and not born here] were allowed to keep either their original African names or names given them elsewhere, as indicated by the frequent use of Spanish and Portuguese names retained by slaves brought from the Caribbean Islands or South America" (Inscoe, p. 529). Peter H. Wood makes a similar point in his book *Black Majority: Negroes in Colonial South Carolina from 1670 Through the Stono Rebellion* (New York: Knopf, 1975), 181–186.

261   landed on Ellis Island with an average of $31.85: Akram Fouad Khater, *Inventing Home: Emigration, Gender, and the Middle Class in Lebanon 1870–1920* (Berkeley: University of California Press, 2001), 56, 209.

262   published lots of newspapers: The number of newspapers published by the community is remarkable. Between 1892 and 1907, the Arab American community published twenty-one Arabic "dailies, weeklies, and monthlies," seventeen of which were based in New York City, for a population not much larger than fifty thousand people. See Akram Fouad Khater, *Inventing Home,* 88.

262   The move to Brooklyn: Ruth Karpf, "Street of the Arabs," *New York Times,* Aug. 11, 1946.

262   The early community thrived: Alixa Naff, *Becoming American: The Early Arab Immigrant Experience* (Carbondale: Southern Illinois University Press, 1985), 128–160.

262   "In the midst of all this riot of the beautiful and odd": "Picturesque Colony," *New York Daily Tribune,* Oct. 2, 1892.

262   "The foreign population in the lower part of this city": "'Sanctified' Arab Tramps," *New York Times,* May 25, 1890.

262   Diego Italians: According to the *Oxford English Dictionary,* "Diego" is a pejorative term, sometimes shortened to "Dago," that was often used to refer to people of Spanish or Italian descent.

263   the growing unrest in Palestine: Lawrence Davidson, "Debating Palestine: Arab American Challenges to Zionism, 1917–1932," in *Arabs in America: Building a New Future,* ed. Michael W. Suleiman (Philadelphia: Temple University Press, 1999), 227–240.

263   whether Arabs could naturalize as American citizens: Ian Haney-Lopez, *White By Law: The Legal Construction of Race* (New York: New York University Press, 1995). Sarah Gualtieri, "Becoming 'White': Race, Religion and the Foundations of Syrian/Lebanese Ethnicity in the United States," *Journal of American Ethnic History* (Summer 2001): 29–58.

263   "Arabs are not white persons": In re *Hassan,* 48 F. Supp. 843 (E.D. Mich. 1942), p. 845.

263   "vital interest [of the United States] as a world power:" Ex parte *Mohriez,* 54. F. Supp. 941 (D.Mass. 1944), pp. 942, 943. Also see "The Eligibility of Arabs to Naturalization," *INS Monthly Review* 4 (October 1943): 12–16.

263   Lend-Lease Act: Michael T. Klare, *Blood and Oil: The Dangers and Consequences of America's Growing Dependency on Imported Petroleum* (New York: Owl Books, 2005), 33. The controversy around the aid stemmed from the fact that Saudi Arabia had not been attacked by the Axis powers, and the Lend-Lease Act was intended to support friendly nations that had.

264   He filed a lawsuit: Nicholas M. Horrock, "New Senate Panel May Study FBI Drive on Arab Terrorism," *New York Times,* Feb. 13, 1975.

264   Operation Boulder: "A Plan to Screen Terrorists Ends," *New York Times,* Apr. 24, 1975. Yvonne Yazbeck Haddad, *Not Quite American? The Shaping of Arab and Muslim Identity in the United States* (Waco, TX: Baylor University Press, 2004), 21.

264   The FBI's Mark Felt: "Ex-Aide Describes FBI Burglaries, Saying He Gave Approval," *New York Times,* Aug. 18, 1976.

265   "complete fabrication": Susan M. Akram and Kevin Johnson, "Race, Civil Rights, and Immigration Law After September 11, 2001: The Targeting of Arabs and Muslims," *New York University Annual Survey of American Law* 58, no. 3 (Nov. 2002): 295–355. The quote by Revell is found on page 315.

265   "indiscriminately lumps together individuals": Jeanne A. Butterfield, "Do Immigrants Have First Amendment Rights?" *Middle East Report* 212 (Autumn 1999): 4–6.

265 "if these individuals had been United States citizens": David Cole, *Enemy Aliens* (New York: New Press, 2003), 162–169. Jeanne A. Butterfield, "Do Immigrants Have First Amendment Rights?" *Middle East Report* 212 (Autumn 1999): 4–6. After twenty years, the L.A. 8 case has finally come to a close in 2007. The federal government, after suffering a harsh rebuke from an immigration judge (who called the case "an embarrassment to the rule of law" and accused the government of "'gross failure' to comply with instructions to turn over to the men 'potentially exculpatory and other relevant information'"), dropped all charges against the last two of the L.A. 8. See Henry Weinstein, "After 20 Years, U.S. Drops Charges Against Men Accused of Ties to Terrorists," *Los Angeles Times*, Oct. 31, 2007.

265 immigration courts expanded their use of "secret evidence": Beth Lyon, "Secret Evidence," Findlaw.com, June 21, 2001. http://writ.news.findlaw.com/commentary/20000621_lyon.html.

266 the agency was unable to name: Susan M. Akram, "The Aftermath of September 11, 2001: The Targeting of Arabs and Muslims in America," *Arab Studies Quarterly* 24 (Spring–Summer 2002): 61–118. Also see Susan M. Akram and Kevin Johnson, "Race, Civil Rights, and Immigration Law After September 11, 2001: The Targeting of Arabs and Muslims," *New York University Annual Survey of American Law* 58, no. 3 (November 2002): 295–355; and David Cole, *Enemy Aliens* (New York: New Press, 2003), 169–179.

266 a new category of "the Muslim": The similarities are striking. Classical anti-Semitism saw the Jewish people as antimodern, atavistically religious, practitioners of strange rites, and thoroughly unwilling to assimilate. Moreover, Jews were said to be manipulating international trade and commerce for their own gain, ultimately interested in world domination, and odd dressers. Particularly with the rise of radical anarchism in the early twentieth century, they were also eyed as dangerous fomenters of terrorist violence. Much the same now applies to Muslims in the West. Moreover, in the same way that European identity had long been constructed in opposition to Judaism, many Europeans (and to a lesser extent Americans) today define themselves against the image of the Muslims in their midst. One article describing the similarities between anti-Semitism and Islamophobia is Maleiha Malik, "Muslims Are Now Getting the Same Treatment Jews Had a Century Ago," *Guardian*, Feb. 2, 2007.

266 First, there was the preventive detention: David Cole, *Enemy Aliens* (New York: New Press, 2003), 25. The 5,000 number comes from Cole, who tabulates it as of May 2003, and includes the 1,182 people arrested in the first seven weeks

following the attacks, the 1,100 or so people detained under the Absconder Apprehension Initiative, and the first wave of arrests under Special Registration. Cole calls the 5,000 number a "conservative estimate" (*Enemy Aliens*, p. 25).

266   The government then sought 19,000 "voluntary" interviews: The "voluntary interviews" came in three waves. First there were 5,000, announced in November, 2001 (Jodi Wilgoren, "Prosecutors Begin Effort to Interview 5,000, but Basic Questions Remain," *New York Times*, Nov. 15, 2001). In March 2002 the Justice Department announced 3,000 more "voluntary interviews" (Philip Shenon, "Justice Dept. Wants to Query More Foreigners," *New York Times*, Mar. 21, 2002). In March 2003 the government sought 11,000 Iraqi Americans for another round of interviews (Danny Hakim and Nick Madigan, "Iraqi Americans: Immigrants Questioned by F.B.I.," *New York Times*, Mar. 22, 2003).

266   They instituted the program of "Special Registration": See Moustafa Bayoumi, "Racing Religion," *New Centennial Review* 6, no. 2 (2006): 267–293. From September 11, 2002, to September 30, 2003, the number of people registered in the United States was 83,519. During the same period, the number of people registered at ports of entries (airports and other border crossings) was 93,741, for a total of 177,260 individuals registered. The number of deportation proceedings initiated by Special Registration is 13,799. See http://www.ice.gov/pi/news/factsheets/nseersFS120103.htm.

267   the infamous Palmer Raids: Louise Cainkar, "The Social Construction of Difference and the Arab American Experience," *Journal of American Ethnic History* (Winter–Spring 2006), 257.

267   None of these policies: There is legitimate concern over future terrorism, but there is also plenty of reason to be skeptical of the claim of widespread terrorist sympathies in the United States. The Justice Department's own internal investigator basically stated as much. In a report released in February 2007, the Department of Justice's inspector general sharply criticized the FBI and other branches of the department for the gross inaccuracies it found in its reporting of terrorism statistics as well as the far too frequent overstatements made regarding terrorism-related cases. (See "The Department of Justice's Internal Controls Over Terrorism Reporting," U.S. Department of Justice, Office of the Inspector General, Feb. 2007.) A few months earlier, New York University's Law and Society Program reached very similar findings. They also cataloged the Justice Department's claims of fighting terrorism and, after their thorough investigation, found that there are in fact "few, if any, prevalent terrorist threats currently within the U.S." ("Terrorist Trial Report Card, US Edition," New York University Center of Law and Security, Dec. 2006, p. 3). The *Washington Post*

had deduced the same thing previously, that the vast majority of prosecutions that are loudly touted as "terrorism-related" are in reality relatively mundane matters of immigration violations, credit-card fraud, or lying to a government official. (Dan Eggen and Julie Tate, "U.S. Campaign Produces Few Convictions on Terrorism Charges: Statistics Often Count Lesser Crimes," *Washington Post*, June 12, 2005.) The inflation of these figures clearly serves other ends, as political gain is being made on the backs of U.S. Muslims. David Cole and James Lobel have argued that virtually all of those who in fact have been convicted of "material support" for terrorism in the United States (around fifty people) have been convicted of "a crime that requires no proof that the defendant ever intended to further a terrorist act." Cole and Lobel also point out that "prosecutors have obtained a handful of convictions for conspiracy to engage in terrorism, [yet] several of those convictions rest on extremely broad statutes that don't require proof of any specific plan or act, or on questionable entrapment tactics by government informants." David Cole and James Lobel, "Why We're Losing the War on Terror," *Nation*, Sept. 24, 2007.

267　At least five major Muslim charities: "Muslim Charities and the War on Terror," OMB Watch, Washington, D.C., Feb. 2006. The highest-profile case launched by the Justice Department was against the Dallas-based Holy Land Foundation. It ended in mistrial in what was seen as a major failure for the government. See Peter Whoriskey, "Mistrial Declared in Islamic Charity Case," *Washington Post*, Oct. 23, 2007.

267　Spies and government informants: Robin Shulman, "The Informer: Behind the Scenes or Setting the Stage?" *Washington Post*, May 29, 2007. Geoff Mulvihill, "Informants' Actions Key in Fort Dix Terror Plot Case: Entrapment Defense Seen as Possible," Associated Press, May 10, 2007.

267　"material witness" warrants: Eric Lichtblau, "Two Groups Charge Abuse of Witness Law," *New York Times*, June 27, 2005. Human Rights Watch and American Civil Liberties Union (joint report), *Witness to Abuse: Human Rights Abuses Under the Material Witness Law Since September 11*, June 2005.

267　immigration hearings were routinely held: Adam Clymer, "Government Openness at Issue as Bush Holds On to Records," *New York Times*, January 3, 2003.

267　dangerous expansion of the use of "secret evidence": Secret evidence today is used mainly in cases the government launches against Muslim charities. See Henry Weinstein, "How Lawyer Navigates Sea of Secrecy in Bizarre Case—Among the Obstacles: Responding to a Filing He Can't See and Writing a Brief with None of His Notes at Hand," *Los Angeles Times*, Aug. 15, 2007. Leslie Eaton, "U.S. Prosecution of Muslim Group Ends in Mistrial," *New York Times*,

Oct. 23, 2007. It has also been used to deny entry to undesirable foreigners and can, of course, be used at any time. See Neil MacFarquhar, "Free Speech Groups Sue Over Visa Denial," *New York Times,* Sept. 26, 2007. Dahlia Lithwick, "The Dog Ate My Evidence: What Happens when the Government Can't Re-create the Case Against You?" *Slate.com,* Oct. 16, 2007, http://www.slate.com/id/2176017/.

267   "reasonably foreseeable": Nina Bernstein, "Judge Rules That U.S. Has Broad Powers to Detain Noncitizens Indefinitely," *New York Times.* June 15, 2006.

267   This is a district court's decision: See David Cole, "Manzanar Redux? In an Echo of Japanese Internment, a Judge's Ruling Allows Foreign Nationals to Be Rounded Up on the Basis of Their Race or Religion," *Los Angeles Times,* June 16, 2006.

267   "Whoever controls the Middle East": Douglas Little, *American Orientalism: The United States and the Middle East Since 1945* (Chapel Hill: University of North Carolina Press, 2002), 126.

268   "colonial war in the postcolonial age": Zbigniew Brzezinski, "Five Flaws in the President's Plan," *Washington Post,* Jan. 12, 2007.

268   "boomerang effects": Hannah Arendt, *The Origins of Totalitarianism* (New York: Harcourt, 1968), 206. Aimé Césaire makes the same point, with the same language ("boomerang effect"), in his *Discourse on Colonialism,* trans. Joan Pinkham (New York: New York University Press, 2000 [1955]), 36.

269   With the passage of the Military Commissions Act: Charlie Savage, *Takeover: The Return of the Imperial Presidency and the Subversion of American Democracy* (New York: Little, Brown and Company, 2007), 321.

269   The government claims a national security exception: See note previous page: dangerous expansion of the use of "secret evidence."

269   Warrantless wiretapping: James Risen and Eric Lichtblau, "Bush Lets U.S. Spy on Callers Without Courts," *New York Times,* Dec. 16, 2005. Scott Shane and Eric Lichtblau, "Wiretapping Compromise Was Months in the Making," *New York Times,* Oct. 20, 2007.

269   "It is indeed a nemesis of Imperialism": J. A. Hobson, *Imperialism* (Ann Arbor: University of Michigan Press, 1965 [1902]), 151–152.

ABOUT THE AUTHOR

Moustafa Bayoumi is an associate professor of English at Brooklyn College, the City University of New York. Born in Zürich, Switzerland, and raised in Kingston, Canada, he completed his Ph.D. in English and comparative literature at Columbia University. A coeditor of *The Edward Said Reader,* he has published academic essays in *Transition, Interventions,* the *Yale Journal of Criticism, Amerasia, Arab Studies Quarterly,* the *Journal of Asian American Studies,* and other places. His writings have also appeared in the *Nation,* the *London Review of Books,* and the *Village Voice.* His essay "Disco Inferno," originally published in the *Nation,* was included in the collection *Da Capo Best Music Writing 2006.* From 2003 to 2006, he served on the National Council of the American Studies Association, and he is currently an editor for *Middle East Report.* He is also an occasional columnist for the Progressive Media Project, an initiative of the *Progressive* magazine, through which his op-eds appear in newspapers across the United States. He lives in Brooklyn.

DATE			